Investigating Pop Psychology

Investigating Pop Psychology provides the basic tools required to make evidence-informed decisions and thoughtfully distinguish science from pseudoscience through the application of scientific skepticism.

Psychologists conduct scientific investigations into a lot of strange things including alien encounters, horoscopes, dream interpretation, superstition, and extrasensory perception (ESP). Through a digestible, open-minded format combined with relevant and topical case studies such as energy psychology, demonic possession, and horoscopes, this book offers an engaging read which encourages students to think critically about the information they are exposed to during their academic careers and beyond. By taking a fresh look into investigations regarding pseudoscience and fringe science in pop psychology, it celebrates the science of psychology while also providing warnings about the problem of pseudoscience in pop psychology.

Providing tips on how to consider evidence regarding the strength of claims in pop psychology, *Investigating Pop Psychology* is an ideal resource for undergraduate introductory psychology students and for students studying science and pseudoscience.

Stephen Hupp, PhD, is a Clinical Psychologist and Professor of Psychology at Southern Illinois University Edwardsville (SIUE) in the United States. In 2015, he won the Great Teacher Award from the SIUE Alumni Association. He has published several books including *Pseudoscience in Therapy* and *Dr. Huckleberry's True or Malarkey? Superhuman Abilities*.

Richard Wiseman, PhD, is a Social Psychologist and Professor of the Public Understanding of Psychology at the University of Hertfordshire in the United Kingdom. He has published over 100 academic papers, written several best-selling psychology books (including *The Luck Factor* and *59 Seconds*) and created psychology-based YouTube videos that have attracted over 500 million views.

D1567106

Investigating Pop Psychology

Other Books in this Series
Investigating Clinical Psychology
Investigating School Psychology
Investigating Paranormal Psychology
Investigating Cognitive Psychology

Investigating Pop Psychology
Pseudoscience, Fringe Science, and Controversies
Stephen Hupp and Richard Wiseman

For more information, please refer to www.routledge.com/Series+Investigating+Psychology/book-series/IPP

Investigating Pop Psychology

Pseudoscience, Fringe Science, and Controversies

Edited by Stephen Hupp and Richard Wiseman

Routledge
Taylor & Francis Group

NEW YORK AND LONDON

Cover image: Getty

First published 2023
by Routledge
605 Third Avenue, New York, NY 10158

and by Routledge
4 Park Square, Milton Park, Abingdon, Oxon OX14 4RN

Routledge is an imprint of the Taylor & Francis Group, an informa business

British Library Cataloguing-in-Publication Data
A catalogue record for this book is available from the British Library

ISBN: 978-0-367-62068-4 (hbk)
ISBN: 978-0-367-60994-8 (pbk)
ISBN: 978-1-003-10779-8 (ebk)

DOI: 10.4324/9781003107798

Typeset in Bembo
by MPS Limited, Dehradun

Dedicated to Scott O. Lilienfeld

Contents

Introduction to the Investigating Psychology Pseudoscience Series

Richard Wiseman PhD

The public are constantly bombarded by information about psychology. Magazines and websites offer quizzes and questionnaires that apparently reveal their real selves; social media posts present fascinating facts about the human mind; and self-development books allegedly describe tips and techniques that can help everyone to improve their lives. Often, these quizzes, factoids, and advice put a smile on people's faces, give them something to talk about with their friends and family, and cause little harm. So far, so good. However, sometimes these websites, social media posts, books, and magazines have a far more significant impact, shaping people's sense of self-identity, changing the way that they perceive and interact with others, and influencing important life decisions. Unfortunately, there are often few, if any, checks and balances in place to ensure that the information that the public receive about psychology is valid. Worse still, researchers examining such claims and ideas have frequently discovered that some of this information is, at best, highly questionable.

Take, for example, the "Yale Goal Study." Spend any time reading psychology-related webpages and you will soon come across an account of this remarkable research. According to most sources, the study took place in the early 1950s. In the first part of the work, researchers asked a class of graduating Yale students whether they knew what they wanted to achieve in life and if they had written down their goals. Only 3% of the graduates fell into this category. Then, 20 years later, the researchers tracked down all of the students and asked them about their personal wealth. Remarkably, the 3% of graduates who had written down their goals 20 years before had a greater level of personal wealth than the remaining 97% of their classmates combined. This astonishing study is frequently cited by self-help gurus and motivational coaches to illustrate the impressive power of goal setting. Journalist Lawrence Tabak tried to track down the source of this widely reported study. He contacted several famous writers who had cited it, the secretary of the 1953 Yale Class, and a research associate at Yale University. Time and again, Tabak drew a blank and eventually concluded that the research had never actually been undertaken. In short, for years, people across the world have been told that goal setting will help to significantly boost their personal wealth based on an entirely fictitious study.

Another example involves whether it's possible to tell whether someone is lying based on their eye movements. Many authors and life coaches promote the notion that liars are more likely to look up to their right and truth tellers are more likely to look up to their left. Some of my own research has examined the relationship between body language and lying, and my colleagues and I put this widely believed claim to the test.

In one study, we asked students to take a mobile phone to a nearby office, and to either put it in a cupboard or to hide it in their pockets. The students were then interviewed on camera about their actions and were asked to state that they had put the mobile phone in the cupboard. As a result, some of the students were lying and some were telling the truth. We carefully counted how often the students looked up to their right and left, and discovered nothing to suggest that lying or truth telling was associated with either pattern of eye movement. Our second study was a more real-world test of the hypothesis. During some missing person cases, family members appear on the media and make public appeals for information about their missing relatives. Occasionally, evidence then emerges that one of the family members committed the crime and was therefore lying when they spoke to the media. We obtained several films of these press conferences and carefully counted how often each person looked up to the left or to the right. Once again, we compared the eye movements of those lying with those telling the truth, and again discovered no evidence to support the notion that lying was associated with either pattern of eye movement. In short, the public have been encouraged to judge the veracity of their friends, partners, and colleagues on an unreliable cue.

Of course, if the Yale Goal Study and the notion of liars looking in a certain direction were the only examples of bad psychology in the public domain, then there wouldn't be a serious problem. However, these examples are just the tip of a sizable iceberg. In fact, similar widely believed claims permeate almost every strata of society. In this series of books, researchers from psychology and academia will shine a much-needed light on many of the most widely believed and popular claims. They will describe the nature of the claim, carefully consider the evidence supporting this notion, and explore why people might believe the claim in the absence of reliable and convincing scientific evidence. Will their analyses be entirely rational and unbiased? No, of course not. Like all of us, researchers and scientists hold beliefs and ideas that influence the way in which they see the world. However, unlike many of the websites, social media platforms, books, and magazines that uncritically promote such claims, they will do their best to take a careful look at key sources of evidence and to reach a balanced and considered viewpoint. This impressive body of work will examine claims associated with almost every area of psychology, including social psychology, personality, learning, and dreaming. Together, it will form an invaluable and highly practical resource for those working in a variety of applied settings, including education, psychotherapy, business, and the courtroom. Perhaps most important of all, this series will illustrate how we can all come to believe what isn't so, emphasize the important role that scientific research plays in helping to sort fact from fiction, and demonstrate how popular psychology has influenced world history and personal lives alike.

Other Books

Other Books in This Series

- *Investigating Clinical Psychology*
- *Investigating School Psychology*
- *Investigating Paranormal Psychology*
- *Investigating Cognitive Psychology*

Other Books by Stephen Hupp

- *Dr. Huckleberry's True or Malarkey? Superhuman Abilities: Game Book for Skeptical Folk*
- *Child and Adolescent Psychotherapy: Components of Evidence-Based Treatments for Youth and Their Parents*
- *Pseudoscience in Child and Adolescent Psychotherapy: A Skeptical Field Guide*
- *Pseudoscience in Therapy: A Skeptical Field Guide*
- *Great Myths of Child Development*
- *Great Myths of Adolescence*
- *Thinking Critically about Child Development: Examining Myths and Misunderstandings*

Other Books by Richard Wiseman

- *Psychology: Why It Matters*
- The *Hocus Pocus* comic series
- *David Copperfield's History of Magic*
- *Laughlab: The Scientific Search for the World's Funniest Joke*
- *The Luck Factor*
- *Did You Spot the Gorilla? How to Recognise Hidden Opportunities in Your Life*
- *Parapsychology*
- *Quirkology: How We Discover the Big Truths in Small Things*
- *59 Seconds: Think a Little, Change a Lot*
- *Paranormality: Why We See What Isn't There*
- *Rip It Up: The Radically New Approach to Changing Your Life*
- *Night School: Wake Up to the Power of Sleep*
- *How to Remember Everything*
- *Shoot for the Moon: Achieve the Impossible with the Apollo Mindset*
- *Deception and Self-deception: Investigating Psychics*
- *Guidelines for Extrasensory Perception Research*
- *Guidelines for Testing Psychic Claimants*

Contributors

James E. Alcock, PhD, is a Registered Clinical Psychologist and Professor of Psychology at York University in Canada. He is author of the book *Belief: What It Means to Believe and Why Our Convictions Are So Compelling*.

Michael I. Axelrod, PhD, is a School Psychologist, the Director of the Human Development Center, and a Professor of Psychology at University of Wisconsin – Eau Claire. He is co-editor of another book in this series – *Investigating School Psychology: Pseudoscience, Fringe Science, and Controversies*.

Tyler R. Black, MD, FRCPC, is a Child and Adolescent Psychiatrist and the Medical Director of the CAPE Unit of BC Children's Hospital and BC Mental Health and Substance Use Services. He is also a Clinical Assistant Professor at the University of British Columbia in Canada.

William Cerbin, PhD, is Professor Emeritus of Psychology and founding Director of the Center for Advancing Teaching and Learning at the University of Wisconsin-La Crosse.

Arlo Clark-Foos, PhD, is an Associate Professor of Cognitive Psychology at the University of Michigan – Dearborn.

Stefano I. Di Domenico, PhD, is an Assistant Professor of Psychology at the University of Toronto Scarborough in Canada.

Christopher C. French, PhD, is an Emeritus Professor of Psychology and Head of the Anomalistic Psychology Research Unit at Goldsmiths, University of London in England. He is co-author of the book *Anomalistic Psychology: Exploring Paranormal Belief and Experience*.

Terence Hines, PhD, is a Professor of Psychology at Pace University (Pleasantville, NY) and an Adjunct Professor of Neurology at New York Medical College (Valhalla, NY). He is author of the book *Pseudoscience and the Paranormal*.

Stephen Hupp, PhD, is a Licensed Clinical Psychologist and Professor of Psychology at Southern Illinois University Edwardsville. He is co-editor of the book *Pseudoscience in Therapy*.

Chelsea Johnson, BS, is a Doctoral Student at the University of Southern Mississippi.

Zachary C. LaBrot, PhD, is an Assistant Professor of School Psychology at the University of Southern Mississippi.

Caleb W. Lack, PhD, is a Licensed Clinical Psychologist and Professor of Psychology at the University of Central Oklahoma. He is author of the book *Critical Thinking, Science, and Pseudoscience: Why We Can't Trust Our Brains*.

Tesia Marshik, PhD, is an Associate Professor of Developmental and Educational Psychology at the University of Wisconsin – La Crosse.

Emily Maxime, BS, is a Doctoral Student at the University of Southern Mississippi.

Carmen P. McLean, PhD, is a Licensed Clinical Psychologist at the Dissemination and Training Division of the National Center for PTSD at the VA Palo Alto Health Care System and a Clinical Associate Professor (Affiliate) at Stanford University School of Medicine. She is co-author of the book *Retraining the Brain: Applied Neuroscience in Exposure Therapy for PTSD*.

J. Thadeus Meeks, PhD, is an Associate Professor of Cognitive Psychology at Southern Illinois University Edwardsville.

Madeleine Miller, BS, is a Doctoral Student at the City University of New York.

Steven Novella, MD, is a Neurologist and an Associate Professor of Neurology at the Yale School of Medicine. He is the host of the Skeptics' Guide to the Universe podcast and co-author of the book *The Skeptics' Guide to the Future: What Yesterday's Science and Science Fiction Tell Us About the World of Tomorrow*.

Anthony R. Pratkanis, PhD, is a retired Professor of Psychology at the University of California. He is co-author (with Elliot Aronson) of the book *Age of Propaganda: The Everyday Use and Abuse of Persuasion*.

M. J. Schneider, BA, is a Social Psychology Researcher and Lab Manager for the Princeton Social Neuroscience Lab.

Jonathan N. Stea, PhD, RPsych, is a Registered Clinical Psychologist and Adjunct Assistant Professor of Psychology at the University of Calgary in Canada. He is co-editor of another book in this series – *Investigating Clinical Psychology: Pseudoscience, Fringe Science, and Controversies*.

Karen Stollznow, PhD, is a Linguist and Researcher for the Griffith Centre for Social and Cultural Research in Australia. She is co-host of the Monster Talk podcast and author of the book *On the Offensive: Prejudice in Language Past and Present*.

Indre V. Viskontas, PhD, is a Cognitive Neuroscientist and Associate Professor at the University of San Francisco. She is the co-host of the Inquiring Minds podcast and author of the book *How Music Can Make You Better*.

Christine C. Vriesema, PhD, is an Assistant Professor of Educational Psychology at the University of Wisconsin – Eau Claire.

Stuart Vyse, PhD, is a Behavioral Scientist and retired Professor of Psychology at Connecticut College. He is author of the book *The Uses of Delusion: Why It's Not Always Rational to Be Rational*.

Richard Wiseman, PhD, is a Social Psychologist and Professor of the Public Understanding of Psychology at the University of Hertfordshire in the United Kingdom. He is author of the book *Shoot for the Moon*.

Preface

The public often find out about psychology via self-help books, social media, podcasts, blogs, videos, shows, and movies. Although science-based ideas sometimes work their way into these types of pop psychology, they often contain information that is not supported by evidence. Worse still, many of these unsupported ideas have the potential to cause harm, both directly (e.g., exacerbating mental health problems) and indirectly (e.g., serving as a substitute for effective therapy). As a result, there's considerable value in being able to spot unsupported claims.

Chapter 1 of this book will explore the concepts of *science* and *pseudoscience,* acknowledging that the boundary between these two concepts is often far from clear, and examining the usefulness of constructs such as *emerging science*, *fringe science*, and *controversies*. This chapter also provides a description of some of the most common sources of false beliefs as well as some of the key hallmarks of false claims. Other chapters that help us understand why we often hold false beliefs include Chapter 5 (which examines superstitious behavior) and Chapter 13 (which reviews how social influence is used by con artists and salespeople). The book's Postscript also provides some tips for helping you become resistant to believing in pseudoscience. The other chapters take a deep dive into specific topics that are commonly characterized as pseudoscience, fringe science, or, at the very least, controversial.

Some chapters provide a fresh look into traditional topics. For example, Chapter 2 investigates the 19th-century practice of phrenology (using the shape of the skull to make predictions about a person's intellectual and personality traits). Long debunked as a pseudoscience, this chapter reviews recent research related to phrenology and examines the degree to which phrenology foreshadowed some modern-day theories about localization in the brain. Other chapters focusing on historical topics include Chapter 4 on Freud's theory of dream interpretation, Chapter 9 on Freud's theory of psychosexual stages, and Chapter 14 on Rorschach ink blots. These ideas greatly influenced the course of psychology, are still used by some therapists, and are presented in an uncritical way in several introductory textbooks.

Several other chapters focus on topics that are controversial. For example, Chapter 8 investigates the brain training industry, Chapter 12 investigates alternative medicine, and Chapter 16 investigates energy psychology. Written by a neuroscientist, a neurologist, and a clinical psychologist, respectively, each of these chapters critically examines these broad topics and helps to demonstrate the value of interdisciplinary perspectives within the same text.

Lastly, some of the remaining chapters focus on other intriguing aspects of fringe psychology. Chapter 3 examines parapsychology, Chapter 6 explores alien encounters, Chapter 10 examines horoscopes, Chapter 11 investigates seemingly romantic experiences with ghosts, and Chapter 15 examines how demonic possessions have sometimes been used to help explain psychological disorders.

In short, this book is designed to help strengthen your critical thinking skills related to pop psychology, and hopefully it will help you apply these same skills to other disciplines as well.

Stephen Hupp

Acknowledgments

I have several people to thank for this book and my way of thinking about psychology. First and foremost, we dedicated this book to Scott O. Lilienfeld because he was a trailblazer in the ways he examined psychology with a skeptical eye. Some of my favorite books include *50 Great Myths of Popular Psychology*, *Science and Pseudoscience in Clinical Psychology,* and *Navigating the Mindfield.* He's also published a textbook for an Introduction to psychology course, a five-volume encyclopedia, and over 500 research articles and book chapters. He was an especially kind person who helped promote the work of many other skeptical minds, and he (along with Steven Jay Lynn) gave me my first book deal. Without that first book, this book would not have been a possibility.

All of the chapter authors for this book deserve a tremendous amount of gratitude. We are extremely thankful for all of the work that went into writing these chapters in a fun and informative way. Each of these authors are leaders in their fields, and their experience and wit really shine. We're also very thankful for the rest of the team that helped make this book a reality. Lucy McClune was the commissioning editor that first contracted the original book proposal while also providing the encouragement that it be expanded into a multi-volume series. Danielle Dyal then helped shape the series by offering feedback and contracting the next two books (*Investigating Clinical Psychology* and *Investigating School Psychology*). Adam Woods guided us through the final steps of completing the book and bringing it to life. Additionally, Neha Shrivastave (the Book Project Manager) and Rakhi Sharma (the Copyeditor) skillfully coordinated and conducted the book's final edits. The whole series is much better thanks to all of their efforts. Many thanks also to Liezel Lindo and Jenna Callantine for their help with reviewing the final draft.

I'd also like to thank my co-editor, Richard Wiseman, for his insights and guidance along the way. His other books have also helped shape the way I (and many others) think about psychology and our world. Some of my favorite books by Richard include *59 Seconds*, *Quirkology*, and *Paranormality*. Additionally, his book *Shoot for the Moon* gave me the final nudge to ask him to get involved with this project.

Lastly, my parents – Deanna and Dennis – worked hard every day to help and support me, and they also helped me view the world in an open-minded way. They, along with my wife and children (Farrah, Vyla, Evan, and Henry) bring me the happiness needed to get through the harder days. They also regularly help me experience what it's like to be on the other side of someone's skepticism.

Stephen Hupp

1 Examining Claims in Pop Psychology

Stephen Hupp

These days, we all have tremendous access to information. Using just our phones, we can learn new languages, discover new dance moves, or find the best place to eat a burger. But we also have tremendous access to *misinformation*. We can learn our horoscope, discover conspiracies, or find the best place to search for Bigfoot. Consequently, we're all exposed to a lot of ideas that appear to be based on science but that are contrary to the scientific consensus. Some academics and writers have referred to such ideas as *pseudoscience*.

Because of frequent exposure to this material, a significant percentage of the public believes strange things. For example, Pew Research found that 41% of adults in the United States believe the claim that psychics have supernatural powers (Gecewicz, 2018). At first glance, this belief seems like harmless fun, but it can have a more serious side including, for example, people turning to psychics for guidance related to their mental health (Held, 2019; Wagner, 2008). Unfortunately, psychics frequently have no formal mental health training, and so they have the potential to cause harm. Other work shows that even licensed therapists often engage in interventions that lack empirical support. For example, 33% of adults believe claims related to living a previous life and so they may seek out a therapist who offers past life regression therapy (Darrisaw, 2019). The problems caused by such unsupported claims extends to many areas of society, and can cause people to think that they are possessed by demons or had a terrifying encounter with aliens. Such beliefs can have serious and negative implications for how people view the world and live their lives.

Examining the Claims

This book has been designed to be useful for those who want to take a skeptical look at these types of claims. I hope that it will interest the public and professionals alike. Of equal importance, it is designed to appeal to students as a supplemental text to an introduction to psychology course.

The authors of the chapters in this book are all experts in their respective fields and were recruited because they already have a history of examining claims from a skeptical viewpoint. They were encouraged to open each chapter by stating claims in a way that fairly represents the arguments of the believers. The goal was to discourage *straw man arguments*, that is, constructing weak versions of claims that are easy to critique. Next, the authors were encouraged to emphasize *investigations* into these topics, to seek evidence that both supports and refutes the claims related to their topic, and to take a fresh look into the topics. Admittedly, the book's subtitle also reveals the inherent bias of this book, a bias you should

DOI: 10.4324/9781003107798-1

keep in mind. All of the chapter topics were chosen because they're all commonly seen as questionable or controversial within mainstream psychology and related fields.

As you'll soon see, there's a real science behind studying some of the topics, such as energy psychology, alternative medicine, and extrasensory perception. In fact, sometimes studying topics like these can lead to important discoveries. And sometimes there may even be benefits to believing in some of the claims described in this book (Vyse, 2022). Of course, beliefs in many of these claims can lead to real harm too. All of these possibilities will be explored, and by the end of the book we'll all hopefully have a better understanding of pop psychology when it comes to science, pseudoscience, and everything in between.

Everything In Between (the Demarcation Problem)

Many believe that it's easy to tell the difference between science and pseudoscience. Relatedly, many also believe that science and pseudoscience are best thought of as a dichotomous variable (or a binary) with only two discrete and opposing options. But to help explore this issue more deeply, let's consider another variable that seems like a clear binary at first glance – hot and cold. You can pretty quickly determine if something is hot or cold, especially when you consider the extreme examples. Boiling water is hot, and ice is cold. But, other times it's a lot trickier. Sometimes water is warm, room temperature, or cool. And what about *lukewarm* – is that warmer or cooler than room temperature?

We have the same challenge with the line between science and pseudoscience, a challenge often called the *demarcation problem* (Pigliucci & Boudry, 2014). Just like the difference between hot and cold water, there's a lot of gray area between scientific and pseudoscientific topics. Darwin's theory of evolution is accepted by the vast majority of the scientific community, but even he got some details wrong. Our understanding of evolution has continued to evolve as the scientific community gathers more data. In fact, that's one of the hallmarks of science itself, forever engaging in self-correction that leads to change in theories and opens the door to future advancements.

There's also *emerging science* that is characterized by new ideas and theories that are being investigated. In the field of clinical psychology, for example, new treatment approaches are being studied all the time. Now, imagine a research study that shows a new type of treatment is effective. Assume that the research design is very strong (e.g., it involved a randomized controlled trial). That new treatment does not yet serve as a good example of an established science. We still need the replication of more similar studies from other research teams.

In the wide space between science and pseudoscience, there are also a lot of *controversies* which come about through different paths. Some claims have mixed evidence. That is, several studies support a claim but other studies fail to do so. Also, a research finding may not be accompanied by a plausible theory. Yet other times, we have controversies based on untested claims. Often these untested claims haven't been tested because there's just no way to study them objectively.

Along our range of possibilities, we also have another interesting type of science to consider. *Fringe science* is characterized by extraordinary claims that are based on an implausible idea that goes against the scientific community's understanding of how the world works. For example, research into Bigfoot can be fairly called a fringe science. There are some reasons why a Bigfoot discovery could be possible. For example, new species of animals, even mammals, are discovered every year. On the other hand, there are also reasons why a Bigfoot discovery is unlikely. For example, the existing Bigfoot evidence has significant problems (e.g., evidence that the large footprints were faked). To the credit of some Bigfoot enthusiasts, though, they often subject their evidence to scientific scrutiny. For example, if they find hair on a tree, they submit it for DNA analysis. Incidentally, in the few episodes of *Finding Bigfoot* that I've seen, it seems that the answer is usually that the hair comes from a bear (and after 100 episodes, they never actually found Bigfoot). Overall, it's fair to say that there was a legitimate scientific investigation into an extraordinary – or fringe – topic.

In short, between the contructs of science and pseudoscience, we have emerging science, controversies, and fringe science. Admittedly, even these concepts aren't discrete categories. They have a lot of overlap and fuzzy lines. Thus, rather than simply categorizing something as a science or pseudoscience, it's often preferable to examine specific claims on a continuum between being supported and unsupported. Both of these options can be helpful ways of considering the demarcation problem, and they also create the great need for the development of critical thinking abilities.

Critical Thinking About Claims

While considering the degree to which a claim is supported, there are a few key concepts to keep in mind. Understanding these key concepts – all tools of critical thinking – will help you interpret new claims while also helping you reconsider some of the claims you currently accept to be true. In fact, if you spend some time learning about the Sagan Standard, the Faker's Dozen, and the Mucky Seven, it will give you a head start as you prepare to read about all of the topics covered in this book.

Extraordinary Evidence: The Sagan Standard

Carl Sagan was an astronomer and science communicator. He helped popularize scientific skepticism through several best-selling books such as *The Demon-Haunted World: Science as a Candle in the Dark* (1996). It's a great book and I often encourage others to read this masterpiece. Scientific skepticism was also on display through Sagan's 1980 television show, *Cosmos*, where he famously said that "extraordinary claims require extraordinary evidence," an idea now known as the *Sagan Standard*. A claim is considered to be extraordinary when it goes against the current scientific consensus. Extraordinary claims need a considerable amount of evidence before most members of the scientific community will come to accept them. Our book will be investigating the evidence related to quite a few extraordinary claims about topics such as demons, aliens, and even g-g-ghosts (topics that Sagan wrote about too). You're encouraged to be open-minded about all of these claims. You're also encouraged to apply the Sagan Standard for each one.

Sources of False Beliefs: The Faker's Dozen

Why do we humans hold so many false beliefs? Somehow, we're simultaneously the smartest creatures on Earth while also being the creatures who are the most susceptible to pseudoscience. It turns out that our brains are like a double-edged sword. On the one side, we have amazing brains that are especially adept at making connections between two things, and when we put enough of these connections together we end up with many of the wonders of this world. For instance, someone once realized that germs on our hands caused people to get sick, and then the rest of us benefited from this connection tremendously. Further, our brains also gave us the ability to create the pyramids, the Internet, and space travel.

On the other side, however, the amazing ability of our brains to make connections also gets us into a lot of trouble. We often think we see a real connection when in fact the connection is not real. For instance, someone once noticed that some children end up showing signs of autism soon after getting a vaccine. Many people were harmed from this false connection because the research is clear – vaccines do not cause autism (Hupp & Jewell, 2015). Another way of demonstrating the faulty connections is through the concept of visual *pareidolia* – the ability to extract a meaningful pattern from an ambiguous set of stimuli. If you see the big dipper in the sky, then you're experiencing pareidolia. If you see a face on the moon, then you're experiencing pareidolia. If you see an elephant in a cloud, then you're experiencing pareidolia. Your brain is making many connections that are not actually real connections.

A lot of our false beliefs come from our ability to make connections, even when the connection is not real. There are also other types of thinking errors that become the sources of our false beliefs. Many of these thinking errors have been identified as *cognitive biases* and *logical fallacies*, and there are several excellent books that explain many of the most common ways that our brain can be deceived. Some prominent examples of these books include *Why People Believe Weird Things* (Shermer, 1997) and *The Skeptics Guide to the Universe* (Novella et al., 2018). These books summarize decades of research, and centuries of philosophy, about how our brains work. Both books deserve a place on your bookshelf.

In another pivotal book, psychology professors – Scott Lilienfeld, Steven Jay Lynn, John Ruscio, and Barry Beyerstein – teamed up to write the book *50 Great Myths of Popular Psychology* (2010), another must-read. In the introduction of that book, they identified ten "sources of psychological myths" (p. 9). I highlighted those same ten sources in my books from the same series – *Great Myths of Child Development* (Hupp & Jewell, 2015) and the sequel *Great Myths of Adolescence* (Jewell et al., 2019). Over time, and inspired by all of the books listed above, that list has evolved into the *Faker's Dozen*, a curated collection of the type of sources that create false beliefs related to pop psychology. There's nothing new or ground-breaking about the Faker's Dozen; these same types of thinking errors are described in many other places. The Faker's Dozen is also not an exhaustive list of all of the different sources of false beliefs, but it's a good starting point for helping us all consider the claims in this book. Here are the Faker's Dozen sources of false beliefs:

- *Post Hoc Ergo Propter Hoc Reasoning* – Believing that one variable caused another variable simply because the first variable occurred *before* the second variable. For example, this is one of the primary sources of the false connection between a child receiving a vaccine one day and the same child later being diagnosed with autism.
- *Assuming Causation from Correlation* – Believing that one variable caused the other just because they are correlated with each other. Sticking with the vaccines example, over the last several decades, rates of autism increased as the amounts of vaccines were also increasing (i.e., these variables represent a *correlation*); however, neither of these variables actually affected each other (i.e., there is no *causation*). Instead, this correlation was an unfortunate coincidence. (Note that this source of false belief is involving large sets of data, whereas the *post hoc* source above was able to be applied to a single case.)

- *Reasoning by Representativeness* – Making a connection between two concepts based on a superficial similarity between them. When it comes to pregnancy, for example, some people falsely believe that a basketball-shaped belly means the baby will be a bouncing baby boy, and a watermelon-shaped belly means the baby will be a sweet baby girl.
- *Argument from Authority* – Arguing that something is true just because an "expert" claimed it to be so (claims made by celebrities are also included in this type of faulty thinking). For example, being a doctor doesn't mean the person is always right, especially when discussing topics outside of their expertise.
- *False Analogy* – Explaining an idea by comparing it to a similar idea while ignoring key unsaid differences. For example, the notion that we develop through "stages" is itself a weak analogy for how most development actually occurs.
- *False Dichotomy* – Depicting only two options when there are actually more than two. For example, it's a false dichotomy to believe that everyone is either good or evil.
- *Nirvana Fallacy* – Assuming that something is completely bad simply because it's not perfect. For example, there are a lot of ways the scientific method can go wrong, but that doesn't mean that science is a worthless endeavor.
- *Grain of Truth Exaggeration* – Making a grand claim based on the fact that only a small aspect of the claim is true. Although it's true that most of us aren't fully using our intellect at all times, that doesn't mean we only use 10% of our brain.
- *Appeal to Nature* – Arguing that a practice is safer because it's natural. For example, some advertisers appeal to a product being "all natural" even though many things found in nature can actually kill you.
- *Appeal to Antiquity* – Arguing that a practice is effective simply because it has been used for a long time. For example, some healers falsely highlight the idea that a treatment must be effective because it has been used since "ancient" times.
- *Biased Sample Misperception* – Believing we have a full picture of a phenomenon even though we've only been exposed to a specific portion of the phenomenon. For example, when we see a person in the news or other media, we are often getting a biased sample of the groups that the person represents.
- *Selective Perception* – Perceiving (and recalling) situations that conform to our ideas while failing to notice (or forgetting) situations that are contrary to our ideas. For example, once a teacher begins to believe a student is a genius, they may start to only attend to (and remember) the times the student said smart things while minimizing the student's mistakes.
- *Confirmation Bias* – Seeking out only information that confirms our beliefs while ignoring information that contradicts our beliefs. For example, when writing about a topic, it's natural for authors to only cite research articles that support their claims while leaving out research articles that go against their claims. This is the queen mother of all sources of false beliefs, and we all really have to work hard to guard against it.

In this book, many of the chapter authors will directly point out these sources of false beliefs as they examine claims related to their topics. Sometimes, though, you'll need to do the work of looking out for these sources. Fortunately, your brain is good at making connections.

Hallmarks of False Claims: The Mucky Seven

When people make false claims, sometimes they know exactly what they are doing, and other times they too have been deceived by the sources of false beliefs described above. Purposeful or not, when people promote false claims, the claims, and the arguments used to support them, share some of the same hallmarks (Hupp, 2019; Lilienfeld et al., 2014; Novella et al., 2018; Sagan, 1996). Being aware of these hallmarks, described here as the *Mucky Seven*, will help make you more resistant to believing in false claims:

- *Meaningless Jargon* – Incorporating scientific-sounding words that don't have any real connection to the proposed concept. For example, words like "quantum," have real meaning in certain situations, but these words are often used to make a pseudoscientific concept sound more scientific.
- *Untestable Idea Promotion* – Endorsing statements that are not able to be studied through sound research designs. For example, there aren't research study designs that can test many of Freud's concepts.
- *Anecdote Overreliance* – Putting anecdotes ahead of research studies. For example, testimonials are one type of anecdotes that are often used to promote questionable treatments.
- *Placebo Exploitation* – Relying on improvements that occur simply because people know they are getting a treatment. For example, people have the expectation that a treatment will help them get better so they start to feel better once the treatment starts regardless of which treatment is being provided.
- *Data Manipulation* – Using problematic practices related to analyzing and reporting data. For example, when people make dubious claims, they often cherry-pick the data that favors their hypothesis and leave out the rest of the data.
- *Burden of Proof Shift* – Offering a defense by suggesting that it's the skeptics that need to prove them wrong. For example, a psychic might suggest that a skeptic cannot point to research that disproves someone had lived a previous life.
- *Science Discreditation* – Offering a defense by attacking different aspects of science. For example, those making dubious claims often harshly critique the peer-review process.

These are some of the key hallmarks to look for as you consider the topic of each chapter. You'll also notice in Chapter 13 that Anthony Pratkanis will provide a deep dive into the social influence tactics that many sellers of pseudoscience use to influence your decisions.

Get to Know the Chapter Authors

One strength of this book is that it will be fun to read. We have entire chapters dedicated to topics such as psychosexual stages, superstitions, and dream interpretations. And that's just a small sampling of the chapters. Each of the other chapters will also provide an in depth look at an intriguing topic. However, the greatest strength of this book involves the people that wrote about each of these topics. We have an impressive lineup from the scientific community. Overall, this mix of contributors includes a neurologist, a neuroscientist, a psychiatrist, a linguist, and at least eight different types of psychologists (i.e., clinical, school, educational, developmental, cognitive, social, behavioral science, and anomalistic). Within this group, we also have best-selling authors, hosts of popular podcasts, and Fellows of the Committee for Skeptical Inquiry.

Moreover, this book has been edited by a social psychologist and a clinical psychologist. The social psychologist – Richard Wiseman – has written several best-selling books, many of which are related to scientific skepticism. For example, the book *Paranormality* (Wiseman, 2010) helps explain why people commonly believe in fortune-telling, communication with spirits, and several other pseudoscientific (or fringe) topics. He also co-authored the book *David Copperfield's History of Magic* (Copperfield et al., 2021) that helps explain how magicians are experts in deception and thus leaders in the skeptical community. For example, did you know that Harry Houdini spent time investigating (and debunking) the claims of psychics?

Hopefully, this lineup of contributors will get you even more excited about all of these already fun topics. However, you may have also noted that by sharing their credentials, I'm trying to influence you by making an *argument from authority* – one of the above sources of false beliefs. And by sharing the popularity of their books and podcasts, I'm trying to influence you by using the *social consensus* tactic (discussed in Chapter 13). Fortunately, Dr. Pratkanis will return at the end of this book in a Postscript that will help strengthen your resistance to false beliefs and social influence tactics.

Summary and Conclusion

Whether you consciously think about it or not, you probably spend a lot of time examining the many pop psychology claims that you're exposed to on a daily basis. Some claims are clearly scientific while others are not. There's also a lot of gray area between the concepts of science and pseudoscience such as emerging science, controversies, and fringe science. Thus, when considering a claim, it's often helpful to think in terms of the continuum between the extent to which the claim is supported and unsupported. Applying the Sagan Standard, which requires extraordinary evidence for extraordinary claims, is usually a good starting point. This chapter also summarized some of the common sources of false beliefs and some of the hallmarks of false claims that will be helpful for you to keep in mind as you consider pop psychology claims. Later, you'll also learn more about social influence tactics and ways to resist believing in false claims.

References

Copperfield, D., Wiseman, R., Britland, D., & Liwag, H. (2021). *David Copperfield's history of magic*. Simon & Schuster.

Darrisaw, M. (2019). By traveling back into my past life, I rediscovered my love for books and writing. Retrieved from www.oprahmag.com

Gecewicz, C. (2018). 'New age' beliefs common among both religious and nonreligious Americans. Retrieved from www.pewresearch.org

Held, L. (2019). Psychic mediums are the new wellness coaches. Retrieved from www.nytimes.com

Hupp, S. (2019). *Pseudoscience in child and adolescent psychotherapy: A skeptical field guide*. Cambridge University Press.

Hupp, S., & Jewell, J. (2015). *Great myths of child development*. Wiley.

Hupp, S., & Santa Maria, C. (2023). *Pseudoscience in therapy*. Cambridge University Press.

Jewell, J., Axelrod, M., Prinstein, M., & Hupp, S. (2019). *Great myths of adolescence*. Wiley.

Lilienfeld, S. O., Lynn, S. J., & Lohr, J. M. (2014). *Science and pseudoscience in clinical psychology*. The Guildford Press.

Lilienfeld, S. O., Lynn, S. J., Ruscio, J., & Beyerstein, B. L. (2010). *50 great myths of popular psychology: Shattering widespread misconceptions about human behavior*. John Wiley & Sons Ltd.

Novella, S., Novella, B., Santa, M. C., Novella, J., & Bernstein, E. (2018). *The skeptics' guide to the universe: How to know what's really real in a world increasingly full of fake.* Grand Central Publishing.

Pigliucci, M., & Boudry, M. (2014). *Philosophy of pseudoscience: Reconsidering the demarcation problem.* University of Chicago Press.

Sagan, C. (1996). *The demon-haunted world: Science as a candle in the dark.* Ballantine Books.

Shermer, M. (1997). *Why people believe weird things.* New York: W.H. Freeman and Co.

Viskontas, I. (2019). *How music can make you better.* Chronicle Books.

Vyse, S. (2022). *The uses of delusion: Why it's not always rational to be rational.* Oxford University Press.

Wagner, A. (2008). Psychics are the new psychologists. Retrieved from www.npr.org

Wiseman, R. (2010). *Paranormality: Why we see what isn't there.* Macmillan.

2 Phrenology and Neuroscience

Jonathan N. Stea, Tyler R. Black, and Stefano I. Di Domenico

Humans are innately curious creatures: curiously mysterious and curious about each other. It is no wonder that systems have been sought to describe the nature of mental life and the ways in which we relate socially – in the realm of modern psychology, these ventures have broadly classed themselves into the scientific disciplines of personality psychology and social psychology, respectively. Phrenology was an early 19th-century attempt to understand mental life by linking personality traits with scalp morphology. While some have argued that phrenology should be considered to be the first scientific study of psychology (because it endeavored to link psychology to underlying physiology) others have argued that phrenology was an early example of a narrow reductionist ethos that is characteristic of modern neurobiology (Renneville, 2020). Either way, from a modern perspective, it is undoubtedly the case that a perusal of phrenology is worthy of study as an exemplar of how to examine claims related to pop psychology.

Examining the Claims

Phrenology was the brainchild of Franz Joseph Gall, a German neuroanatomist and physician. Gall had always maintained that his theories had developed as a result of his own observations and experiences: for example, he noticed that students with protruding eyes were notable for their excellent memory (Renneville, 2020). Gall piggybacked from the assumption (widely contested at the time) that the brain was the seat of cognition, and he hypothesized that mental skills could be linked to external contours of the head (Finger, 2019). He then embarked on a vast empirical project to identify distinctive traits in both animals and humans, surveying a wide range of people with varying skills, including "poets, mathematicians, musicians, actors, cooks, the insane, thieves, and murders" (Renneville, 2020, p. 18). Gall's method of identifying cranial sites of particular "faculties" involved identifying a subject with a "prominent" mental trait and then matching it to a physical location on the head; alternatively, he also sometimes worked from head to traits (Renneville, 2020). Ultimately, Gall originally proposed a list of 27 brain functions or "faculties" that included a range of proclivities (Parker Jones et al., 2018). Some examples include circumspection (i.e., *cautiousness*), friendliness (i.e., *adhesiveness*), aptness toward education (i.e., *eventuality*), compassion (i.e., *benevolence*), ambition (i.e., *love of approbation*), and murder (i.e., *destructiveness*). Image 2.1 provides an example of a phrenology chart by another well-known phrenologist (Fowler & Fowler, 1859).

DOI: 10.4324/9781003107798-2

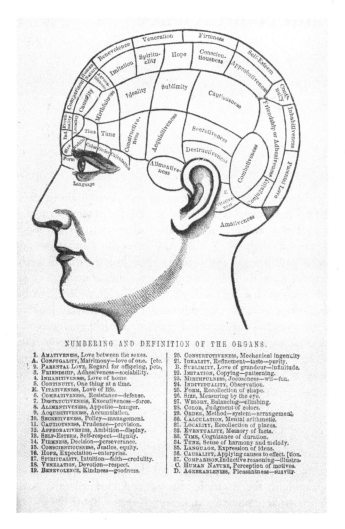

NUMBERING AND DEFINITION OF THE ORGANS.

1. AMATIVENESS, Love between the sexes.
A. CONJUGALITY, Matrimony—love of one. [etc.
2. PARENTAL LOVE, Regard for offspring, pets,
3. FRIENDSHIP, Adhesiveness—sociability.
4. INHABITIVENESS, Love of home
5. CONTINUITY, One thing at a time.
E. VITATIVENESS, Love of life.
6. COMBATIVENESS, Resistance—defense.
7. DESTRUCTIVENESS, Executiveness—force.
8. ALIMENTIVENESS, Appetite—hunger.
9. ACQUISITIVENESS, Accumulation.
10. SECRETIVENESS, Policy—management.
11. CAUTIOUSNESS, Prudence—provision.
12. APPROBATIVENESS, Ambition—display.
13. SELF-ESTEEM, Self-respect—dignity.
14. FIRMNESS, Decision—perseverance.
15. CONSCIENTIOUSNESS, Justice, equity.
16. HOPE, Expectation—enterprise.
17. SPIRITUALITY, Intuition—faith—credulity.
18. VENERATION, Devotion—respect.
19. BENEVOLENCE, Kindness—goodness.

20. CONSTRUCTIVENESS, Mechanical ingenuity
21. IDEALITY, Refinement—taste—purity.
B. SUBLIMITY, Love of grandeur—infinitude.
22. IMITATION, Copying—patterning.
23. MIRTHFULNESS, Jocoseness—wit—fun.
24. INDIVIDUALITY, Observation.
25. FORM, Recollection of shape.
26. SIZE, Measuring by the eye.
27. WEIGHT, Balancing—climbing.
28. COLOR, Judgment of colors.
29. ORDER, Method—system—arrangement
30. CALCULATION, Mental arithmetic.
31. LOCALITY, Recollection of places.
32. EVENTUALITY, Memory of facts.
33. TIME, Cognizance of duration.
34. TUNE, Sense of harmony and melody.
35. LANGUAGE, Expression of ideas.
36. CAUSALITY, Applying causes to effect. [tion.
37. COMPARISON, Inductive reasoning—illustra
C. HUMAN NATURE, Perception of motives.
D. AGREEABLENESS, Pleasantness—suavity.

Image 2.1 Example of a Phrenology Chart from The Illustrated Self-Instructor in Phrenology and Physiology (Fowler & Fowler, 1859). [credit: iStock from Getty Images].

The early development of phrenology highlights the notorious perils of putting too much stock into anecdotal evidence. As many astute students of science are well aware, anecdotes are often a good starting point to generate research into the reliability and validity of scientific claims, but they confer low-quality evidence. Worse, the methodology underpinning phrenology was dubious even by the standards of the 19th century (Parker Jones et al., 2018). For example, phenologists ascertained the physical location on the skull of the "Amativeness" faculty – describing sexual desire – by probing the heads of "emotional" young and widowed women; and they hypothesized the location of the "Combativeness" faculty by looking for flat regions on the heads of easygoing "Hindoos and Ceylonese" (Parker Jones et al., 2018). Thus, this approach used tenuous and outright offensive stereotypes about particular social groups.

Nevertheless, specific claims could be derived from phrenology. The broadest and most fundamental claim is that measuring the contours of the head can provide a reliable method for inferring constructs related to personality and mental capacities. A corollary claim is that local scalp morphology reflects underlying brain morphology. The reason for this claim is that "phrenologists believed that inspecting the outer surface of the head provided an indirect measure of brain shape based on the assumption that the softness of the skull during development should allow it to yield under the pressure of locally expanding cortical structures"(Parker Jones et al., 2018; p. 27). In other words, phrenologists believed that the brain was like a muscle insofar as those parts that were frequently used would hypertrophy (grow larger) and push local areas of the skull outward, whereas those functions that were neglected would atrophy (shrink) and depress local areas of the skull. In a fascinating study that will be reviewed later in this chapter, Parker Jones et al. (2018) tested these 19th-century claims of phrenology with the use of 21st-century scientific methods, thus offering a new investigation into an old set of claims.

Pop Psychology, Pop Culture, and Public Perception

Phrenology was wildly popular in the 19th century, peaking in the 1830s. Phrenological societies sprang up in Britain and France, and support for Gall's ideas could be found in Scandinavia, Spain, Germany, the United States, and Canada (Renneville, 2020). True believers consulted phrenology for vocational, marriage, and child rearing advice, whereas those more skeptical consumed phrenology as a way to experiment and test its validity against their own self-knowledge and against their own beliefs about race and gender (Bittel, 2019). Allusions to phrenology can be found in the works of popular figures of the 19th century, including Edgar Allan Poe, Walt Whitman, Ralph Waldo Emerson, and Herman Melville (Scherlinder Morse, 1997). Image 2.2 also shows that phrenology was even used as a carnival attraction.

Image 2.2 Photo from the carnival attraction of a phrenology reader from London, Ohio in 1938. [credit: Shutterstock].

One of phrenology's most enthralled and fiercest skeptics was Mark Twain (Finger, 2019). For example, Twain underwent two phrenological examinations by Lorenzo Fowler – first without identifying himself and then a second with his identity known. Displeased with the contrasting results following his "test," Twain went on to ridicule phrenology in *Tom Sawyer, Huckleberry Finn,* and in other works (Finger, 2019). Twain described this event in his autobiography with much snark, particularly with reference to Fowler's suggestion that the "cavity" on Twain's skull indicated that he was incapable of humor:

> However, he found a cavity, in one place; a cavity where a bump would have been in anybody else's skull. That cavity, he said was all alone, all by itself, occupying a solitude, and had no opposing bump, however slight in elevation, to modify and ameliorate its perfect completeness and isolation. He startled me by saying that that cavity represented the total absence of the sense of humor! He now became almost interested. Some of his indifference disappeared. He almost grew eloquent over this America which he had discovered. He said he often found bumps of humor which were so small that they were hardly noticeable, but that in his long experience this was the first time he had ever come across a cavity where a bump ought to be.
>
> (Quote from 1906 as cited in Twain, 2013, p. 336)

Present day, the popularity of phrenology has obviously fizzled, but throwbacks to its hype remain in popular culture. For example, in *The Simpsons*, Mr. Burns accuses Mona Simpson of being a career criminal by way of phrenology, to which Mr. Smithers states, "Phrenology was dismissed as quackery 160 years ago." Much more disturbingly, phrenology is often remembered in pop culture for its racist and sexist history. This history is perhaps best exemplified by allusion to Quentin Tarantino's movie, *Django Unchained*, whereby the rhetoric of scientific racism is evoked during a monologue by a southern slave owner when he announces, "The science of phrenology is crucial to understanding the separation of our two species" (Holmes, 2016). Indeed, concepts within phrenology survived into the 20th century but became distorted, hijacked, and associated with pseudoscientific racial science ideas, such as genocide and Nazi eugenics (Andre, 2018; Bank, 1996; Hilts, 1982). While one would be hard pressed to find phenology devotees in modern times, some do indeed still exist, albeit without any supporting evidence (Van den Bossche, 1998).

The Evidence

For nearly two centuries, phrenology has been mocked and attacked by opponents as being atheistic, immoral, and pseudoscientific; as scientific evidence against phrenology accumulated. In 1845, Marie Jean Pierre Flourens experimentally demonstrated with pigeon brains that large portions of the brain could be destroyed without functional impairment (Yildirum & Sarikcioglu, 2007). In 1861, Paul Broca demonstrated without a shadow of a doubt that the faculty of speech was located in the temporal region of the brain rather than near the eye, as Gall had maintained (Broca, 1861). To be charitable, phrenology foreshadowed the idea that the brain is in part organized around functionally discrete modules. Its nonsensical Achilles' heel, however, was the conviction that the brain's soft tissue could exert a significant effect on skull shape.

In the most comprehensive and rigorous evaluation of phrenological claims to date, Parker Jones et al. (2018) employed 21st-century scientific methods among almost 6,000 participants to test whether local changes in scalp morphology correlated with the "faculties" that Gall described. The authors also assessed whether local scalp morphology reflected the brain's underlying morphology. Specifically, the authors turned to the world's largest brain-imaging study to relate neuroimaging data from MRI results to questionnaires that tapped features of personality and cognition. In perhaps what is the greatest and shortest results section of all time, the authors wrote in its entirety: "The phrenological analyses produced no statistically significant or meaningful effects" (p. 31).

Thinking – Really Thinking! – About Phrenology

At this point, you will not be surprised to read that character traits do not correlate with bumps and lumps on people's heads as Gall had proposed. Still, it would be too easy to write off the effort behind phrenology as being entirely misguided and phrenology itself as being entirely wrong. You may be familiar with the concept of *attacking the strawman*, a fallacious type of argument in which a proposition is portrayed in the weakest possible terms so it can be easily refuted. We will not be strawmanning phrenology here; instead, we will *steelman* it by generously considering any positive aspects of this practice, its related theories, and the scientific investigations into its validity. That is, we will consider the evidence against phrenology's propositions as stated in their strongest possible terms.

We will start with the obvious. Phrenology proposed that the contents of people's character was related to biological matter. We might take this notion for granted. You might even exclaim, "Oh come on! Of course people's minds, character traits, and behavior is related to their brains!" But people did not always think this was so, even the well-informed. René Descartes (1596–1650), for example, famously argued that although the body is "like a machine," the mind is a nonphysical entity. This was Descartes' philosophical perspective called *mind-body dualism*. Phrenology, with its insistence on mapping character traits onto the shape of the skull, can be seen as an early attempt to move us away from mind-body dualism and toward the modern neuroscience perspective in which the mind is seen as being the product of the brain: That's one point for Franz Josef Gall, zero points for René Descartes.

Phrenology also proposed that different areas of the skull were related to specific behaviors. As described above with Paul Broca's experiments, phrenology anticipated what we today refer to as *localization of function*, the observation that different parts of the brain do indeed appear to play an important role for specific cognitive, emotional, and behavioral functions. Indeed, even though many parts of the brain are involved in most functions, neuroscientists today still subscribe to the idea of localization of function in many ways. Actually, to be precise, with the advent of functional neuroimaging techniques such as functional magnetic resonance imaging (fMRI), neuroscientists have come to see our cognitive, emotional, and behavioral functions as being dependent upon multiple brain regions working together (Cabeza & Moscovitch, 2013). Still, even with respect to the complex interactions among different parts of the brain, distinct structures in the brain do appear to play important, distinct roles. For example, the ventral lateral prefrontal cortex (VLPFC) works with the amygdala when people control their emotions – the VLPFC can dampen the amygdala's automatic responses to emotional stimuli (Ochsner & Gross, 2005); interestingly, the VLPFC also works with the hippocampus when people encode new information into episodic memory – the VLPFC organizes the incoming information that is subsequently stored in the hippocampus (Simons & Spiers, 2003). The point is that in both cases, the VLPFC plays a "control" function, though the way this function is used depends upon the other structures with which VLPFC interacts. Phrenology's adherents did not envision localization of function as we know it today – as a set of neuronal computations that are supported by relatively discrete brain regions – they did not have fMRI equipment, know how neurons work, or even what neurons are. However, their efforts to map distinct operations of the mind to distinct regions of the skull was directionally correct.

In the early 20th century, a German neurologist named Korbinian Brodmann put thin slices of tissue from the cerebral cortex, the outer "bark" of the brain, under a microscope – a technique called *histology*, which allows neuroscientists to examine the cells of the brain. He noticed that tissues from different regions of the cortex differed in their cellular compositions. Painstakingly, Brodmann was able to distinguish 52 separate areas and reasoned that distinct areas may be important for specific tasks. Brodmann's system for classifying different parts of the cortex is still widely used today, though it has been refined several times. However, what is most relevant for the present discussion is that Brodmann's areas and Gall's phrenological bust bear a visual resemblance to each other. The similarities may only be superficial, but they further underscore how prescient the phrenologists were with their proposal of localized functioning, a notion that they shared with Brodmann.

There is yet another way in which Gall and other phrenologists working in the 19th century were surprisingly prescient. They proposed a comprehensive taxonomy of traits for understanding human personality. It would only take more than 100 years before the personality trait researchers would develop consensus on a taxonomy of traits for describing individual differences, the "Big Five" personality traits (Goldberg, 1993). Alternative trait taxonomies continue to be developed and used (Ashton & Lee, 2007), but the bulk of research on personality traits now centers on the Big Five (Soto & John, 2017).

The Big Five personality traits represent one of the most, if not *the* most, psychometrically robust discoveries of the past 50 or so years of psychological science. The most common technique for measuring personality traits is to directly ask people about their typical thoughts, feelings, and behaviors. Using a technique called *factor analysis*, personality psychologists have been able to examine how large numbers of different questionnaire items are interrelated and "group" together under common statistical factors. Over the years, study after study, the results of factor-analytic work repeatedly converged on five broad traits for capturing a large swathe of individual differences – the Big Five traits. Below you will find a brief description for each Big Five trait, and as you read through them, recall some of the traits examined by phrenologists (e.g., cautiousness, friendliness, aptness toward education, compassion, and ambition).

- **Neuroticism:** High scorers tend to be anxious, defensive, and moody; low scorers tend to be relaxed, calm, and easy going.
- **Extraversion:** High scorers tend to be sociable, enthusiastic, and reward-seeking; low scorers tend to be reserved, serious, and passive.
- **Openness:** High scorers tend to be intellectual, curious, and creative; low scorers tend to be traditional and conventional.
- **Agreeableness:** High scorers tend to be compassionate, polite, and helpful; low scorers tend to be tough, demanding, and critical.
- **Conscientiousness:** High scorers tend to be organized, responsible, and achievement-oriented; low scorers tend to be disorganized, forgetful, and leisurely.

The Big Five traits framework is the choice framework of contemporary personality research and a multitude of studies have examined the correlates and outcomes of the Big Five. The Big Five traits are reliably linked to many important life outcomes including occupational success, physical health, relationship quality, and psychological wellness (Soto, 2019).

Research has also begun to examine the neural correlates of the Big Five – and here we find fascinating points of convergence with phrenology. Reviewing this entire body of research is well beyond the scope of this chapter, so we will consider the results from an illustrative study.

Recall that phrenologists believed that one's character traits can be inferred by the size of the bumps on their skull. A larger bump meant that the trait had been "exercised." Structural MRI scans enable modern-day neuroscientists to measure the volumes of different brain regions with exquisite precision. If we are being charitable to phrenology – remember, we are steelmanning! – we may consider such structural imaging scans to be contemporary analogues of what the phrenologists were up to when they measured the size of the bumps on people's skulls.

DeYoung et al. (2010) conducted a structural neuroimaging study to examine how the Big Five traits may be correlated with the volumes of different brain regions. They reasoned that inter-individual variation with respect to each of the Big Five traits would be associated with structural differences in brain regions associated with trait-relevant cognitive, emotional, and behavioral functions. For example, DeYoung et al. hypothesized that Neuroticism would be associated with the volumes of brain regions associated with processing threat and punishments (e.g., regions of the cingulate cortex). The results of their study largely supported their hypotheses. For example, higher scores on Extraversion were found to be positively associated with the volume of the medial orbitofrontal cortex, a region associated with processing rewards; higher scores on Neuroticism were associated with reduced volumes in the hippocampus, which has been previously associated with stress and depression; higher scores on Agreeableness were associated with greater volumes of the superior temporal sulcus, an area associated with interpreting others' actions and intentions; finally, Conscientiousness was positively associated with the volume of the middle frontal gyrus, a structure that is important for carrying out planned actions.

Of course, if we had a time machine to bring phrenologists to the present day and present them with DeYoung et al.' findings, they would not be able to explain these associations – they simply would not know enough about the nature of personality traits or the workings of the brain to make sense of these associations. Still, these covariations between people's scores on the Big Five traits and the brain volumes of distinct regions are a kind of "proof of concept" for the basic phrenological proposition that character traits can be mapped onto different parts of the head. A modern reader may even have some sympathy for old phrenologists: if they had the psychometric tools of modern personality researchers and the neuroimaging technology of today's neuroscientists, their basic ideas may have eventually led them to make similar discoveries.

Understanding Beliefs

Now our steelmanning approach to this chapter must come to an end. Phrenology was always predicated on highly controversial ideas, even in the 19th century. While Gall's lectures attracted much interest from colleagues and the general public who believed in what he had to say, Catholic conservatives of the time objected to the undertones that phrenology supported philosophical determinism and obviated metaphysical notions of the human soul – which implied that even heinous criminal acts could be attributed to faulty brain organization rather than free will, serving to challenge long-held legal precedents (Eling & Finger, 2020). And while Gall knew that phrenology was controversial, he also remained convinced that he was right about his new science, as he believed it was based on sound empirical data as opposed to the armchair philosophizing about the human mind that came before him (Eling & Finger, 2020).

So how did Gall and his followers come to believe so adamantly in their convictions? Well, as with rigid adherence to any pseudoscientific ideology, belief is often underpinned by combinations of myriad, general logical fallacies and cognitive biases, as well as poor science literacy and motivated reasoning processes. But with respect to phrenology, perhaps the strongest bias at play is the illusion of accuracy produced by a method known as cold reading, which capitalizes on the Barnum effect: the tendency for people to accept vague statements as representitive of their unique traits (Dickson & Kelly, 1985; Novella, 2000).

More specifically, cold reading is a technique that involves making general statements about a target subject that are likely to be somewhat true of almost anyone (Novella, 2000). A dynamic cold reading (e.g., in a psychic reading) uses feedback from the subject to make increasingly more accurate and specific claims that focus on the hits and ignore the misses, so to speak, whereas a static cold reading (e.g., in an astrological chart, fortune cookie, or palm reading) uses a limited set of pre-written statements concerning the subject, such as "You like to be admired by others" or "Sometimes you're forgetful" (Novella, 2000). Phrenology cold readings could be practiced both dynamically and statically. In dynamic readings, phrenologists read the bumps on a subject's skull with their hands, allowing for the process of dialogue, feedback, and refinement. An interesting application of phrenological cold static readings was the invention of the psychograph in 1931 by Henry C. Lavery, which was an automated machine that made 32 skull measurements to produce a set of statements that were selected from 160 different possibilities and printed on small pieces of ticker tape (Novella, 2000). Whether dynamic or static, cold readings can be so powerful that they not only fool the subject, but phrenologist as well, as illusions of accurate feedback become mutually and positively reinforced.

Belief in phrenology is not and has not been innocuous. In the broadest sense, belief in pseudoscientific systems can be harmful via their exploitative deprivation of time and financial resources from supported systems, as well as their complicity in the erosion and trust of the scientific enterprise (Lilienfeld et al., 2015). Unfortunately, belief in phrenology more specifically was also directly harmful, as its tenets were used to justify scientific racism ideology, such as genocide and Nazi eugenics (Andre, 2018; Bank, 1996; Hilts, 1982).

Phrenology and Racism

As phrenological science developed, it became heavily influenced by societal beliefs and used in many cases to reinforce them. No greater example of this reciprocal bias exists than the use of phrenology to justify racist beliefs, segregations, and slavery. One of the largest proponents of phrenology in America, Orson Fowler, published a textbook entitled *Self Instructor in Phrenology and Physiology*, complete with diagrams of cranial proportions that emphasized racial stereotypes (Fowler, 1849). He wrote extensively about various measurements and the implications of these on what were essentially the ethnocentric views of his time. Declaring phrenology a "universal fact," he had stereotyped cartoons which explained the inferiority of nonwhite races and emphasized white superiority. On the basis of these measurements, and after making other extremely offensive remarks about other races, Fowler wrote that "the Caucasian race is superior in reasoning power and moral elevation to all the other races, and, accordingly, has a higher and bolder forehead, and more elevated and elongated top-head" (p. 72). This is just one example of many racist quotes that can be attributed to Fowler.

Similarly, in his book, James Montgomery argued that the historical discoveries and accomplishments of Hindu and African people contradicted the pronouncements of phrenologists on racial limitations (Montgomery & Thompson, 1829). In doing so, he made many racist claims. For example, when talking about Hindu people, he wrote that based on "the recession of the forehead ... a skillful phrenologist might be tempted to pronounce it the head of some nondescript animal, approaching to humanity, but far inferior, not to the European only, but to any other species of genuine men" (p. 398). Also, the American physician Charles Caldwell expressed extreme African inferiority in his *Elements of Phrenology* (1827), writing that the "African figure occupies an intermediate station between the figure of the Caucasian and the Ourangoutang" (p. 253; see also Branson, 2017).

As slavery and anti-slavery debates raged in the Americas in the 1800s, phrenological arguments were used to both justify and refute the inferiority of those of African descent (Hamilton, 2008). Phrenology had captured both a broad general and popular foothold, and discussions using phrenological concepts were used to emphasize the importance of racial distinctions but also the concept of education and environment influencing a person's development and capabilities. In arguing for abolition, Vermont Governor William Slade challenged the application of the science of phrenology to the debate by stating: "The science of phrenology ... in its present and imperfect state ... can hardly be trusted with so grave a matter as this ..." (p. 5; Union Herald, 1838). Overall, phrenology serves as an early example of a harmful pseudoscience and also an early opportunity for skepticism.

Summary and Conclusion

Phrenology is often used as a textbook example of a pseudoscience. The scientific evidence against its tenets unequivocally undermines its credibility as a reliable and valid scientific system. And yet, at its broadest level of analysis, phrenology foreshadowed ideas in personality psychology and neuroscience insofar as there exists support for relationships between individual differences and brain morphology. While phrenology is easily dismissed as a fad of antiquity, it had influences in the development of psychology, criminology, health care, and neurology. Its rich history also contains a powerful message about how pseudoscience can be abused to justify nefarious ideologies. It is important to understand these historical roots and connections, as they laid some of the groundwork of the very institutions that still harbor institutional and systemic racism to this day.

References

Andre, C. (2018). Phrenology and the Rwandan genocide. *Arquivos de Neuro-Psiquiatra, 76*, 277–282.

Ashton, M. C., & Lee, K. (2007). Empirical, theoretical, and practical advantages of the HEXACO model of personality structure. *Personality and Social Psychology Review, 11*, 150–166. doi:10.1177/ 1088868306294907

Bank, A. (1996). Of 'native skulls' and 'noble Caucasians': Phrenology in colonial South Africa. *Journal of Southern African Studies, 22*, 387–403.

Bittel, C. (2019). Testing the truth of phrenology: Knowledge experiments in Antebellum American cultures of Science and Health. *Medical History, 63*, 352–374.

Branson, S. (2017). Phrenology and the science of race in antebellum America. *Early American Studies, 15*(1), 164–193.

Broca, P. (1861). Remarques sur le siege de la faculte du langage articule; suivies d'une observation d'aphemie (perte de la parole). *Bulletins de La Societe Anatomique (Paris), 6*, 330–357, 398–407.

Cabeza, R., & Moscovitch, M. (2013). Memory systems, processing modes, and components: Functional neuroimaging evidence. *Perspectives on Psychological Science, 8*(1), 49–55. doi:10.1177/1745691612469033

DeYoung, C. G., Hirsh, J. B., Shane, M. S., Papademetris, X., Rajeevan, N., & Gray, J. R. (2010). Testing predictions from personality neuroscience: Brain structure and the Big Five. *Psychological Science, 21*, 820–828.

Dickson, D. H., & Kelly, I. W. (1985). The "Barnum effect" in personality assessment: A review of the literature. *Psychological Reports, 57*, 367–382.

Eling, P., & Finger, S. (2020). Gall and phrenology: New perspectives. *Journal of the History of the Neurosciences, 29*, 1–4.

Finger, S. (2019). Mark Twain's life-long fascination with phrenology. *Journal of the History of the Behavioral Sciences, 55*, 99–121.

Fowler, O. S. (1849). *Self-instructor in phrenology and physiology*. Fowler and Wells.

Fowler, O. S., & Fowler, L. N. (1859). *The illustrated self-instructor in phrenology and physiology*. Fowler and Wells Publishers.

Goldberg, L. R. (1993). The structure of phenotypic personality traits. *American Psychologist, 48*(1), 26–34. doi:10.1037/0003-066X.48.1.26

Hamilton, C. S. (2008). Am I not a man and a brother?' Phrenology and anti-slavery. *Slavery and Abolition, 29*, 173–187.

Hilts, V. L. (1982). Obeying the laws of hereditary descent: Phrenological views on inheritance and eugenics. *Journal of the History of the Behavioral Sciences, 18*, 62–77.

Holmes, D. G. (2016). Breaking the chains of science: The rhetoric of empirical racism in Django Unchained. *Black Camera, 7*, 73–78.

Lilienfeld, S. O., Lynn, S. J., & Lohr, J. M. (Eds.). (2015). *Science and pseudoscience in clinical psychology* (2nd edition). The Guilford Press.

Montgomery, J., & Thompson, C. (1829). *An essay on the phrenology of the Hindoos and Negroes*. E. Lloyd.

Novella, S. (2000). Phrenology: History of a pseudoscience. *The New England Skeptical Society.* Retrieved from https://theness.com/index.php/phrenology-history-of-a-pseudoscience/

Ochsner, K. N., & Gross, J. J. (2005). The cognitive control of emotion. *Trends in Cognitive Sciences, 9*, 242–249.

Parker Jones, O., Alfaro-Almagro, F., & Jbabdi, S. (2018). An empirical, 21st century evaluation of phrenology. *Cortex, 106*, 26–35.

Renneville, M. (2020). Matter over mind? The rise and fall of phrenology in nineteenth-century France. *Journal of the History of the Neurosciences, 29*, 17–28.

Scherlinder Morse, M. (1997). Facing a bumpy history: The much-maligned theory of phrenology gets a tip of the hat from modern neuroscience. *Smithsonian Magazine.* Retrieved from https://www.smithsonianmag.com/history/facing-a-bumpy-history-144497373/

Simons, J. S., & Spiers, H. J. (2003). Prefrontal and medial temporal lobe interactions in long-term memory. *Nature Reviews Neuroscience, 4*, 637–648.

Soto, C. J. (2019). How replicable are links between personality traits and consequential life outcomes? The Life Outcomes of Personality Replication Project. *Psychological Science, 30*, 711–727.

Soto, C. J., & John, O. P. (2017). Short and extra-short forms of the Big Five Inventory–2: The BFI-2-S and BFI-2-XS. *Journal of Research in Personality, 68*, 69–81.

Twain, M. (2013). *Autobiography of Mark Twain* (Vol. 2). Edited by B. Griffin & H. E. Smith. Berkeley, CA: University of California Press.

Union Herald. (May 18, 1838). *Anti-slavery speech of Mr. Slade of Vermont, on the abolition of slavery and the slave trade in the District of Columbia.* Delivered in the House of Representatives of the U.S., December 20, 1837. Cazenovia, NY.

Van den Bossche, P. (1998). The loose foundations of criticism against phrenology. Retrieved from https://www.phrenology.org/kritiek.html

Yildirum, F. B., & Sarikcioglu, L. (2007). Marie Jean Pierre Flourens (1974-1867): An extraordinary scientist of his time. *Journal of Neurology, Neurosurgery, and Psychiatry, 78,* 852.

3 Extrasensory Perception, Psychokinesis, and Sensation

James E. Alcock

The conversation lulls as Harry and Martha stroll down a busy street. For no particular reason, Harry begins to think about the beach party they attended in Jamaica a decade earlier and the man from the Bronx who collapsed in a gale of laughter while trying to dance under a limbo stick. He is about to ask Martha if she remembers this character when she poses that very same question first! Unable to think of any rational explanation, they conclude that they have experienced extrasensory perception (ESP).

Rebecca visits her elderly uncle, who looks fine and reports being in good health. That night, she dreams about his death only to be stunned in the morning to learn that he had died in his sleep. Absent any rational explanation, she too concludes that she has experienced ESP.

And at a casino, Peter urges a spinning roulette ball to land on red, and it does! Although he "doesn't really" believe in psychokinesis, he repeats his urging on the next spin of the wheel.

Belief in *extrasensory perception* – mind to mind communication (telepathy), exploration of objects hidden from view (clairvoyance), foreseeing the future (precognition) – and *psychokinesis* – influencing objects through "mind power" alone – is widespread among the public. This chapter will examine the evidence regarding beliefs like these, with an emphasis on claims related to ESP and psychokinesis.

Examining the Claims

Formal efforts to use science to demonstrate the reality of the paranormal were triggered, somewhat ironically, by scientific discoveries such as Darwin's theory of evolution that threw post-mortem survival into doubt. This aroused existential anxiety in many people, among them esteemed Cambridge philosopher Henry Sidgwick who, although having abandoned the religion in which he had been reared, continued to believe in post-mortem survival. He argued that there can be no basis for a moral system of values without an afterlife in which rewards and punishments are meted out. He was impressed by the power of science and was determined to use it to prove that we survive bodily death (Cerullo, 1982). Spiritualism was sweeping the Western world at the time, and its claims that mediums could communicate with the dead offered a promising avenue of research. And so, in 1882, Sidgwick, along with Cambridge scholars Frederic Myers and Edmund Gurney and several spiritualists, established the *Society for Psychical Research* with the specific goal of putting post-mortem survival on a scientific footing. Proving the reality of ESP was considered an important steppingstone that would demonstrate the separate existence of body and mind.

DOI: 10.4324/9781003107798-3

Early research focused on the collection and analysis of anecdotal reports of telepathic experiences, precognitions, and other paranormal experiences (Myers et al., 1886). However, critics were not impressed by this evidence, considering the reports unreliable because of likely distortions of memory, the lack of corroborating evidence, and the scant attention paid to the possible role of perceptual illusions, dream states, and even deception. Ultimately, the researchers themselves came to recognize the unreliability of anecdotal evidence. Studies of communication with the dead also led to disappointment, for mediums were either unable to produce their feats under controlled conditions or were caught cheating. However, the researchers did not give up.

Enter American botanist, Joseph Banks Rhine. Like Sidgwick, he viewed the religion in which he had been reared as little more than mythology but could not accept a strictly materialistic view of the world. And again, like Sidgwick, he wanted to put post-mortem survival on a scientific footing and considered the demonstration of the reality of ESP as an important first step. Impressed by the progress that psychologists were making through statistical analysis of data from laboratory experiments, he established a para-psychology laboratory in 1930 with the intent to harness psychological methodology in the study of the paranormal.

Psychological experiments typically involve comparisons of data from an experimental group and a control group, but adapting this methodology to parapsychology was not straightforward. Rhine recognized that it was not possible to set up a "no-ESP/ psychokinesis" control group given the belief that ESP and psychokinesis cannot be blocked by any known barrier. Nor can control group participants be instructed to "turn off" such abilities, for it was believed that they can operate without conscious intent or awareness. Rhine's solution was to employ chance itself to provide the necessary comparison, and he developed forced-choice guessing tasks that allowed contrasting a participant's success rate with what would be expected by chance alone. Thus, a "sender" concentrates on one of a limited number of targets and a "receiver" makes a guess about that target, or a participant predicts (precognition) or attempts to influence (psychokinesis) the throw of a die. A success rate significantly higher (or lower) than chance expectation is then taken to reflect a paranormal influence. In addition, mirroring the approach of mainstream psychology, researchers systematically varied experimental conditions in the search for factors that might influence the occurrence of such phenomena.

Elegant in its simplicity, this methodology became the dominant approach in para-psychology. Thus, the research focus shifted from reports of emotionally powerful and personal "psychic" experiences to laboratory tasks in which the participants, even when scoring significantly above or below chance, are unable to identify which "hits" are attributable to ESP or psychokinesis and which only to chance. Early studies had involved using ordinary playing cards as targets, with the sender focusing on a randomly chosen card and the receiver reporting whatever card came to mind. However, Rhine recognized a potential bias: because of past experience with playing cards, some cards (for example, Ace of spades or Queen of hearts) are more likely to come spontaneously to a receiver's mind than others, thereby distorting the statistical analysis of outcomes. Rhine's colleague Karl Zener presented a solution: a deck of 25 cards, five each bearing either a circle, a star, a square, a cross, or wavy lines (see Image 3.1). This "Zener deck" overcame the problem of familiarity and bias, while also greatly simplifying the statistical analysis of results. While the Zener deck played a mainstay role in parapsychological research for many years, card guessing and dice-rolling eventually fell out of favor as a number of new paradigms emerged.

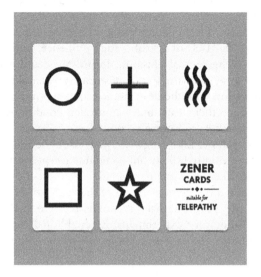

Image 3.1 Zener Cards [credit: Shutterstock].

Evidence for the Paranormal

By the mid-1930s, Rhine was confident that he had scientifically confirmed the existence of ESP and psychokinesis (Rhine, 1934), but critics were unconvinced and pointed to significant flaws and weaknesses in his methodology. Although his use of cards and dice now seems simplistic and his data are rarely cited as evidence of the paranormal, there has been a succession of other supposed "breakthroughs" in the quest to establish the reality of ESP and psychokinesis, including the following.

In the 1930s, British mathematician S. G. Soal became a harsh critic of parapsychological research after failing to find evidence of psychic ability in his own large series of studies using methodology similar to Rhine's. However, persuaded to take up this research again in the early 1940s, and employing procedures described as tightly controlled and fraud-proof, he produced what appeared to be outstanding evidence of ESP. His findings were even more persuasive in light of his former skepticism. However, subsequent investigation revealed that his impressive data had been generated through simple but clever fraud (Marwick, 1978).

In the 1970s, physicists Russell Targ and Hal Puthoff conducted a series of *remote-viewing* (essentially, ESP) studies in which a participant wandered about a randomly selected geographical site while another remained at the laboratory and described whatever images came to mind, with the goal of demonstrating some kind of mind-to-mind transfer of information. After a series of such trials, judges assessed the correspondence between the reported mentations and the targets. The procedures were claimed to be extremely well-controlled, and remarkable results were reported as evidence of ESP (Targ & Puthoff, 1975; Tart et al., 1980). However, when other researchers were finally able to assess the raw data, serious methodological flaws were identified that were able to account for the above-chance results (Marks & Kamman, 1980).

From the late 60s through to the early 80s, physicist Helmut Schmidt studied the ability of participants (human, animal, and even insect!) to predict or influence the radioactive emission of subatomic particles. His investigations initially won high regard from other parapsychologists (Beloff, 1980). However, careful examination revealed a disjointed research program rife with flawed methodology, belying his claims of having demonstrated ESP and psychokinesis (Alcock, 1987).

Beginning in 1979, physicist Robert Jahn supervised a long series of studies that convinced him that he had established the reality of paranormal phenomena. But once again, careful scrutiny revealed several serious flaws in his methodology, including poor control against cheating (Alcock, 1987; Hansen et al., 1992; Palmer, 1985).

Another major methodological initiative, one still in use, involves the *Ganzfeld* technique through which normal sensory stimulation is reduced to a minimum to allow greater sensitivity to possible psychic influences in an ESP experiment. This typically involves seating a participant in a comfortable chair in a quiet room, wearing earphones that carry white noise, and with eyes covered by half ping-pong balls illuminated by soft lighting. Charles Honorton conducted a large series of Ganzfeld studies and, after combining the results through meta-analysis, he concluded that he had demonstrated ESP beyond any reasonable doubt. However, an extensive critical review of all available Ganzfeld research, including Honorton's, revealed significant methodological flaws in all the studies, leading to the conclusion that Ganzfeld research had failed to demonstrate the reality of ESP (Hyman, 1985). Honorton disputed that conclusion but later prepared a joint paper with Hyman (Hyman & Honorton, 1986) in which the two agreed upon specific methodological criteria for future Ganzfeld research. Honorton continued his research until his premature death, after which psychologist Darryl Bem, confident that Honorton had indeed established the reality of ESP, published his research in a major psychological journal (Bem & Honorton, 1994). Hyman (1994) again responded with cogent criticism, pointing to a number of important inconsistencies with Honorton's earlier findings. Several meta-analyses were subsequently conducted in the attempt to replicate the results of Bem and Honorton (1994). Some analyses (Milton & Wiseman, 1999; Ritchie et al., 2012) found no effect, although there were others that reported successful replication (Storm & Ertel, 2001).

Bem (2011) subsequently published his own parapsychological research in another mainstream psychological journal. He claimed to have demonstrated, among other amazing things, that events in the present can be influenced by actions one takes in the future! However, a number of attempts to replicate ended in failure (Galak et al., 2012; Ritchie et al., 2012) and close examination of his methodology revealed an astonishing number of fundamental flaws (Alcock, 2011a, 2011b). Bem initially rejected all criticism, but later conceded that he viewed his experiments only as "rhetorical devices," adding that he was not concerned about rigor (Engber, 2017). Bem subsequently carried out two large-scale attempts at replication, both of which failed (Schlitz et al., 2021).

Cardeña (2018) reviewed a wide swath of parapsychological research that included Bem's. Again relying heavily on meta-analysis, he argued that the evidence for ESP and other psychic abilities is comparable to that for established phenomena in psychology and other disciplines. However, critics rejected that conclusion (Reber & Alcock, 2020). First of all, meta-analysis is a very unreliable tool, since weaknesses in individual studies cannot be eliminated by examining them as a group (Ioannidis, 2016). In addition, phenomena that are considered established in psychology and other disciplines fit well within a well-tested scientific framework, rather than standing in gross exception to it as is the case with parapsychology.

This reflects an overall pattern in parapsychology. A new methodology appears impressive at first but gradually loses its shine as its shortcomings became apparent, although that may take years. It is then replaced by another new and promising methodology, and the cycle continues.

Reasons for Skepticism

Repeatability is a keystone of laboratory science, providing a check against sloppy research, self-delusion, and fraud. However, in the near century since Rhine began his experimental research, there has yet to be a single demonstration of ESP, psychokinesis, or other psychic phenomenon that can be reliably replicated by neutral scientists. As a result, the larger scientific world remains as doubtful about the reality of paranormal phenomena as it was when Rhine began. As damning as this is, there are other important reasons to doubt the reality of paranormal phenomena (Alcock, 2003).

Murky concept. The entire concept of ESP, psychokinesis, and other psychic phenomena is extremely problematic. Unlike the concepts of mainstream science, paranormal phenomena are defined only negatively; for example, information transfer is deemed to be ESP only if all normal means can be ruled out. Yet, one can never be certain of having eliminated all possible flaws and biases. In addition, one cannot clearly distinguish various forms of ESP from psychokinesis and from each other. For example, is the receiver in a telepathy experiment receiving information from the sender, or instead using clairvoyance to see the target list? Or is the receiver employing precognition to foresee the target sequence that will be presented to the sender? And is a participant predicting the outcomes of a random event generator through precognition, or using psychokinesis to influence those outcomes?

Murky data. Statistical analysis of the correspondence between two sets of data is central to parapsychological research: How well do a receiver's responses correspond with the sender's targets? How well do a participant's attempts at psychokinesis correspond to the outcomes of a random process? Above chance (or below chance) scoring rates are taken to reflect the operation of ESP or psychokinesis. However, a statistical difference says nothing about the *cause* of the difference. While parapsychologists attribute it to a paranormal influence, it may simply be due to unrecognized methodological flaws or the vagaries of chance itself.

Given the large numbers of trials typically used by these researchers, even a tiny bias in the methodology is enough to produce statistical significance. And consider the pattern of results that would be expected if paranormal phenomena do *not* exist and methodological flaws alone are responsible for the observed statistical deviations. In that case, no barrier of any kind between sender and receiver or between participant and random event generator would have any effect. It would make no difference whether sender and receiver know each other's location, nor would knowing the location of a random event generator be necessary in precognition or psychokinesis experiments. Distance between sender and target would have no effect and it would make no difference whether the presumed influence is operating in the present, the past, or the future. It would not matter (harking back to Helmut Schmidt's research) whether the participants were human, animal, or even insect. Improving the methodology by tightening the conditions to minimize the possibility of error would lead to a diminution of observed statistical effect size. And of course, all of this is descriptive of parapsychological findings across the decades.

Murky theory. In mainstream science, phenomena are circumscribed by identification of their causal links with observable effects. No such links have been established in parapsychology (Reber & Alcock, 2020). There is no well-defined theory that predicts or accommodates paranormal phenomena, and while some parapsychologists have sought to bend interpretations of quantum mechanical theory to allow for the paranormal, such interpretations run counter to mainstream scientific understanding. Other theoretical efforts to explain paranormal have been made, for example, in terms of dissociated "thought-forms" that can develop an autonomous existence (Parker, 2021). Fascinating as these attempts are, they remain only speculations in the absence of reliable data to support them.

Modern science generally relies upon hypotheses that are falsifiable, but parapsychologists cannot suggest any pattern of empirical outcomes that would dampen their belief in the paranormal. Failures to find supportive evidence are explained away in terms of ad hoc labels that are then taken to represent characteristics of the psychic phenomena. For example, when a parapsychologist repeats another's experiment and fails to obtain similar results, this does not weaken confidence in the original finding. Instead, it is concluded that this failure to replicate is evidence of a characteristic of the paranormal, the *experimenter-psi effect* through which experimenters' personalities or even their own psychic abilities are said to play a key role in the outcome.

Murky boundaries. Parapsychological processes apparently have no limits, and as a result, parapsychologists cannot tell us when paranormal events will *not* occur. That being said, there is one domain that has proven completely immune to paranormal influence: the laboratories of mainstream science. Were psychic phenomena such as ESP real, one would expect that the expectations and motivations of individual scientists would bring some psychic influence to the extremely delicate and precise experiments of modern physics, something that has never been observed.

Inconsistency with mainstream science. Biology does not contradict physics. Chemistry is not at odds with genetics. However, claims of ESP are completely inconsistent with well-established findings in normal science, and if the claims of parapsychology are true, much of modern science is simply wrong. While that is possible, it is unlikely, and the insubstantial evidence provided by parapsychologists is no match for the large pool of strongly replicable data of mainstream science (Reber & Alcock, 2020).

Lack of interest in normal explanations. When scientific efforts to find evidence of ESP and other psychic phenomena began in the 1880s, very little was known about the functioning of the brain. Perception was assumed to be veridical, and memory was viewed as a reliable record of experienced events. Today, we know that nonconscious influences play a huge role in thinking, perception, and memory, and that at times we are incapable of distinguishing between stimulation from the outside world and that originating in another part of own brains. Yet, parapsychologists show virtually no interest in exploring normal explanations of supposedly paranormal phenomena.

Lack of progress. Except for parapsychology, every research domain that claims scientific status progresses over time. Constructs become more sharply defined, methodologies are improved, theories are expanded, greater effect sizes are produced, and repeatability is increased. Parapsychology's failure is not because it deals with difficult-to-detect and imagination-defying phenomena. Physicists, during the 140 years that parapsychologists have conducted formal research, have made enormous progress in understanding their own difficult-to-detect and imagination-defying phenomena, among them radio wave transmission (1886); X-rays (1895); radioactivity (1896); the electron (1897); radioactive elements radium and polonium (1898); alpha and beta particles (1899); general relativity (1916); the proton (1919); the neutron (1932); the anti-electron (positron, 1932); cosmic radio waves (1933); "artificial radiation" (positron emission, 1934); microwave background radiation from the Big Bang (1965); quantum teleportation (1992); the neutrino mass (1998); the Higgs boson (2012); gravitational waves (2015); and the demonstration of quantum entanglement (2015). And during all that research, using the most sensitive of instruments, there has never been a hint of anything paranormal.

Understanding Beliefs

Paranormal belief is rooted in both personal experience and culturally shared folk knowledge. It is relatively easy to understand why such belief is widespread among the public, given how it is reified by much of the media. Books, movies, television, and the Internet often promote paranormal belief, and their impact is even greater when it jibes with personal experience (Sparks & Miller, 2001). In recent years, a new genre of reality TV, "paranormal television" that claims to present factual investigations of ghosts and other paranormal phenomena has become popular. Even though the methodology depicted typically reflects ignorance or even rejection of sound science, its producers strive to make it appear "sciencey" (Hill, 2017), for mimicking science provides a false sense of legitimacy that enhances a program's appeal (Blancke et al., 2017).

But an even more important contributor to belief in the paranormal is the fact that most people, given that the way our brains work, are likely to have experiences from time to time that *seem* to be paranormal (Alcock, 1981, 2018). As noted earlier, one reason for this is that not all information from the outside world is processed consciously, and non-conscious influences can mislead us into thinking that we have experienced ESP. Recall the opening examples: perhaps the same limbo music that Harry and Martha heard at the beach party was playing over a music store's loudspeakers as they strolled down the street, but they were not consciously aware of it because it was mixed in with background street noise. However, enough information reached their ears to trigger similar memory streams in each of them, and so it is not so surprising that they both think of the limbo incident at about the same time. And as for Rebecca, perhaps her brain picked up that her uncle did not smile as much as usual or that his breathing was a little labored but she was not conscious of this observation, leaving her feeling slightly anxious but unclear as to why. This low-level anxiety may have triggered the dream of his demise. As for Peter and the roulette wheel, our brains automatically associate events that occur closely together in time, leaving us vulnerable to causal inferences when only coincidence is at play. Other seemingly paranormal phenomena such as out-of-body experiences or apparitions can occur naturally when perceptions originating in another part of the brain are mistakenly perceived as coming from the outside world. Individuals with a deficit in reality testing are more vulnerable to such errors (Dagnall et al., 2010).

But how do parapsychologists maintain their belief in the face of continuing rejection by mainstream science? Cognitive dissonance is reduced through a variety of assertions, such as that this lack of acceptance is due to "gatekeeper" skeptics who persuade scientists that parapsychology does not merit consideration; or that scientists shun parapsychology for fear of losing the respect of their colleagues (Tart, 2016); or that scientists deliberately avoid examining phenomena that threaten the current scientific model; or that paranormal phenomena are capricious, making them difficult to capture in a laboratory and suggesting that the experimental controls of normal science are not appropriate. Some even suggest that scientists' skepticism reflects an emotional stance akin to religious conviction (Targ & Harary, 1984), that scientists deny the existence of ESP because they fear the implications of telepathic influence (Braude, 1993), or that their denial stems from having suppressed their own ESP in childhood because of the distress experienced upon telepathically sensing their mother's anger underlying her kindly outward presentation (Tart, 1982, 1984). Such ad hominem characterizations are unhelpful in the evaluation of parapsychological claims.

Summary and Conclusion

While normal science is driven forward both by well-articulated theory and by reliable data that challenge such theory, parapsychology is based only on the earnest convictions of its researchers that paranormal phenomena exist. However, their efforts over the past 140 years have failed to yield even a single demonstration that is repeatable by neutral scientists.

However, belief in the paranormal is unlikely to go away anytime soon. Because of the many non-conscious influences on perception and cognition, we are all vulnerable to baffling experiences that seem to call for a paranormal explanation. In consequence, it is all too easy to fall into the nominal fallacy of assigning a label such as ESP to the experience and then using the label to *explain* the experience.

Personal experience is at times a very poor guide to reality, and historical recognition of that fact led to efforts to find methods to minimize error and self-delusion, which paved the way for the development of modern science. Parapsychology runs in the opposite direction, giving precedence to experience. It is a case of belief in search of supportive data rather than reliable data in search of explanation.

References

Alcock, J. E. (1981). *Parapsychology: Science or magic?* Oxford: Pergamon Press.

Alcock, J. E. (1987). A comprehensive review of major empirical studies in parapsychology involving random event generators and remote viewing. In D. Druckman & J. Swets (Eds.), *Enhancing human performance: Issues, theories and techniques* (Vol. 2). Washington, DC: National Academy Press.

Alcock, J. E. (2003). Give the null hypothesis a chance: Reasons to remain doubtful about the existence of psi. *Journal of Consciousness Studies, 10,* 29–50.

Alcock, J. E. (2011a). Back from the future: Parapsychology and the Bem Affair. *Skeptical Inquirer, 35,* 31–39.

Alcock, J. E. (2011b). Response to Bem's comments. *Skeptical Inquirer* [online]. https://skepticalinquirer.org/exclusive/response-to-bems-comments/

Alcock, J. E. (2018). *Belief: What it means to believe and why our convictions are so compelling.* Amherst, NY: Prometheus Books.

Beloff, J. (1980). Seven evidential experiments. *Zetetic Scholar, 6,* 91–94.

Bem, D. J. (2011). Feeling the future: Experimental evidence for anomalous retroactive influences on cognition and affect. *Journal of Personality and Social Psychology, 100*(3), 407–425.

Bem, D. J., & Honorton, C. (1994). Does psi exist? Replicable evidence for an anomalous process of information transfer. *Psychological Bulletin, 115,* 4–18.

Blancke, S., Boudry, M., & Pigliucci, M. (2017). Why do irrational beliefs mimic science? The cultural evolution of pseudoscience. *Theoria*, *83*, 78–97.

Braude, S. E. (1993). The fear of psi revisited, or it's the thought that counts. *ASPR Newsletter*, *XVIII* (1), 8–11.

Cardeña, E. (2018). The experimental evidence for parapsychological phenomena: A review. *American Psychologist*, *73*(5), 663–677.

Cerullo, J. (1982). *The secularization of the soul*. Philadelphia: Institute for the Study of Human Issues.

Dagnall N., Drinkwater, K., Parker, A., & Munley, G. (2010). Reality testing, belief in the paranormal and urban legends. *European Journal of Parapsychology*, *25*, 25–55.

Engber, D. (2017, May 17). Daryl Bem proved ESP is real: Which means science is broken. Retrieved from https://slate.com/health-and-science/2017/06/daryl-bem-proved-esp-is-real-showed-science-is-broken.html

Galak, J., LeBoeuf, R. A., Nelson, L. D., & Simmons, J. P. (2012). Correcting the past: Failures to replicate. *Journal of Personality and Social Psychology*, *103*(6), 933–948.

Gardner, M. (1957). *Fads and fallacies in the name of science*. New York: Dover.

Gurney, E., Myers, F. W. H., & Podmore, F. (1886). Phantasms of the living (2 vols.). Trübner.

Harris, W. S., Gowda, M., Kolb, J. W., Strychacz, C. P., Vacek, J. L., Jones, P. G., Forker, A., O'Keefe, J. H., & McCallister, B. D.,(1999). A randomized, controlled trial of the effects of remote, intercessory prayer on outcomes in patients admitted to the coronary care unit. *Archives of Internal Medicine*, *159*, 2273–2278.

Hansen, G. P., Utts, J., & Markwick, B. (1992).Critique of the PEAR remote-viewing experiments. *The Journal of Parapsychology*, 56(2), 97–113.

Hill, S. A. (2017). *Scientific Americans: The culture of amateur paranormal researchers*. Jefferson, NC: McFarland.

Hyman, R. (1985). The ganzfeld psi experiment: A critical appraisal. *Journal of Parapsychology*, *49*, 3–49.

Hyman, R. (1994). Anomaly or artifact? Comments on Bern and Honorton. *Psychological Bulletin*, *115*, 19–24.

Hyman, R., & Honorton, C. (1986). A joint communiqué: The psi ganzfeld controversy. *Journal of Parapsychology*, *50*, 351–364.

Ioannidis, J. P. A. (2016). The mass production of redundant, misleading, and conflicted systematic reviews and meta-analyses. *The Milbank Quarterly*, *94*(3), 45–514.

Marks, D., & Kamman, R. (1980). *The psychology of the psychic*. Buffalo, NY: Prometheus Books.

Marwick, B. (1978). The Soal-Goldney experiments with Basil Shackleton: New evidence of data manipulation. *Proceedings of the Society for Psychical Research*, *56*, 250–280.

Milton, J., & Wiseman, R. (1999). Does psi exist? Lack of replication of an anomalous process of information transfer. *Psychological Bulletin*, *125*(4), 387–391.

Palmer, J. (1985). An evaluative report on the current status of parapsychology. Prepared for the United States Army Research Institute for the Behavioral and Social Sciences.

Parker, A. (2021). Thought-forms gone rogue. A theory for psi-critics and parapsychologists. *Journal of Scientific Exploration*, *85*, 55–132.

Reber, A. S., & Alcock, J. E. (2020). Searching for the impossible: Parapsychology's elusive quest. *American Psychologist*, *75*(3), 391–399.

Rhine, J. B. (1934). *Extra-sensory perception*. Boston: Boston Society for Psychic Research.

Ritchie, S. J., Wiseman, R., & French, C. C. (2012). Failing the future: Three unsuccessful attempts to replicate Bem's 'retroactive facilitation of recall' effect. *PloS One*, 7 (3), e33423.

Schlitz, M., Bem, D. *et al.* (2021). Two replication studies of a time-reversed (psi) priming task and the role of expectancy in reaction times. *Journal of Scientific Exploration*, *35* (1), 65–90.

Sparks, G. G., & Miller, W. (2001). Investigating the relationship between exposure to television programs that depict paranormal phenomena and beliefs in the paranormal. *Communication Monographs*, *68* (1), 98–113.

Storm, L., & Ertel, S. (2001). Does psi exist? Comments on Milton and Wiseman's (1999) meta-analysis of Ganzfeld research. *Psychological Bulletin*, *127*(3), 424–433.

Targ, R., & Harary, K. (1984). *The mind race*. New York: Random House.

Targ, R., & Puthoff, H. (1975). Information transfer under conditions of sensory shielding. *Nature, 251*, 602–607.

Tart, C. (1982). The controversy about psi: Two psychological theories. *Journal of Parapsychology, 46*, 313–320.

Tart, C. (1984). Acknowledging and dealing with the fear of psi. *Journal of the American Society for Psychical Research, 78*, 133–143.

Tart, C. T. (2016, November 9). Fear of psi: An interview. *New thinking allowed foundation*. https://www.newthinkingallowed.org/fear-of-psi-with-charles-t-tart/

Tart, C., Puthoff, H., & Targ, R. (1980). Information transmission in remote viewing experiments. *Nature, 284*, 191.

4 Dream Interpretation and Consciousness

Caleb W. Lack

For about two decades, I have had a reoccurring dream. In it, I am driving a vehicle down a perfectly normal road, and then I start to cross a very tall bridge suspended over a body of water. As I drive across, my hands slowly turn the steering wheel to the right, against my own will. Panicked, I try to force them to turn back to the left, away from the edge of the bridge, but it doesn't work. Next thing I know, the car – with me inside – crashes through the side of the bridge and starts slow-motion diving toward the water. My hands are still locked on the steering wheel, and all I can do is watch as the water gets closer … and closer … and closer … and then I inevitably wake up right before I hit the water, startled, my heart racing, and covered in sweat. Why do I have this dream over and over again? What does it mean about me, my future, or my loved ones? Or does it even mean anything at all? The answer to those questions varies widely, depending on who you ask, and when you might have asked them.

Having your dreams decoded and explained has never been easier than it is in the 21st century. A quick Google search for "dream interpretation" yields countless websites promising to tell you what the most common dreams mean (Regan, 2021), the "secret meaning" of them (Daniel, 2021), or even providing an entire "dream dictionary" at your fingertips. A trip to the library will turn up dozens of books promising to decode your dreams, you can download apps and podcasts to help you figure out what they mean, or you can see someone in person to help you understand the meanings of your dreams.

Or, that's how the story goes, anyway.

Examining the Claims

It turns out that dreams, dreaming, and figuring out what they mean is a lot more complicated than just opening up an app or a dream dictionary and going "I knew that dreaming of an out-of-control car meant I don't have enough control over my road to success and that I need to allow my fundamental instincts and drives steer the best path for me!" (that is, by the way, a common interpretation of my reoccurring dream). But apparently a bridge means you need to make a change, and falling means I am holding on too tight to something and need to relax, but falling into water means there might be a sudden change in my life soon. So, for 20 years, I have been needing and having sudden changes in my life and I need to just relax and let my instincts help me ride it out. Or maybe, that's all just conjecture.

DOI: 10.4324/9781003107798-4

A Brief History of Dream Interpretation

Dreams are something that we all experience on a nightly basis, although how much you remember them greatly varies according to many factors (Bloxham, 2018). For example, children under age nine tend to have fewer dreams and remember them less often than older children and adults (Sándor et al., 2015). How often you wake during the night also impacts recall, as the more periods of wakefulness you have (even if very brief), the more you remember (Vallat et al., 2017). What kind of dreams you remember the next day may even be impacted by what foods you eat, or at least what you believe about how food impacts dreams (Nielsen & Powell, 2015). But even if you aren't remembering them well (or at all), research has found we spend around two hours per night dreaming, in REM and non-REM sleep, which can add up to around six *years* spent dreaming across an average lifespan (Schneider & Domhoff, 2021). Even if you just remembered a fraction of what those dreams were upon waking, that's still a huge amount of dreams across your life! As such a major life experience for humans, it makes intuitive sense that we as a species would be intrigued and fascinated by why we dream and what they mean.

Dreams and dreaming play a prominent role in many of the world's major religious traditions, with some scholars even hypothesizing that dreams are partially responsible for the development of religion itself (Bulkeley, 2016). The earliest recorded dreams and subsequent interpretation come from Babylonian tablets dating back 5,000 or more years, with the oldest known being the dream of Dumuzi of Uruk, interpreted by his sister Geshtin-anna, who foresaw in the dream his downfall and death (Hoffman, 2004). Much of recorded early Babylonian dream interpretation focused on *oniromancy*, using dreams to foretell the future (Langdon, 1917), but other cultures placed more emphasis on dreams as communication from various gods and goddesses, seen in writings and stories from ancient world. Almost all major world religions have had guides to dreams and their meaning. Examples include the 3,000-year-old Egyptian papyri referred to as the "Dream Book" that details over 100 dreams and what they mean; the story of Joseph interpreting Pharaoh's dreams in the Jewish Torah; the *Somniale Danielis* that Christians in the Middle Ages used; the 16th-century *Lofty Principles of Dream Interpretation* by Chinese scholar Chen Shiyuan; and many more. Humankind has had a long fascination with understanding what dreams mean.

Modern attempts at understanding dreams, especially in the realm of psychology and psychotherapy, stem from the seminal work of Sigmund Freud, a physician and neurologist who developed psychoanalysis, which included extensive theories of personality, psychopathology, treatment of mental health problems, and (most relevant to this chapter) dreams. Although many other researchers and clinicians were publishing work about dreams, including many that directly influenced his writing (Borch-Jacobsen & Shamdasani, 2012), it was Freud's specific ideas that would become most well-known and widespread. In *The Interpretation of Dreams*, first published in 1899 (though it was given 1900 as a publication year) and revised seven times before his death in 1939, Freud outlined what he thought caused dreams, types of dreams, and what they meant about one's self and life. For him, dreams were the "royal road to a knowledge of the unconscious activity of the mind" and provided a way to access parts of the mind that were not normally accessible to our conscious selves. Freud's hypothesis was that, if someone could properly understand their dreams, they would then truly know what was at the root of their mental health problems. This level of insight would subsequently cause us to become more mentally healthy, better able to adapt to the world around us.

Based on analysis of both his own dreams and those of his patients, Freud concluded that all dreams were driven by *wish fulfillment*, ways that we wanted things to have been different in the past or ways that we wanted our lives to be in the future. We might be consciously aware of these wishes, but in almost all cases there were significant unconscious or repressed desires at play as well. This played out in what he called the *manifest content* and *latent content* of dreams. Manifest content is what is actually remembered about the dream – what happened in it, other people, objects, or animals, the setting, and so on. Latent content, on the other hand, would be the hidden meaning of the dream that reveals your unconscious, normally inaccessible (and maybe even personally or socially unacceptable) desires and thoughts.

In his psychoanalysis, Freud would not just tell his patients what their dream meant by relying on some sort of collection. In fact, he thought such universal symbols ("If you dream about riding a horse, it always means you want to escape your problems, no matter who you are!") didn't really exist, and that instead the symbols were exclusive to the specific patient. As such, a trained psychoanalyst would need to lead you through the process of interpreting *your* dreams, rather than dreams in general. This was typically done via *free association*, where the psychoanalyst would ask their patient to clear their mind and just share whatever pops into their head, not trying to make sense of it, just letting it happen. The psychoanalyst might have the patient describe a dream they had, and then would give them ideas or words from that dream to free associate on. The idea was that the first word or words that came to mind would be coming from your unconscious rather than conscious mind, which could help the patients and psychoanalyst understand the symbolic content of the dream and what wish fulfillment it was truly representing. For Freud, that was most often some sort of sexual wish or desire, in line with his emphasis on repressed sexual energy fueling a large part of our mind. Interestingly, despite his emphasis on individualized dream interpretation, Freud seems to have frequently done the opposite, and instead at least implicitly endorsed universal symbols and their associated latent meaning when interpreting his patient's dreams (Lilienfeld et al., 2009).

Successors to Freud's ideas, especially Carl Jung, continued to place an emphasis on the use of dreams within psychoanalysis. Jung called them "the guiding words of the soul" (2009, p. 233) and, like his mentor Freud, considered them to be products of one's unconscious mind. His method of dream analysis followed Freud's to a degree, in that first the dream needed to be described in detail and then free association needed to take place. But Jung was also heavily focused on what he called "archetypes," or symbols in dreams that he considered to be shared by all of humanity, and such could be interpreted the same regardless of the individual. Jung's system was much more *prospective* as well, and he believed that dreams were more representative of what the dreamer was moving toward in their life, as opposed to Freud's *retrospective* view that dreams primarily represented past events.

Psychoanalysis as a means to help people with anxiety, depression, and other mental health struggles has fallen out of favor. For example, while there are roughly 180,000 psychologists and 26,000 psychiatrists in the United States (Bureau of Labor Statistics, 2021), the American Psychoanalytic Association only has approximately 3,500 members (APsaA, n.d.). But that doesn't mean that dreams or interpreting them has become less popular. The use of "dream work" in psychotherapy today is varied, ranging from more well-elucidated models such as the cognitive-experiential model (Hill & Knox, 2010) to specifically targeting nightmares in treatment (Davis & Balliett, 2013). This is not surprising, as large numbers of both laypeople and mental health professionals still believe that dreams can reveal hidden truths or even predict the future. In their study of college students in three countries, Morewedge and Norton (2009) found that 56% of the students in the United States agreed that dreams had important meaning. Also, 65% of the South Korean student sample and 74% of Indian student sample reported believing in the importance of meaning in dreams.

Dreams and dreaming are frequently featured heavily in movies and television series, such as Christopher Nolan's film *Inception*, Richard Linklater's *Waking Life*, Stanley Kubrick's *Eyes Wide Shut*, or the *Nightmare on Elm Street* series. And, as we saw earlier in the chapter, the popularity of books, websites, and even apps that supposedly tell you what they mean indicates that anyone can find out what their dreams "mean" with a simple online search. But what does modern psychological science have to say about all this? Are there hidden meanings to dreams? Will understanding them help you become healthier?

Research on Dreams and Dreaming

Psychological research since Freud and Jung's time has expended a lot of energy attempting to understand dreams and dreaming, from the neurobiological processes behind them to the evolutionary reasons for them to what the content of them means or where it is drawn from. Many hypotheses and theories have been developed across the past 150 years, some more supported by the evidence than others (Morgese & Lombardo, 2017). A consistent theme, though, is that modern research has poked huge holes into psychoanalytic assumptions about the mind and dreams, as well as the overall idea of the usefulness of dream interpretation (Domhoff, 2001).

First, contrary to Freud's ideas of latent content, most of our dreams don't have hidden, secret meanings, but instead are about our daily lives. Much more in line with Jung's ideas that dreams are transparent in their meaning, the vast majority of dream content is "far more coherent, patterned, and thoughtful" than is portrayed in the media or would be predicted by Freud (Domhoff, 2007, p. 2). Carefully collected dream reports dating back to the 1960s repeatedly show that the setting, characters, and events in dreams tend to be overwhelmingly familiar to the dreamer (Schredl, 2019). Several lines of research show that following an individual's dreams across long periods of time reveals incredible consistency across time in themes, settings, and characters in dreams, even across decades of one's life (Domhoff, 2007). Most dreams are about normal, everyday activities and only a small number are described as having bizarre or unusual content, both in laboratory and home studies. While there are higher amounts of oddities that occur in REM dreams compared to non-REM (maybe twice as much, up to 10%; Dorus et al., 1971), even those can often be traced back exaggerations of what you were talking about, watching, reading, or playing on a given day. Interestingly, the dreams of children are even less bizarre and more commonplace than those of adults (Strauch, 2005), although by adolescence they become similar to adults (Foulkes, 1982).

Second, most emotionally charged dreams are negative (50% or more), rather than being positive or enjoyable (only 25%) as would be expected from Freud's ideas of dreams as wish fulfillment (Strauch & Meier, 1996). The high amount of repetitive negative or terrifying dreams seen in individuals with post-traumatic stress disorder (PTSD) alone, from 60% to 72% (Kilpatrick et al., 1998; Leskin et al., 2002), pokes holes in the idea of dreams as wish fulfillment. Providing further problems for Freud's theory is that laboratory studies have found anywhere from 25% to 35% of adult dreams do not have *any* emotional content (Fosse et al., 2001), with a whopping 75% of dreams in children and early adolescents having no emotions reported (Strauch, 2005). Additionally, relatively few of our dreams involve sexual activity, which Freud considered to be the most common type of desire that would manifest in dreams. Although almost all adults report that they have had a dream involving sex at some point (Schredl et al., 2004), studies find them to be of low frequency. Controlled studies show rates of sex-related dreams anywhere from 1% (Snyder, 1970) to 8% (Zadra, 2017), although we see all the way up to 20% based on retrospective self-report (Schredl et al., 2019). Given that wish fulfillment and sexual desires form the basis of psychoanalytic dream interpretation, this is another major reason to doubt Freud's views.

Third, there are many well-understood problems with human memory and recall. Rather than just recording everything that we see, feel, and do similar to the way a video camera works, memory is primarily reconstructive. This means that we do not simply "play back" our memories, experiencing them in the exact same way each time. Instead, we quite literally recreate our memories each time we bring them to mind and how accurate they are is therefore subject to many, many variables. For instance, our past experiences, current emotional state, and even the social situation can all change what information we are able to recall about events (Burton, 2020). Shermer (2002) describes memory as "a complex phenomenon involving distortions, deletions, additions, and sometimes complete fabrication" (p. 96). This is not to say that we just "make up" our memories, but instead that we can (and often do) remember events and experiences in ways that are not entirely true, even if such things seem very important at the time (Neisser & Harsch, 1992). It's been shown for several decades that dreams are not immune to such recall and forgetting issues (Goodenough, 1991). As such, it's quite likely that most of the dreams we can remember have only a passing resemblance to the actual dream we experienced, especially if recalling it later to a therapist. Further, we remember remarkably few of our dreams the next day, let alone multiple days later. Try it yourself—how many of your dreams do you recall from last night? How about two nights ago? How accurate can an interpretation of a dream be, if what we are saying we dreamed may not be all that accurate in the first place *and* is only a very small sample of the total number of dreams we had that night?

Finally, there is no evidence that understanding or interpreting dreams has a positive impact on one's mental health. Good evidence shows that the state of one's mental health can impact the quality and quantity of sleep (Mellman, 2006) and can even impact the content and frequency dreams (Sikka et al., 2018). For example, people diagnosed with PTSD frequently report distressing nightmares on a very regular basis, and when people are feeling anxious and nervous during the day they are likely to have dreams with more negative, anxious content. However, there is little to suggest the free association in Freudian dream analysis (or any other kind) is either free of the biases of suggestion and persuasion of the analyst or even that it truly helps understand dream content (Domhoff, 2019). The very idea of "repression" of memories, which would then be somehow released during dreaming, has been thoroughly debunked for decades (Loftus et al., 1998). And even the basic idea that there is some sort of hidden symbolism in many or most dreams has been found quite wanting (Domhoff, 2015). Further, the inconsistency with which analysts or various dream dictionaries interpret the same dream shows a severe lack of inter-rater reliability and the consistency needed to establish a sound clinical procedure (Kramer, 2000). There is good news, though, for those that do have unpleasant and bad dreams: effective treatment of anxiety, depression, and PTSD using evidence-based approaches such as cognitive-behavioral therapy has repeatedly shown to impact dreams, leaving the dreamer with happier and more fulfilling sleep (Nadorff et al. 2014; Nappi et al., 2010).

Summary and Conclusion

A century's worth of research has shown that "dreams are for the most part reasonable simulations of waking life that contain occasional unusual features in the form of distorted settings and objects, highly unusual characters, inexplicable activities, strange images and metamorphoses, and sudden scene shifts" (Domhoff, 2007, p. 24). Despite the ongoing fascination in the public and media, there is little evidence to suggest dreams have hidden meanings or that understanding them can make you more mentally healthy. Like many popular but untrue myths about psychology, large numbers of people still accept many dream myths to be true and allow them to impact their daily lives in terms of the money they spend, the choices they make, and the potentially effective help they may not seek.

References

American Psychoanalytic Association. (n.d.). ApsaA mission & vision. Retrieved September 13, 2021, from https://apsa.org/content/apsaa-mission-vision

Bloxham, A. (2018). Relationships between dream recall, motivation to remember dreams, and waking memory ability: A preliminary investigation. *International Journal of Dream Research*, *11*(2), 141–153.

Borch-Jacobsen, M., & Shamdasani, S. (2012). *The Freud files: An inquiry into the history of psychoanalysis* (p. 43, 111). Cambridge: Cambridge University Press.

Bulkeley, K. (2016). *Big dreams: The science of dreaming and the origins of religion*. Oxford University Press.

Bureau of Labor Statistics. U.S. Department of Labor, Occupational Outlook Handbook, OOH Data Access and Republishing Information. Retrieved from https://www.bls.gov/ooh/about/ooh-developer-info.htm (visited September 08, 2021).

Burton, H. (2020). *The malleability of memory: A conversation with Elizabeth Loftus*. Open Agenda Publishing.

Daniel, A. (2021). The secret meaning of 60 common dreams, according to experts. Retrieved September 6, 2021, from https://bestlifeonline.com/dream-interpretation/ on September

Davis, J. L., & Balliett, N. E. (2013). Treating nightmares. In L. Grossman & S. Walfish (Eds.), *Translating research into practice: A desk reference for practicing mental health professionals*. Springer Publishing.

Domhoff, G. W. (2001). Why did empirical dream researchers reject Freud? A critique of historical claims by Mark Solms. *Dreaming*, *14*, 3–17.

Domhoff, G. W. (2007). Realistic simulation and bizarreness in dream content: Past findings and suggestions for future research. In D. Barrett & P. McNamara (Eds.), *The new science of dreaming: Content, recall, and personality characteristics* (Vol. 2, pp. 1–27). Westport, CT: Praeger Press.

Domhoff, G. W. (2015). Dreaming as embodied simulation: A widower dreams of his deceased wife. *Dreaming*, *25*, 232—256. doi:10.1037/a0039291

Domhoff, G. W. (2019). The neurocognitive theory of dreams at 20: An assessment and comparison with four other theories of dreaming. *Dreaming*, *29*(4), 265–302. doi:10.1037/drm0000119

Dorus, E., Dorus, W., & Rechtschaffen, A. (1971). The incidence of novelty in dreams. *Archives of General Psychiatry*, *25*, 364–368.

Fosse, R., Stickgold, R., & Hobson, J. A. (2001). The mind in REM sleep: Reports of emotional experience. *Sleep*, *24*, 947–955.

Foulkes, D. (1982). *Children's dreams*. New York: Wiley.

Goodenough, D. (1991). Dream recall: History and current status of the field. In S. Ellman & J. Antrobus (Eds.), *The mind in sleep: Psychology and psychophysiology* (2nd ed., pp. 143—171). New York, NY: Wiley.

Hill, C. E., & Knox, S. (2010). The use of dreams in modern psychotherapy. *International Review of Neurobiology, 92*(10), 291–317. doi:10.1016/S0074-7742(10)92013-8

Hoffman, C. (2004). Dumuzi's dream: Dream analysis in ancient mesopotamia. *Dreaming, 14*(4), 240–251. doi:10.1037/1053 0797.14.4.240

Jung, C. G., & Shamdasani, S. (Ed.). (2009). *The red book: Liber novus.* Translated by M. Kyburz & J. Peck. W W Norton & Co.

Kilpatrick, D. G., Resnick, H. S., Freedy, J. R., Pelcovitz, D., Resick, P., Roth, S., & van der Kolk, B. (1998). Post-traumatic stress disorder field trial: Evaluation of the PTSD construct—criteria A through E. In T. A. Widiger, A. J. Frances, H. A. Pincus, R. Ross, M. B. First, W. Davis, & M. Kline (Eds.), *DSM-IV sourcebook* (Vol. 4, pp. 803–846). Washington, DC: American Psychiatric Press.

Kramer, M. (2000). Does dream interpretation have any limits? An evaluation of interpretations of the dream of "Irma's injection". *Dreaming 10*, 161–178. doi:10.1023/A:1009486324024

Langdon, S. (1917). A Babylonian dream tablet on the interpretation of dreams. *The Museum Journal, 8*(2), 116–122. Retrieved from https://www.penn.museum/documents/publications/journal/08-2/babylonian_tablet_dreams.pdf

Leskin, G. A., Woodward, S. H., Young, H. E., & Sheikh, J. I. (2002). Effects of comorbid diagnoses on sleep disturbance in PTSD. *Journal of Psychiatric Research, 36*(6), 449–452. doi:10.1016/s0022-3956(02)00025-0

Lilienfeld, S. O., Lynn, S. J., Ruscio, J., & Beyerstein, B. L. (2009). *50 great myths of popular psychology.* Wiley-Blackwell.

Loftus, E., Joslyn, S., & Polage, D. (1998). Repression: A mistaken impression? *Development and Psychopathology, 10*, 781–792. doi:10.1017/S0954579498001862

Mellman T. A. (2006). Sleep and anxiety disorders. *The Psychiatric Clinics of North America, 29*(4), 1047–1058. doi:10.1016/j.psc.2006.08.005

Morewedge, C. K., & Norton, M. I. (2009). When dreaming is believing: The (motivated) interpretation of dreams. *Journal of Personality and Social Psychology, 96*(2), 249–264. doi:10.1037/a0013264

Morgese, G., & Lombardo, G. P. (2017). Empirical research and literature review of the experimental and systematic study of dreams in the late 19th and early 20th century: The important role of general psychology. *Dreaming, 27*(4), 311–333. doi:10.1037/drm0000065

Nadorff, M. R., Porter, B., Rhoades, H. M., Greisinger, A. J., Kunik, M. E., & Stanley, M. A. (2014). Bad dream frequency in older adults with generalized anxiety disorder: Prevalence, correlates, and effect of cognitive behavioral treatment for anxiety. *Behavioral Sleep Medicine, 12*(1), 28–40. doi:10.1080/15402002.2012.755125

Nappi, C. M., Drummond, S. P., Thorp, S. R., & McQuaid, J. R. (2010). Effectiveness of imagery rehearsal therapy for the treatment of combat-related nightmares in veterans. *Behavior Therapy, 41*(2), 237–244. doi:10.1016/j.beth.2009.03.003

Neisser, U., & Harsch, N. (1992). Phantom flashbulbs: False recollections of hearing the news about Challenger. In E. Winograd & U. Neisser (Eds.), Affect and accuracy in recall: Studies of "flashbulb memories." Cambridge University Press.

Nielsen, T., & Powell, R. A. (2015). Dreams of the Rarebit Fiend: Food and diet as instigators of bizarre and disturbing dreams. *Frontiers in Psychology, 6*, 47. doi:10.3389/fpsyg.2015.00047

Regan, S. (2021). A beginner's guide to dream interpretation & 8 common dreams. Retrieved September 6, 2021, from https://www.mindbodygreen.com/articles/beginners-guide-to-dream-interpretation

Sándor, P., Szakadát, S., Kertész, K., & Bódizs, R. (2015). Content analysis of 4 to 8 year-old children's dream reports. *Frontiers in Psychology, 6*, 534. doi:10.3389/fpsyg.2015.00534

Schneider, A., & Domhoff, G. W. (2021). The quantitative study of dreams. Retrieved September 6, 2021, from http://dreamresearch.net/

Schredl, M. (2019). Typical dream themes. In K. Valli & R. J. Hoss (Eds.), *Dreams: Understanding biology, psychology, and culture* (pp. 173–180). Greenwood Press/ABC-CLIO.

Schredl, M., Ciric, P., Götz, S., & Wittmann, L. (2004). Typical dreams: Stability and gender differences. *Journal of Psychology, 138*, 485–494.

Schredl, M., Geißler, C., & Göritz, A. S. (2019). Factors influencing the frequency of erotic dreams: An online study. *Psychology & Sexuality*, 10(4), 316–324.

Shermer, M. (2002). *Why people believe weird things: Pseudoscience, superstition, and other confusions of our time*. New York, NY: Henry Holt.

Sikka, P., Pesonen, H., & Revonsuo, A. (2018). Peace of mind and anxiety in the waking state are related to the affective content of dreams. *Scientific Reports, 8*(1), 12762. doi:10.1038/s41598-018-30721-1

Snyder, F. (1970). The phenomenology of dreaming. In L. Madow & L. Snow (Eds.), The psychodynamic implications of the physiological studies on dreams (pp. 124–151). C.C. Thomas.

Strauch, I. (2005). REM dreaming in the transition from late childhood to adolescence: A longitudinal study. *Dreaming, 15*, 155–169.

Strauch, I., & Meier, B. (1996). *In search of dreams: Results of experimental dream research*. State University of New York Press.

Vallat, R., Lajnef, T., Eichenlaub, J. B., Berthomier, C., Jerbi, K., Morlet, D., & Ruby, P. M. (2017). Increased evoked potentials to arousing auditory stimuli during sleep: Implication for the understanding of dream recall. *Frontiers in Human Neuroscience, 11*, 132. doi:10.3389/fnhum.2017.00132

Zadra, A. (2017, March 20). *How common are sex dreams?* Antonio Zadra. Retrieved October 1, 2021, from https://antoniozadra.com/en/node/28

5 Superstition and Learning

Stuart Vyse

No one is born superstitious. All our superstitions are acquired during the course of our lives. It's also true that many people never become superstitious. So, superstition is not an instinct nor is it an inevitable outcome of growing up. For those who acquire them, superstitions are learned, and we now know quite a bit about how that happens.

Superstitions come in two broad categories, and the methods of acquiring them are also different. When we think about superstitions, often the first things to come to mind are black cats, walking under ladders, and the number 13. These and many other common examples are what psychologist Gustav Jahoda (1970) called *socially shared* superstitions. In contrast, there are many superstitions that are unique to the individual, such as the lucky silver dollar that Uncle Frank keeps in his pocket, Barack Obama's belief that he must play in a pickup basketball game on election days (Obama, 2020), and tennis player Serena Williams' practice of bouncing the ball exactly five times before each first serve (Rhue, 2018). These are *personal superstitions* that appear to grow out of direct experience, and those who have them tend to hold them close without encouraging others to use the same approach. Although there are many common threads to the psychology of these two forms of superstition, there are differences in how they develop.

Examining the Claims

Socially Shared Superstitions

Many superstitions come to us as part of our family and cultural education. The sociology of superstition is not widely studied, but we know that there are a few demographic characteristics that predict whether you will be superstitious or not (Jarvis, 1980; Vyse, 2013). Studies consistently find that women are more superstitious than men. People also tend to be less superstitious as they age. Most studies find that young adults have stronger belief than older adults.

Socialization within a family and culture clearly has a powerful effect. Socialization in a religion typically involves an institutional framework that provides a number of social and personal incentives for sustained belief and involvement, none of which apply to superstition. But for those who believe, it is likely that a similar socialization process was an important force. Research suggests that parents are the strongest "agents of influence" on religion of their children – particularly in the early years – and people who change denominations often choose one with a similar theology and worship style to their religion of origin (Sherkat, 2003, p. 160). Marriage is one of the most common reasons for adopting a new religion. Although the analogy is not perfect, belief in superstition is

DOI: 10.4324/9781003107798-5

undoubtedly fostered by similar family influences. Where parents and other family members practice superstitions, children are more likely to carry on these traditions.

The effect of regional and cultural differences on the acquisition of socially shared superstition is obvious from the different superstitions people acquire in different places. In the United Kingdom, one of the most popular superstitions centers around random encounters with a particular species of bird: the magpie. The superstition is based in this traditional English nursery rhyme:

> One for sorrow,
> Two for joy,
> Three for a girl,
> Four for a boy,
> Five for silver,
> Six for gold,
> Seven for a secret never to be told.
>   – Traditional nursery rhyme

Consistent with the rhyme, seeing a single magpie is considered bad luck, and there are a number of countermeasures that are used to avoid harm. On encountering a lone magpie, people salute the magpie or say a special phrase, such as, "Good morning Mr. Magpie, how is your lady wife today?" Within the United Kingdom, there are many regional differences in beliefs surrounding magpies, but in the United States, the magpie superstition is all but unknown. Part of the explanation may be that magpies are far less common in the United States, but the role of the nursery rhyme and the elaborate stories surrounding magpies are evidence of a deep cultural foundation. Similarly, the evil eye is an envy-based superstition found in varying forms throughout large areas of South Asia, the Middle East, and South America, but growing up in a default protestant family in the middle west of the United States, I'd never heard of it. I was well into my 50s when a student from Peru first told me about the evil eye.

Merely by breathing the air of your native region during the formative years, you acquire knowledge of the popular superstitions. Most people learn the superstitions of their culture, but believing in and exercising them requires an extra step. As in the case of religious belief, our parents' acceptance or rejection of superstition undoubtedly has a strong influence on our later belief.

Personal Superstitions

Personal superstitious are far more idiosyncratic than socially shared superstitions, and we know much more about how these strange quirks and rituals come about. The classical beginning of this story is B. F. Skinner's most famous experiment, "'Superstition' in the Pigeon" (1948). Skinner placed individual hungry pigeons into a conditioning chamber (a Skinner box) and offered brief opportunities to eat grain through a hole in the chamber wall every fifteen seconds. The birds were under no obligation to do anything to get the food. They could simply have waited by the hole in the wall for the food to arrive, but none of them did this. Instead, the birds who went through this training were typically very active. They each developed a distinctive ritual or repeated behavior. One turned in counterclockwise circles; another pecked at a corner of the chamber; and a third bobbed its head repeatedly. None of these actions was required to get the food, but in Skinner's view, each bird had been conditioned by the coincidence of reinforcement arriving just as the bird made some random action. Whatever the action taken, the birds tended to do it again, as if their behavior had made the food arrive. Of course, this repetition made additional coincidences more likely.

Skinner likened this behavior to human superstitions, but he put the word superstition in quotes because these were birds, not humans. The concept of magical thinking does not really apply to nonhuman species. The connection to human superstition was further challenged when two researchers replicated the experiment and suggested that Skinner was not seeing what he thought he saw in the quirky movements of his pigeons. According to this new account, the pigeons were engaging in "interim behaviors" that were more instinctive than learned (Staddon & Simmelhag, 1971). The birds were just doing what birds do when there is food around but they have to wait for it.

So, Skinner's pigeons were merely a metaphor for human superstition, but a number of later experiments using humans suggested that the metaphor was apt. For example, Wagner and Morris (1987) placed preschool age children in a cubicle with a mechanical clown named "Bobo" whose name was inspired by the classic inflatable clown from Albert Bandura's research. Instead of passively taking a beating, however, this Bobo actively dispensed marbles from his mouth. The children were told that if they collected enough marbles, they could earn a small toy. Mimicking Skinner's (1948) conditions, 12 children were exposed to a situation in which Bobo either spat out a marble every 15 seconds or every 30 seconds. Although not all of the children developed a distinctive superstitious response under these circumstances, seven of the children did. Two of the children stood in front of Bobo and wiggled or swung their hips; one girl kissed Bobo repeatedly on the nose; and four children either smiled or grimaced at Bobo.

In another experiment by Ono (1987), when Japanese college students were provided with points that came irrespective of their behavior, they developed several very elaborate superstitious responses, including, in one woman's case, jumping up and down while touching the ceiling of the experimental room with her shoe. Humans are far less influenced by instinct than pigeons – certainly there is no jumping up to touch the ceiling with your shoe instinct – and as a result, it seems more plausible that the kind of coincidental reinforcement that Skinner imagined influenced his birds was the source – or, as we will see, *one* of the sources – of these unusual human behaviors.

Nine years after his initial superstition experiment, Skinner and colleague William H. Morse identified a different kind of superstition (Morse & Skinner, 1957). The first kind of superstition had been about a specific action that was stamped in by the arrival of a reinforcer: grain for the pigeon or a marble from Bobo's mouth for the children in the Wagner and Morris's (1987) experiment. But operant conditioning has three components: a discriminative stimulus (S^D); a response (R); and a reinforcing stimulus (S^R). The S^D is a feature of the context that signals that reinforcement is available or not. For example, when a rat is pressing a lever for food in a Skinner box, a light on the wall of the chamber might indicate when reinforcement is available: pressing the lever when the light is on produces food but pressing when the light is off does nothing. Under these conditions, the rat's behavior will quickly come under "stimulus control": the rat will press when the light is on but not when it is off.

Morse and Skinner's (1957) second kind of superstition was less about the response – the behavior the animal produced – and more about the S^D. They placed three hungry pigeons in chambers and trained them to peck at a small disk on the wall to obtain a small amount of grain. The pigeons were on a very lean schedule of reinforcement that *averaged* one reinforcement every 30 minutes, with the interval between reinforcements varying randomly between 1 and 59 minutes. Under this schedule, the birds produced a slow, somewhat variable pattern of pecking at the disk. They never stopped altogether, but they pecked at a slow pace. Most of the time the disk was illuminated an orange color, but after the birds were well trained on this schedule, Morse and Skinner changed the color of the light from orange to blue for a 4-minute period, then back to orange. In this case, the color of the light had nothing to do with the schedule of reinforcement. The timers that determined when a response would be reinforced continued their work irrespective of the color of the light, a condition that should have led to the birds ignoring the color of the light because it had no informative value, but that is not what happened. All of the birds behaved as if the light change had special significance. Some suddenly started to press faster when the blue light arrived, and other birds pressed slower. The experiment was conducted over a long period of time, and through the course of the experiment the appearance of the blue light gradually alternated its effect on the birds, changing from a positive sign to a negative one, or vice versa, for all three birds. But throughout the experiment the light actually had no special significance at all.

Taken together, these two types of experimentally produced superstitions encompass many of the personal superstitions seen in everyday life. The business person who wears a lucky bracelet to an important meeting is using the second type of superstition, re-establishing a context that has been associated with good outcomes in the past. The football player who lays out his uniform, including his underwear, helmet, and cleats on the floor in front of his locker before he dresses for the game – as the Baltimore Ravens place kicker Justin Tucker reportedly does – is using the first kind of superstition: an idiosyncratic action that is associated with success (ESPN, 2019). The tennis star Serena Williams employs a combination of both types of superstitions, reportedly tying her shoelaces in the same way, using the same shower before each match and bouncing the ball five times before the first serve and twice before the second (Camber & Newling, 2007).

Human behavior is more complicated than that of pigeons, and as a result, there are a number of additional factors that go into acquiring a personal superstition. In a subsequent pair of experiments with pre-school children, Edward Morris and colleagues demonstrated how superstitions could be learned through imitation (Higgins et al., 1989). Once again Bobo the clown was recruited to dispense marbles. In the first experiment, children were taught that pressing Bobo's nose produced a clicking sound, but unbeknownst to the children, pressing the nose had no effect on the schedule of marble delivery, which, as in the previous experiment, occurred on a variable schedule that averaged 15 seconds between marbles. Given this introduction to Bobo, many of the children engaged in superstitious nose pressing. In a second experiment, preschoolers were broken into two groups, each of which viewed a different videotape. For one group, the video showed a child superstitiously pushing Bobo's nose, and for the other group, the video just showed an image of Bobo alone. Later, when the children were left alone with Bobo, a third of the children who had seen another child pressing Bobo's nose imitated that behavior. None of the children in the other group pressed Bobo's nose.

These were not overwhelmingly powerful results, but they show that superstitions can be acquired through imitation. Indeed, Justin Tucker's uniform-arranging superstition is patterned after a similar practice of his childhood idol, football star Deion Sanders. Furthermore, the socialization process of acquiring socially-shared superstition undoubtedly involves imitation of our parents or other family members. Children who see their parents applying the principles of feng shui in their homes in an effort to bring luck are likely to imitate that behavior later on.

Superstitious Beliefs

At its core, a superstition is a mistaken idea about a cause and effect relationship. *My rabbit's foot brings me luck at the roulette table.* B. F. Skinner put the word superstition in quotes in the title of his experiment, "'Superstition' in the pigeon," because it is unclear what if anything his pigeons believed, but according to his view, the birds behaved *as if* they believed their actions caused the food to come. When humans acquire personal superstitions by trial and error, they often describe the superstition in the form of a rule: "If I bounce the ball five times, I serve better." Indeed, for humans, acquiring a personal superstition appears to be a process of figuring out the rule – the superstitious belief – and then following it. Some researchers have explored how this process of rule discovery works.

In a series of studies, college students were asked to play simple video games without being told how points were obtained (Heltzer & Vyse, 1994; Rudski et al., 1999; Vyse, 1991). For example, in one study, students sat at a computer screen that showed a 5 × 5 matrix of boxes with a circle in the upper left-hand corner (Heltzer & Vyse, 1994). Pressing the "Z" key moved the circle down one square, and pressing the "/" key moved the circle one square to the right. Any combination of four presses on both keys moved the circle from the upper left-hand corner to the lower right-hand corner, and getting the circle to the lower right-hand corner was occasionally rewarded with a point. Any fifth press on a key ended the trial and brought up a new board with the circle back at the starting point. For one group of participants, points were given *on every other* successfully completed trial on a strictly alternating basis. For a second group, points were given on an *average* of 50% of successfully completed trials, but the actual sequence of points was random.

Most participants in both groups figured out they needed to move the circle to the lower right-hand corner of the matrix to get points, and almost all participants in the every-other-trial group described the game accurately. But most of the students in the random point group developed interesting superstitious rules to describe how points were delivered. For example, one participant claimed that there was a series of four paths through the matrix that must be completed in sequence, only three of which they had worked out by the time the experiment ended (Heltzer & Vyse, 1994, p. 168). Another said you had to move the circle through the top half of the matrix on one trail and the bottom half on the next. Of course, none of these rules were accurate because the path used to get from upper left to bottom right was irrelevant. A similar study varied the probability of reinforcement from 25% of responses to 75% and found that superstitious rule statements were most prominent in the group who experienced 75% reinforcement (Rudski et al., 1999).

This relationship of random successes to the development of superstitious rules is symbolic of the larger context of superstitious belief. Superstitions only emerge at times when we care about something but lack complete control over it. Humans are tremendous problem solvers, and when we can establish a rule that accurately describes events – as was the case for the people in the alternating trials group of the matrix experiment – all is well. But when we lack an accurate rule and adequate control over the outcome, we are likely to generate a superstitious explanation to fill the void.

In the ancient world, much of daily life was a dark and frightening place. Weather was enormously important for survival and yet for most of human history, it was almost completely unpredictable. Similarly, the causes of disease were poorly understood, and there were few effective medical treatments. Infant mortality was common, and life expectancy for those who survived infancy was short by today's standards. As a result, many methods of foretelling the future that today we would call superstitions have been popular throughout human history (Vyse, 2019). Many of these methods of divining the future involved attempting to read something meaningful in a random process. *Augury* was a method of foretelling the future from the flight of birds; the ancient Chinese *I Ching* or *Book of Changes* was used in combination with dried Yarrow stalks which were tossed to form different combinations; and the earliest use of dice or the casting or drawing of lots was often to foretell the future. Even today, people tell fortunes by reading tea leaves or coffee grounds in the bottom of a cup or by the fall of Tarot cards. Each of these methods parallels the larger project of attempting to pull meaning and predictability out of the random uncertainties of life. A random world is difficult to accept, and like the video game playing college students in the matrix study, we are often willing to impose a superstitious order where we have failed to find a truer rule (Vyse, 2021).

Do Superstitions Work?

When a human learns a superstition, there are many forms of reinforcement that might contribute to the process. In socially shared superstitions, imitation is thought to involve *vicarious reinforcement*, in which observing someone else being rewarded for a particular behavior increases the likelihood that you will engage in that behavior in a similar circumstance (Kazdin, 1973). For example, if you witness your father always keeping a lucky stone in his pocket and he says it has always brought him luck – and perhaps you even observe some of this good luck – then you are likely to be similarly inclined in the future. In addition, many superstitions are learned from *direct instruction* when parents prompt and reward superstitious behavior: "Johnny, take that hat off the bed. That's bad luck!" Presumably, once a superstition is adequately instilled through these methods, it becomes intrinsically reinforcing to do it (Scott et al., 1988), and you even feel bad if you don't.

In the case of personal superstitions, once you have identified a lucky object or action, it must also be sustained by some intrinsic reinforcement or psychological benefit. Of course, in order to develop a personal superstition, you need to be the kind of person for whom superstition is an option, which typically involves some prior socialization. But once it becomes a habit, superstitions are self-sustaining. In those situations when control is lacking, superstitions provide sufficient psychological benefit to keep people wearing lucky ties and performing pre-game rituals.

One of the burning questions of superstition research has been, might there be another source of reinforcement? Is it possible superstitions actually work? Not in a direct magical sense. There is no magic, and as a result, superstitions cannot help you win at the roulette table or in the bingo parlor. These are games of pure chance. But could there be an indirect effect on skilled activities? Could it be that whatever psychological benefit Serena Williams derives from her tennis superstitions translates into better play? Undoubtedly many athletes believe their superstitions help them, and even without resorting to magical thinking, it makes a kind of sense. If superstitious behaviors are sustained by the psychological benefits they provide, might those psychological or emotional benefits lead to better performance? It seems plausible, but unfortunately, the evidence for this kind of indirect benefit has been somewhat mixed.

For quite a while no one bothered to test this hypothesis. Superstition research centered on why people believe and how superstitions are acquired. But in 2010, a group of researchers at the University of Cologne in Germany published a study that seemed to show the benefits of superstition. In a famous experiment that came to be called "the golf ball study," individual people were invited into a lab room to putt a golf ball into a cup (Damisch et al., 2010). The participants in this very simple study were divided into two groups. For one group, as the experimenters handed the person the golf ball, they said "Here is your ball. So far it has turned out to be a lucky ball." For the other group, the experimenter simply said, "This is the ball everyone has used so far." The researchers had previously determined that approximately 80% of their participants believed in the concept of luck, and miraculously, the participants in the lucky ball group were significantly more successful at getting the ball into a cup. This was the first study to show a benefit of superstition on performance of a skill, but that was not the end of the story.

In science, we place great value on a phenomenon being repeatable. If only one group of researchers can make something happen in a single laboratory but others cannot reproduce it using the same procedures, we cannot put much faith in the phenomenon. Perhaps because the golf ball study received quite a bit of attention, a group of researchers at Dominican University in the United States attempted a replication (Calin-Jageman & Caldwell, 2014). They used a much larger group of participants and communicated with the German researchers to make certain they were using comparable methods. In addition, they established that their American participants' level of belief in luck was similar to that of the German participants. But this time, using a far more powerful and controlled study, the researchers found no difference in the putting scores of the lucky and non-lucky groups. So we are left with a muddle. It seems plausible that the psychological benefit of a superstition might boost performance, but at this point we don't have good evidence that it does.

The news is a bit more positive in the case of a related form of behavior: rituals. As we have seen, some superstitions are beliefs about an object (e.g., lucky ball) or a relatively discrete action (e.g., knocking on wood). But other superstitions involve a much longer sequence of actions. Justin Tucker arranging his uniform in the locker room before a game would fall into this category. Recent research has found more compelling evidence that rituals do have beneficial effects in a number of contexts. In one cleverly designed experiment, unsuspecting participants arrived at the laboratory and were told that they would be singing the song "Don't Stop Believing" by the 80s rock band Journey in front of a small audience of strangers. Half the participants were randomly assigned to do a ritual prior to performing, and the other half were asked to just sit quietly for a minute. The ritual instructions were as follows:

> Please do the following ritual: Draw a picture of how you are feeling right now. Sprinkle salt on your drawing. Count up to five out loud. Crinkle up your paper. Throw your paper in the trash. (Brooks et al., 2016, p. 6)

Then all the participants, whether they were in the ritual condition or not, sang the song with the help of a karaoke machine that automatically scored the accuracy of their singing. The results showed that ritual performers were less anxious and sang better than people who merely sat quietly. Other studies have shown that rituals can improve performance in timed math tests and in dealing with loss (Brooks et al., 2016; Norton & Gino, 2014). The authors in this line of work suggest that the requirements of a ritual are that it (a) be a fixed sequence of actions, (b) have some symbolic features (e.g., "Draw a picture of how you are feeling right now"), and (c) have no practical connection to the activity it is paired with. So, actually practicing singing or rehearsing the lyrics to "Don't Stop Believing" could not qualify as part of a ritual. There is growing evidence that these rituals produce a psychological benefit that translates into better performance (Hobson et al., 2018). But there is a hitch. The ritual doesn't have to be either religious or superstitious. Unless the user attributes magical or supernatural significance to it – creating a false cause and effect narrative – it isn't a superstitious ritual. Thus, we are left with good evidence that superstitious rituals can be both psychologically beneficial in the moment and lead to better performance in a subsequent skilled activity, but it's the ritual that does the work, not the superstition. As a result, if a person employs a personal superstition in the form of a pre-job interview ritual, it just might make them give a better interview than if they didn't employ it. Furthermore, if a superstitious ritual did help performance, this could reinforce the use of the ritual and make it more likely to crop up in future situations.

Summary and Conclusion

As the foregoing suggests, there are many ways to learn a superstition. Early socialization is particularly important, but in the case of personal superstitions, operant conditioning and superstitious rules learned through direct experience can also play a role. Given all these paths to magical thinking, it is not surprising that superstitions similar to those used by ancient peoples remain popular in our modern world.

References

Brooks, A. W., Schroeder, J., Risen, J. L., Gino, F., Galinsky, A. D., Norton, M. I., & Schweitzer, M. E. (2016). Don't stop believing: Rituals improve performance by decreasing anxiety. *Organizational Behavior and Human Decision Processes*, *137*, 71–85. doi:10.1016/j.obhdp.2016.07.004

Calin-Jageman, R. J., & Caldwell, T. L. (2014). Replication of the superstition and performance study by Damisch, Stoberock, and Mussweiler (2010). *Social Psychology*, *45*(3), 239–245. doi:10.1027/1864-9335/a000190

Camber, R., & Newling, D. (2007, July 3). Superstitions That Serve Me Well, by Serena Williams. *Daily Mail Online*. https://www.dailymail.co.uk/news/article-465726/Superstitions-serve-Serena-Williams.html

Damisch, L., Stoberock, B., & Mussweiler, T. (2010). Keep your fingers crossed! How superstition improves performance. *Psychological Science*, *21*(7), 1014–1020. doi:10.1177/0956797610372631

ESPN. (2019, October 2). "Tabasco shots, baths and gross gloves: The best rituals and superstitions on all 32 NFL teams." ESPN. https://www.espn.com/nfl/story/_/id/27699107/tabasco-shots-baths-gross-gloves-best-rituals-superstitions-all-32-nfl-teams

Heltzer, R. A., & Vyse, S. A. (1994). Intermittent consequences and problem solving: The experimental control of "superstitious" beliefs. *Psychological Record*, *44*, 155–169.

Higgins, S. T., Morris, E. K., & Johnson, L. M. (1989). Social transmission of superstitious behavior in preschool children. *The Psychological Record*, *39*, 307–323.

Hobson, N. M., Schroeder, J., Risen, J. L., Xygalatas, D., & Inzlicht, M. (2018). The psychology of rituals: An integrative review and process-based framework. *Personality and Social Psychology Review*, *22*(3), 260–284. doi:10.1177/1088868317734944

Jahoda, G. (1970). *The psychology of superstition*. New York: Jason Aronson.

Jarvis, Peter. (1980). Towards a sociological understanding of superstition. *Social Compass* 27(2–3), 285–295. doi:10.1177/003776868002700209

Kazdin, A. E. (1973). The effect of vicarious reinforcement on attentive behavior in the classroom 1. *Journal of Applied Behavior Analysis, 6*(1), 71–78.

Lees, N. B., & Tinsley, B. J. (2000). Maternal socialization of children's preventive health behavior: The role of maternal affect and teaching strategies. *Merrill-Palmer Quarterly, 46*(4), 632–652.

Morse, W. H., & Skinner, B. F. (1957). A second type of superstition in the pigeon. *The American Journal of Psychology, 70*(2), 308–311.

Norton, M. I., & Gino, F. (2014). Rituals alleviate grieving for loved ones, lovers, and lotteries. *Journal of Experimental Psychology: General, 143*(1), 266–272. doi:10.1037/a0031772

Obama, B. (2020). *A promised land*. New York: Crown.

Ono, K. (1987). Superstitious behavior in humans. *Journal of the Experimental Analysis of Behavior, 47*(3), 261–271. doi:10.1901/jeab.1987.47-261

Rhue, Holly. (2018, July 13). "11 celebrities on their weird superstitions." *ELLE*. https://www.elle.com/culture/celebrities/g22071946/celebrity-superstitions/

Rudski, J. M., Lischner, M. I., & Albert, L. M. (1999). Superstitious rule generation is affected by probability and type of outcome. *Psychological Record, 49*(2), 245–260. doi:10.1007/BF03395319

Scott, W. E., Farh, J. L., & Podsakoff, P. M. (1988). The effects of "intrinsic" and "extrinsic" reinforcement contingencies on task behavior. *Organizational Behavior and Human Decision Processes, 41*(3), 405–425. doi:10.1016/0749-5978(88)90037-4

Sherkat, D. E. (2003). Religious socialization. In M. Dillon (Ed.), *Handbook of the sociology of religion* (pp. 151–163). Cambridge: Cambridge University Press.

Skinner, B. F. (1948). "Superstition" in the Pigeon. *Journal of Experimental Psychology, 38*(2), 168–172. doi:10.1037/11324-029

Staddon, J. E., & Simmelhag, V. L. (1971). The "superstition" experiment: A reexamination of its implications for the principles of adaptive behavior. *Psychological Review, 78*(1), 3–43. doi:10.1037/h0030305

Vyse S. A. (2013). Believing in magic: The psychology of superstition - Updated. Oxford University Press

Vyse, S. (2019). *Superstition: A very short introduction*. Oxford: Oxford University Press.

Vyse, S. (2021). Les êtres humains peuvent-ils tolérer un monde aléatoire? (Can humans tolerate a random world?). In *Pourquoi moi? Le hazard dans tous ses états* (p. 45–51). Paris: Belin.

Vyse, S. A. (1991). Behavioral variability and rule generation: General restricted, and superstitious contingency statements. *The Psychological Record, 41*, 487–506.

Wagner, G. A., & Morris, E. K. (1987). "Superstitious" behavior in children. *The Psychological Record, 37*(4), 471–488. doi:10.1007/BF03394994

6 Alien Encounters and Memory

J. Thadeus Meeks and Arlo Clark-Foos

In 1966, only 7% of Americans believed in the existence of Unidentified Flying Objects (UFOs), but by about 50 years later this figure rose to 56% (Costa, 2017). Across those 50 years, a growing number of people have also reported seeing, or even being abducted by, aliens. Although it can be easy to dismiss some reports of UFOs and other alien encounters, other reports are more believable. For example, in 2021, the U.S. Air Force reported about 144 unidentified aerial phenomena, only one of which they were able to explain – a deflating balloon. An author of the report stated, "we absolutely do believe what we're seeing are not simply sensor artifacts. These are things that physically exist." Overall, the reports of sightings and abductions range from mild to frightening. While most people report seeing lights in the sky, others recall abductions and intrusive probing. Additionally, pop culture has widely embraced alien encounter culture with movies such as *Independence Day,* and TV shows such as *X-Files,* making encounters central to their plots. It's safe to say, society has an interest and belief in aliens that is so ubiquitous that we all know the alien stereotype – skinny gray creatures that fly in disc-like saucers.

Examining the Claims

To examine claims related to alien encounters, a good starting point is some of the earlier accounts that captured the imagination of the public. Prior to the 1960s, reporting of UFOs and encounters with aliens were rare and generally positive. This changed in 1961 when Barney and Betty Hill reported being followed by a strange saucer-like craft with aliens that knocked them unconscious, abducted them, experimented on them, and released them with little recollection of the experience (Lacina, 2020). In addition to strange dreams of encounters with aliens following the abduction, the Hills also received hypnotherapy from a therapist who allegedly helped them to recover detailed memories about their abduction. Their story was reported in the media and tabloids and even inspired a 1975 movie starring James Earl Jones. Some have claimed that their story also resulted in a dramatic rise in abduction reports. Furthermore, many of these reports contained negative elements, such as descriptions of saucers, gray creatures, and probing.

Then in November of 1975, a crew of lumberjacks in Arizona claimed to have come across a craft in the woods and went to investigate. One of the men, called Travis Walton, noted that as he got close, the craft suddenly started to move (Spiegel, 2015, para. 4). Walton said that he was then struck by a beam of light. His friends, apparently thinking he was killed, drove off, Walton was found five days later and spoke of a chilling encounter with bald gray creatures that had abducted him, fought with him on an examining table, and caused him to lose consciousness. In the years since, some have

DOI: 10.4324/9781003107798-6

reported odd growth patterns on the side of the trees that faced the clearing where Walton was abducted. Walton has said he believes the aliens were only healing him after he was inadvertently hurt during their own research. Like the Hill's, Walton's case drew huge media attention and was also made into a film, *Fire in the Sky*.

What really happened in these famous examples? How can we interpret these accounts and many others like them? Are there any alternative explanations that need to be considered?

The Evidence

Researchers estimate anywhere between two thousand (Bullard, 1994) to nearly four million (Kristof, 1999) people believe that they have been abducted by aliens. One out of every four Americans say they know someone who claims to have seen a UFO and roughly one in five believe abductions happen (Costa, 2017). In fact, of those who believe in abductions, nearly half believe it is because of alien interest in human anatomy, reflecting the experience of many abductees. There is obvious similarity in the stories of the Hills, Travis Walton, and many others experiencing alien abductions. The consistency across abduction stories is one of the hallmark features suggesting they are real accounts of genuine experiences (Bullard, 1989). In many cases, the experiencers have passed polygraph tests. Perhaps also supporting their claims, experiencers are not generally found to be suffering any mental illness (McNally & Clancy, 2005). When the U.S. Air Force corroborated the existence of unexplainable flying objects, this helped to add some legitimacy to claims about UFOs. Moreover, given the astronomically large amount of planets in the universe, it's plausible that life – even intelligent life – exists somewhere out there.

On the other hand, there is also evidence against the authenticity of these claims. For example, sometimes people simply make up stories. Doug Bower and Dave Chorley, who first reported crop circles near Stonehenge in 1976, later admitted their story was made up and they had manufactured the evidence themselves. In fact, skeptics commonly point out that whenever lifeforms have been caught making crop circles, they always turn out to be human. Just as people pass polygraph tests about their encounters, they also fail them, and polygraph tests themselves have been shown to be unreliable and can even be deceived (Lilienfeld et al., 2010).

Although there is a large amount of unexplained footage of objects in the sky, there is still no definitive physical evidence of saucers, aliens, or abductions. Instead, much of our knowledge of abductions comes from the abductees' own memories. Lastly, even though it's plausible that intelligent life exists in other solar systems, it's considerably less plausible that the life could travel to Earth in a reasonable amount of time. The closest solar system is about four light years away, and traveling at the speed of light itself is quite a challenge, if not impossible. Thus, it would take so long for aliens to visit Earth, that they are very unlikely to have ever done so, much less on a regular basis.

Alternative Explanations

If we take the position that at least some of these experiences are not the result of genuine abductions, then we need to consider alternative explanations. For example, they could either be the result of a false memory for an event that never happened or a false belief that led to misinterpretation of an event that *really did* happen. But how can false memories and false beliefs be created?

Hypnotherapy

Many people who experience an abduction have been found to be under considerable stress and sometimes seek help from a therapist. The methods that some therapists use to help their clients to understand their experiences may strengthen the belief and confidence in alien abduction. Rather than being spontaneously recovered, reports of alien abduction experiences could be incidentally reinforced by means of hypnotherapy (Clark & Loftus, 1996; Newman & Baumeister, 1996). Hypnosis was common at the time the Hills reported their story but has since been criticized for its potential to encourage the formation of false memories (Loftus, 1996). Hypnotists often ask patients to repeatedly revisit a past memory, with some false memory researchers arguing that this procedure has implanted false memories (more on this below). As a result, some researchers strongly suggest that similarity between these procedures casts doubt on the legitimacy of memories recovered through hypnosis (Kihlstrom, 2004). In support of this notion, an analysis of memories recovered through therapy versus those recovered spontaneously by the individual shows that far more of the latter can be corroborated by external evidence (Geraerts et al., 2007). Both the Hills (Lacnia, 2020) and Travis Walton (Spiegel, 2015) reportedly believed that they had been abducted by aliens before undergoing hypnosis, and the hypnosis sessions appeared to have helped clarify and piece together their memories of the experience.

Lynn and Kirsch (1996) suggest that hypnosis may not play a critical role in alien abduction recovery because there are elements that are at the core of alien abduction experience, independent of hypnotic procedures. According to this argument, these may be the result of a person seeking out a therapist that is open to the idea of alien abduction, and the therapist then reinforcing the belief of alien abduction to reduce the anxiety of the patient. This need for explanatory power and relief likely could foster an environment in which one could come to accept that they were abducted. This argument is supported by the notion that some therapists have interests and/or beliefs in alien abduction and related phenomenon, and often believe in the veracity of the abduction story (Newman & Baumeister, 1996). This explanation does not apply to every instance, as is evidenced by the Hill's case. While the Hill's therapist concluded their memories began as dreams by Betty that were later adopted into Barney's memory, he did not doubt that the Hills believed their stories (Lacina, 2020).

Sleep Paralysis

Some of the stereotypical characteristics of alien abductions (e.g., inability to move, visual and auditory hallucinations) are also highly common experiences in sleep paralysis or following anesthesia. Indeed, many point to sleep paralysis as the event that is tied to the alien abduction experience (Cheyne, 2003; McNally & Clancy, 2005). As one can imagine, being awake and conscious, and yet not being able to move is a frightening experience. But there are other characteristics of sleep paralysis to note. Cheyne (2003) describes three types of hallucinations that occur as a result of sleep paralysis. First, the person may experience the presence of another entity in their presence. Second, there is the sensation of bodily damage or harm. Finally, there is the feeling of moving, which is related to the feeling of flying and falling. These characteristics of sleep paralysis share a striking resemblance to what experiencers of alien abduction often report. Further connecting these two concepts, individuals reporting alien abduction are more likely to have had experiences of sleep paralysis (French et al., 2008; McNally & Clancy, 2005). After such confusing and frightening experiences, people will use their known cultural narratives to interpret what occurred to them (Lynn & Kirsch, 1996; McNally & Clancy, 2005). The alien abduction experience is one common cultural narrative that is known by many.

These can be confusing experiences that blur the line between reality and imagination. When this happens, one's imagination and memory work together to construct their own reality. As psychologist Allan Cheyne said:

> People will draw on the most plausible account in their repertoire to explain their experience. Trolls or witches no longer constitute plausible interpretations of these hallucinations. The notion of aliens from outer space is more contemporary and somewhat more plausible to the modern mind. So a flight on a broomstick is replaced by a teleportation to a waiting spaceship.
>
> (Allan Cheyne, as quoted in Kristof, 1999, para. 12)

The history of humankind is filled with experiences that are difficult for individuals to explain. In these instances, we draw on the familiar to construct an explanation. In the past, this was witches and broomsticks and in the 20th and 21st centuries, it's aliens and UFOs.

Even if sleep paralysis is often the basis for the formation of alien abduction memories, it is not the whole story. There are many people that experience sleep paralysis that do not claim to be abducted by aliens. McNally and Clancy (2005) report that 30% of the population have had at least one experience of sleep paralysis. Research shows that there are indeed several individual difference factors that may predispose a person to interpret their experience in this way. For example, experiencers are more likely to have preexisting beliefs related to alien abduction and other paranormal phenomenon (French et al., 2008; McNally & Clancy, 2005). This idea is related to the confirmation bias – a tendency to selectively attend to information that confirms our held beliefs (Lord et al., 1979; Wason, 1960). This can occur below the person's level of awareness and further strengthen the belief and memory of the experience. They may also have a higher tendency to dissociate (French et al., 2008; Holden & French, 2002) and may be more prone to fantastical thought (French et al., 2008; McNally & Clancy, 2005). In addition, some evidence suggests that those reporting alien abduction experiences have higher levels of depression (Clancy et al., 2002; McNally & Clancy 2005). Based on these findings, there is a profile that emerges of someone that might interpret something that is unfamiliar to them (e.g., sleep paralysis) as a supernatural occurrence.

False Memories

Much of what is called into question are false beliefs, and not necessarily false memories. For example, a person may believe extraterrestrial beings created crop circles, but that does not mean that the person has a memory of their creation. The same would apply to more general beliefs about aliens visiting Earth in UFOs. Even an encounter with a UFO at night is not really a memory that can be questioned as false. Rather, it is a probable misinterpretation of an event. Thus, it is not the memory that may be false, but the belief related to the memory. Some experiencers of UFO abductions, however, not only come to believe in the event occurrence but also form *memories* for the event that they believe occurred. This differs from someone *remembering* that they saw that UFO on the way home because alien abductions are *remembered* with much more detail, such that it is more difficult to explain away as merely a false belief or misinterpretation.

If the fact that false memories can be created by suggestions after the experience sounds unlikely, there is much research that demonstrates that information presented after an event can become erroneously incorporated into a previous memory. This phenomenon, known as the *misinformation effect*, has been shown to occur frequently in the context of laboratory and naturalistic studies (see Ayers and Reder (1998) for a review). The strengthening of these false memories by various recovery attempts is also consistent with the constructive nature of memory. Memory does not operate like a tape recorder in which the memory is retrieved exactly as it was encoded. Instead, memory is more like a jigsaw puzzle – we construct our memories from different experiences (Clancy et al., 2002; Lindsay & Read, 1994; Loftus, 1993; Schacter, 1999, 2012). In this construction, we often mis-combine elements, both real and created, resulting in false memories. Our prior beliefs affect these false memories because we tend to reconstruct our memories with a bias toward our own personal view of the world. Clark and Loftus (1996) cite the misinformation effect as one of the sources of alien abduction memory formation. When one experiences a strange, and seemingly unexplainable event, they will use what they know to fill in the pieces. This information may come from past exposure to media, suggestions from a therapist, or other sources. The overarching point here is that there is plenty of material that people may unconsciously use to interpret what they do not understand, and when these pieces are put together, sometimes they may look like an alien abduction.

Source monitoring is another component of memory that may help explain reports of alien abduction (Clark & Loftus, 1996). This concept does not refer to the memory for information itself, but rather the origin or source of the information (Johnson et al., 1993; Schacter et al., 1998). A source misattribution occurs when one incorrectly attributes the information to a different source. While source misattributions do not always cause major problems for an individual, these memory errors could be detrimental (e.g., assessing the credibility of the source). Regarding alien abductions, someone may remember details about an abduction experience and incorrectly attribute the source of the details to the original event rather than suggestions and details provided after the event occurred (e.g., hypnotherapy). A specific type of source monitoring may be especially relevant for cases of alien abduction. Reality monitoring involves discriminating between an event that occurred in the external environment from something that was generated internally in our minds (Johnson & Raye, 1981). When we make such judgments, we may confuse elements of our imagination with similar events that actually occurred (Henkel & Franklin, 1998). Thus, memories of exposure to the culturally consistent narrative of alien abduction may be incorporated into an individual's recollection of an actual event such as sleep paralysis, blurring the lines between reality and fantasy.

But can such false memories be created merely through suggestion? The evidence seems to suggest so. In one well-known example, Loftus and Pickrell (1995) introduced false descriptions to adults about getting lost in a shopping mall when they were young. Five out of 24 participants in the study subsequently falsely recalled having had this experience. It is important to note that this suggestion was subtle and in no way involved coercion. But it is not out of the norm of common belief that people can get lost in a shopping mall. Alien abduction, on the other hand, is a much more implausible event. Surely these types of memories cannot be created by mere suggestion. Or can they?

Mazzoni et al. (2001) successfully created an equal amount of implausible as plausible false memories in undergraduate students. More specifically, the researchers told the participants that demonic possession was more common than previously thought. These participants were just as likely to form false autobiographical memories about demonic possession as compared to a more plausible scenario. More specific to the current topic, Otgaar et al. (2009) found a significant number of false memories created for alien abduction in children. Taken together and combined with the predisposing factors associated with experiencers of alien abduction, it is not that improbable that memory recovery attempts can serve to create memories with false details.

It is possible that experiencers of alien abduction are generally more susceptible to false memories. Clancy et al. (2002) examined this possibility using the Deese-Roeidger Memory (DRM) procedure (Roediger & McDermott, 1995). In this procedure, participants study lists of words that all semantically relate to an unpresented critical lure. For example, a study list might consist of such words as *bed, wake, dream,* and so on. All the words relate to the critical lure of *sleep,* but this lure is never presented at study. Research shows people will often recall and/or recognize the critical lure as having been studied. Using these DRM lists, Clancy et al. found that experiencers of alien abduction had higher false memory rates as compared to non-experiencers. In contrast, French et al. (2008) failed to find this same difference using a DRM procedure. This discrepancy could be because more of the participants in Clancy et al.'s study went through a hypnosis procedure, thus accounting for differences across the separate studies (French et al., 2008).

There is also more general research using the DRM paradigm that can be applied to the experience of alien abduction. For example, false memories can be created by nonconscious processes during memory formation (Seamon et al., 1998). In addition, people are often very confident in their false memories (Roediger & McDermott, 1995). Taken in combination, these two factors may help explain why individuals maintain their staunch position on their alien abduction experience.

One may guess that being required to elaborate on a false memory would bring the falsity of the details to light. Often, the opposite occurs. Research shows that elaboration increases the amount of, and sometimes confidence in, false memories. This applies for various types of elaboration, including perceptual elaboration (Drivdahl & Zaragoza, 2001), conceptual elaboration (Zaragoza et al., 2011), and emotional elaboration (Drivdahl et al., 2008). In this context, encouraging and confirmatory comments by others could serve to strengthen the confidence in a false memory (Zaragoza et al., 2011). Thus, it is no wonder that beliefs in alien abduction do not dissipate over time and retellings of the story. In addition, false memories are not merely remembered with some vague sense of familiarity, but rather are often remembered with false contextual, re-collective detail (Roediger & McDermott, 1995; Zaragoza et al., 2011). What about being forewarned about the possibility of a false memory? Research using the DRM paradigm suggests that sometimes warnings can be ineffective in reducing the occurrence of false memories (Gallo et al. 1997, 2001; McDermott & Roediger, 1998). All these findings give some insight on why one may confidently and persistently believe in an alien abduction experience.

Summary and Conclusion

Belief in UFOs and alien abductions has been around for some time, and there is no sign that these beliefs will fade into obscurity anytime soon. There has been a recent resurgence of interest in these phenomena, perhaps due to the attention from the U.S. Air Force; however, just because members of Air Force could not identify an object, that doesn't mean the object must have aliens inside. There are many simpler explanations that are from Earth.

Our society has long held a fascination with UFO and alien abduction occurrences. These phenomena are often associated with rich detail that can seem convincing. But are these memories real? Many people have strong and consistent beliefs in their abductions and confidently reject alternative explanations. Research on false memories, however, makes it clear that experiencers of alien abduction may be unconsciously creating and subsequently reporting false details. These details could be based solely on imagination, but also could be due to the misinterpretation of actual occurrences (e.g., lights in the sky). False memories are not unique to these individuals. To the contrary, false memories are common and can be formed in numerous ways. Although false beliefs and memories of alien abduction may not seem harmful, these beliefs pose potential psychological harm for the individual. Thus, when asking whether one really went aboard that spaceship, perhaps careful thought about the nature of how that memory came to be is warranted.

References

Ayers, M. S., & Reder, L. M. (1998). A theoretical review of the misinformation effect: Predictions from an activation-based memory model. *Psychonomic Bulletin & Review, 5*(1), 1–21. doi:10.3758/bf03209454

Bullard, T. E. (1989). UFO abduction reports. *Journal of American Folklore, 102,* 147–170.

Bullard, T. E. (1994). The influence of investigators on UFO abduction reports: Results of a survey. In A. Pritchard, D. E. Pritchard, J. E. Mack, P. Kasey, & C. Yapp (Eds.), *Alien discussions: Proceedings of the Abduction Study Conference held at M.I.T* (pp. 571–619). Cambridge, MA: North Cambridge Press.

Cheyne, J. A. (2003). Sleep paralysis and the structure of waking-nightmare hallucinations. *Dreaming, 13*(3), 163–179. doi:10.1037/1053-0797.13.3.163

Clancy, S. A., McNally, R. J., Schacter, D. L., Lenzenweger, M. F., & Pitman, R. K. (2002). Memory distortion in people reporting abduction by aliens. *Journal of Abnormal Psychology, 111,* 455–461. doi:10.1037/0021-843x.111.3.455

Clark, S. E., & Loftus, E. F. (1996). The construction of space alien abduction memories. *Psychological Inquiry, 7,* 140–143. doi:10.1207/s15327965pli0702_5

Costa, C. (August 4, 2017). UFOs, aliens, and abductions survey. *New York Skies: A UFO blog. Seattle New Times.* https://syracusenewtimes.com/ufos-aliens-and-abductions-survey/

Drivdahl, S. B., & Zaragoza, M. S. (2001). The role of perceptual elaboration and individual differences in the creation of false memories for suggested events. *Applied Cognitive Psychology, 15,* 265–281. doi:10.1002/acp.701

Drivdahl, S. B., Zaragoza, M. S., & Learned, D. M. (2008). The role of emotional elaboration in the creation of false memories. *Applied Cognitive Psychology, 23,* 13–35. doi:10.1002/acp.1446

French, C., Santomauro, J., Hamilton, V., Fox, R., & Thalbourne, M. (2008). Psychological aspects of the alien contact experience. *Cortex, 44,* 1387–1395. doi:10.1016/j.cortex.2007.11.011

Gallo, D. A., Roberts, M. J., & Seamon, J. G. (1997). Remembering words not presented in lists: Can we avoid creating false memories? *Psychonomic Bulletin & Review, 4,* 271–276. doi:10.3758/bf03209405

Gallo, D. A., Roediger, H. L., & McDermott, K. B. (2001). Associative false recognition occurs without strategic criterion shifts. *Psychonomic Bulletin & Review, 8,* 579–586. doi:10.3758/bf03196194

Geraerts, E., Schooler, J. W., Merckelbach, H., Jelicic, M., Hauer, B. J. A., & Ambadar, Z. (2007). The reality of recovered memories: Corroborating continuous and discontinuous memories of childhood sexual abuse. *Psychological Science, 18,* 564–568. doi:10.1111/j.1467-9280.2007.01940.x

Henkel, L. A., & Franklin, N. (1998). Reality monitoring of physically and conceptually related objects. *Memory & Cognition, 26*(4), 321–335.

Holden, K. J., & French, C. C. (2002). Alien abduction experiences: Some clues from neuropsychology and neuropsychiatry. *Cognitive Neuropsychiatry, 7*, 163–178. doi:10.1080/13546800244000058

Johnson, M. K., Hashtroudi, S., & Lindsay, D. S. (1993). Source monitoring. *Psychological Bulletin, 114*, 3–28. doi:10.1037/0033-2909.114.1.3

Johnson, M. K. & Raye, C. L. (1981). Reality monitoring. *Psychological Review, 88*(1), 67–85.

Kihlstrom, J. F. (2004). An unbalanced balancing act: Blocked, recovered, and false memories in the laboratory and clinic. *Clinical Psychology: Science and Practice, 11*, 34–41. doi:10.1093/clipsy.bph057

Kristof, N. D. (1999). Alien abduction? Science calls it sleep paralysis. *The New York Times.* https://www.nytimes.com/1999/07/06/science/alien-abduction-science-calls-it-sleep-paralysis.html

Lacina, L. (2020). How Betty and Barney Hill's alien abduction story defined the genre. *The History Channel.* https://www.history.com/news/first-alien-abduction-account-barney-betty-hill

Lilienfeld, S. O., Lynn, S. J., Ruscio, J., & Beyerstein, B. L. (2010). *50 great myths of popular psychology: Shattering widespread misconceptions about human behavior.* John Wiley & Sons Ltd.

Lindsay, D. S., & Read, J. D. (1994). Psychotherapy and memories of childhood sexual abuse: A cognitive perspective. *Applied Cognitive Psychology, 8*, 281–338. doi:10.1002/acp.2350080403

Loftus, E. F. (1993). The reality of repressed memories. *American Psychologist, 48*, 518–537. doi:10.1037/0003-066x.48.5.518

Loftus, E. (1996). Memory distortion and false memory creation. *Applied Cognitive Psychology, 24*, 281–295.

Loftus, E. F., & Pickrell, J. E. (1995). The formation of false memories. *Psychiatric Annals, 25*, 720–725. doi:10.3928/0048-5713-19951201-07

Lord, C. G., Ross, L., & Lepper, M. R. (1979). Biased assimilation and attitude polarization: The effects of prior theories on subsequently considered evidence. *Journal of Personality and Social Psychology, 37*, 2098–2109. doi:10.1037/0022-3514.37.11.2098

Lynn, S. J., & Kirsch, I. I. (1996). Alleged alien abductions: False memories, hypnosis, and fantasy proneness. *Psychological Inquiry, 7*, 151–155. doi:10.1207/s15327965pli0702_8

Mazzoni, G. A. L., Loftus, E. F., & Kirsch, I. (2001). Changing beliefs about implausible autobiographical events: A little plausibility goes a long way. *Journal of Experimental Psychology: Applied, 7*, 51–59. doi:10.1037/1076-898x.7.1.51

McDermott, K. B., & Roediger, H. L. (1998). Attempting to avoid illusory memories: Robust false recognition of associates persists under conditions of explicit warnings and immediate testing. *Journal of Memory and Language, 39*, 508–520. doi:10.1006/jmla.1998.2582

McNally, R. J., & Clancy, S. A. (2005). Sleep paralysis, sexual abuse, and space alien abduction. *Transcultural Psychiatry, 42*, 113–122. doi:10.1177/1363461505050715

Newman, L. S., & Baumeister, R. F. (1996). Not just another false memory: Further thoughts on the UFO abduction phenomenon. *Psychological Inquiry, 7*, 185–197. doi:10.1207/s15327965pli0702_14

Otgaar, H., Candel, I., Merckelbach, H., & Wade, K. A. (2009). Abducted by a UFO: Prevalence information affects young children's false memories for an implausible event. *Applied Cognitive Psychology, 23*, 115–125. doi:10.1002/acp.1445

Roediger, H. L., & McDermott, K. B. (1995). Creating false memories: Remembering words not presented in lists. *Journal of Experimental Psychology: Learning, Memory, and Cognition, 21*, 803–814. doi:10.1037/0278-7393.21.4.803

Schacter, D. L. (1999). The seven sins of memory: Insights from psychology and cognitive neuroscience. *American Psychologist, 5*, 182–203. doi:10.1037/0003-066x.54.3.182

Schacter, D. L. (2012). Adaptive constructive processes and the future of memory. *American Psychologist, 67*, 603–613. doi:10.1037/a0029869

Schacter, D. L., Norman, K. A., & Koutstaal, W. (1998). The cognitive neuroscience of constructive memory. *Annual Review of Psychology, 49*, 289–318. doi:10.1146/annurev.psych.49.1.289

Seamon, J. G., Luo, C. R., & Gallo, D. A. (1998). Creating false memories of words with or without recognition of list items: Evidence for nonconscious processes. *Psychological Science, 9*(1), 20–26. doi:10.1111/1467-9280.00004

Spiegel, L. (April 23, 2015). UFO-alien abduction still Haunts Travis Walton. HuffPost Weird News Podcast. https://www.huffpost.com/entry/travis-walton-still-haunted-by-ufo_n_7119910

Wason, P. C. (1960). On the failure to eliminate hypotheses in a conceptual task. *Quarterly Journal of Experimental Psychology, 12*, 129–140. doi:10.1080/17470216008416717

Zaragoza, M. S., Mitchell, K. J., Payment, K., & Drivdahl, S. (2011). False memories for suggestions: The impact of conceptual elaboration. *Journal of Memory and Language, 64*, 18–31. doi:10.1016/j.jml.2010.09.004

7 Learning Styles and Cognition

Tesia Marshik and William Cerbin

Have you ever tried explaining a concept to someone, and the person you're speaking to replies, "Oh, sorry, I'm a visual learner" as an explanation for why they aren't understanding? Or have you ever provided a similar explanation for why you enjoyed a particular class, or why you are good at some subjects and not others?

These examples illustrate the concept of a "learning style." Many people believe they have a learning style that determines the way they prefer to learn, and the way they learn best. Over 70 different versions of learning styles have been proposed (Cassidy, 2004; Coffield et al., 2004a). To name a few, theorists have suggested that learners differ based on whether they are convergers vs. divergers, verbalizers vs. imagers, globalists vs. analysts, and accommodators vs. assimilators. But the most popular versions of learning styles are distinguished by sensory modalities (e.g., visual, auditory, and kinesthetic). For example, a person who claims to be a visual learner would prefer to have new information presented in a visual format such as pictures, diagrams, videos, graphics, and maps. An auditory learner would prefer to listen to new information, such as audiobooks, podcasts, TED Talks, and lectures. In addition, and this is a key point, many people believe that they not only prefer learning in a particular way, but they actually learn best when the new information is presented in a way that matches or meshes with their learning style. The assumption is that visual learners thrive on visual information and auditory learners on verbal information, and this chapter will examine the evidence about this claim and other claims related to learning styles.

Examining the Claims

Pop Psychology, Pop Culture, and Public Perception

International surveys suggest that as many as 93% of the general public believe that "individuals learn better when they receive information in their preferred learning style" and 88% believe that "children have learning styles dominated by particular senses" (Macdonald et al., 2017). Learning styles are commonly applied in many settings including healthcare, management, and industry, but are especially prominent in education. A review of 37 studies in 18 countries found that on average 89% of educators believe in learning styles (Newton & Salvi, 2020).

A quick Internet search for "learning styles" produces an enormous mix of resources heralding the benefits of discovering one's learning style and companies marketing tests and trainings. The same search also reveals numerous reviews, commentaries, blogs, and videos debunking the myth and denouncing wasted time and effort. As with many

DOI: 10.4324/9781003107798-7

things, it is easy to fall victim to confirmation bias and attend to sources that support your initial view, but it is also easy to become frustrated or overwhelmed by the sheer amount of conflicting information online. Of course, the *way* you search also matters. Searching for "types of learning styles" or "how to accommodate learning styles" prioritizes different results compared to searching "are learning styles real" or "learning styles myth." These varied results both reflect and add to confusion.

Importantly though, similar conflicting messages also exist in academic sources. For example, a recent review indicated that 89% of published journal articles on learning styles provided generally positive views or otherwise directly endorsed the use of learning styles in education without providing empirical evidence (Newton, 2015) and the majority of teacher education textbooks advocate for the use of learning styles accommodations and/or present the theory as widely accepted and verified (Cuevas, 2015; Wininger et al., 2019). Furthermore, a study conducted by the National Center on Teacher Quality found that 67% of teacher-education programs required students to account for learning styles in their lesson-plans (Pomerance et al., 2016) and learning styles are frequently included in formal teacher certification and state licensing standards and exams (Furey, 2020). Given the popularity of learning styles among teachers, it is perhaps unsurprising that approximately 90% of students believe in them too (Dandy & Bendersky, 2014; Riener & Willingham, 2010). The idea is so common that few people even think to question it.

The Evidence

Much of the evidence in favor of learning styles stems from common, anecdotal experiences. Once you've been told that you have a certain learning style, it is relatively easy to remember times when that style seemed to work better than other styles. For example, someone who believes they are a visual learner may easily recall a time that they struggled to grasp a concept until they saw a table or graphic in the textbook and suddenly it "clicked." Similarly, someone who thinks they are an auditory learner may recall times that they were especially dependent on verbal explanations provided by a teacher to clarify content they read about in the textbook. It is not uncommon for people to blame poor performance on a lack of a match between their preferred learning style and their teachers' instructional methods – e.g., "I just don't learn that way." The same confirmation process happens from other perspectives as well: for instance, when a parent observes their child struggling to learn something until they are given something to physically manipulate, or when they have a child who is good at crafting, they assume their child must be a hands-on or kinesthetic learner. Learning styles offer a relatively simple and intuitive explanation for why we experience success in some contexts but not others.

There are also a number of published articles and books that argue for the idea that people have learning styles. For instance, there are over 50 publications centered on one popular model (Dunn & Dunn, 1992), including review papers supposedly providing evidence that teaching to students' preferences increased their academic achievement (Dunn et al., 1995; Lovelace, 2005). In one of those reviews, the author concluded that the data "overwhelmingly supported the position that matching students' learning-style preferences with complementary instruction improved academic achievement" (Lovelace, 2005, p. 181). However, these works have been challenged by a host of other researchers who found that most of the studies did not undergo external peer review and, when scrutinized, had significant methodological flaws (Kavale et al., 1998; Kavale & LeFever, 2007; Pashler et al., 2009).

If one takes a critical and comprehensive look at the learning style literature as a whole, three major problems emerge: a lack of coherence and clarity among learning styles conceptions, inadequate ways to assess or determine learning styles, and a dearth of support for the idea that teaching to individuals' modality preferences significantly improves their learning. The first two issues are related. In order to claim that learning styles exist and are important psychological qualities, you need to be able to define what a learning style is and then measure it to see whether a person possesses the characteristic. However, there is yet no scientific consensus on how many or what types of learning styles exist. As previously noted, over 70 different frameworks have been proposed, but the associated research is largely fragmented and isolated, with little dialogue happening between proponents of individual learning styles models (Coffield et al., 2004a). Coffield (2012) described the literature as "incoherent and conceptually confused" (p. 220); with its array of poorly defined and overlapping categories, and distinctions that lack scientific basis, even among the 13 most popular models. So perhaps unsurprisingly, studies have shown that most instruments designed to assess learning styles have poor reliability and validity (Coffield et al., 2004a), meaning they don't clearly measure what they purport to measure, and participants scores often vary significantly from one measurement to the next.

Aside from the basic definitional issues, one of the major problems with measuring learning styles is that it is usually done via self-report questionnaires. For example, surveys may ask whether one prefers to learn something by looking at pictures, vs. through reading, vs. listening to a lecture, or through doing. Individuals learning "styles" are then determined by summing the scores for each category, with higher scores indicating a stronger style preference. In other words, learning styles "measurements" are derived from subjective judgments that people make about themselves. But the major flaw of such self-report methods is that such judgments may be unstable and differ from one time to the next, and there is no guarantee that one's stated preferences are accurate, or that they reflect a distinct style or aptitude for learning. One may *prefer* certain methods, or *think* that one learns best through certain methods, but that doesn't make it so. Preferences do not necessarily equate to abilities, and we are not always good judges of our abilities to boot. (Imagine if students' learning in school was assessed via self-ratings of how well they thought they understood the content, as opposed to having them demonstrate their understanding in some way.)

Another major limitation of learning styles questionnaires is that they ignore differences in participants' experiences across contexts. So the end result of a learning style classification is largely a function of what kinds of questions and scenarios were included in the questionnaires. But our preferences often change in light of what we are trying to learn (Riener & Willingham, 2010). For example, if you are learning how to recognize the songs of different birds, then it makes sense to use auditory methods. If, however, you are learning how to distinguish poisonous from non-poisonous plants in the wild, then visual methods would likely work best. Moreover, most content is best taught through interactive, multimodal experiences (Moreno & Mayer, 2007). For instance, when learning how to play basketball, visuals and auditory feedback might be very helpful – but you also need to practice those skills (kinesthetically) on the court. You would never expect so-called "auditory learners" or "visual learners" to become skilled players only by listening to instructions or looking at photos all day.

The significance of context may be demonstrated with a simple thought experiment (as described by Riener and Willingham, 2010, and paraphrased here): if a friend said they wanted to teach you something, and asked how you wanted to learn it … would you be able to answer that question without knowing WHAT was going to be taught? Might your answer change if the topic was "how to ride a bike" compared to "trends in access to healthcare in the 21st century" or "how to talk to your kids about sex?" How easily could you pick just <u>one</u> of those options? And wouldn't your learning ultimately depend more strongly on the *quality* of demonstrations, readings, charts and/or the extent to which you connect with the speaker and content? This is probably why studies have found that most people have bimodal or multimodal preferences, as opposed to having a clear or strong preference for a single modality (Fleming, 2012; Husmann & O'Loughlin, 2019; Prithishkumar & Michael, 2014). Further, research suggests that even when people do report a strong, single learning style preference, most do not actually study in a way that aligns with their stated preference, and those that do experience no benefit to their learning (Husmann & O'Loughlin, 2019). In sum, the measurement of learning styles is plagued by inconsistencies in conceptual definitions, subjectivity, and a lack of real-world correspondence to behavior and learning outcomes.

And that brings us to the second major criticism of learning styles, which is the lack of evidence that teaching to individuals' modality preferences significantly improves their learning. Learning style advocates often rely on people to judge for themselves whether they learn more in one modality than another. But this type of evidence is weak at best because people are not always adequate judges of their learning and because it is impossible to determine how much of one's learning is actually influenced by a learning style preference vs. any other factor (such as background knowledge, or motivation). What's needed are controlled experiments that directly measure participants' learning. Here is how a typical experiment works. First, participants are evaluated to determine their learning styles[1] and then assigned randomly to a learning condition in which they are presented with new information to learn. (Randomly placing participants into the different instructional conditions is important because it controls for other individual factors that could impact their learning – such as background knowledge and motivation.) Some individuals receive instruction that matches or meshes with their learning style and others receive information that matches a different learning style. For example, an experiment might test visual and auditory learners. Half the visual learners would receive "visual instruction" and half would receive "auditory instruction." Similarly, half the auditory learners would receive "auditory instruction" and half would receive "visual instruction." If matching instruction to learning styles really matters, then the results should show that people who were taught with instruction that matched their learning style would learn more/perform better than those taught with instruction that did not match their style. That is, visual learners would learn more from visual instruction than from auditory instruction, and auditory learners would learn more from auditory instruction than from visual instruction.

However, decades of research, and reviews of research, show that people do not learn better when taught in a mode consistent with their learning style. As early as the 1970s, which is arguably when the idea of learning styles first took hold, researchers were already noting this lack of confirmatory evidence. For instance, Tarver and Dawson (1978), Arter and Jenkins (1979), and Kampwirth and Bates (1980) published a series of review papers covering between 12 and 22 studies on the topic, all of which concluded that there was little support for the learning styles hypothesis. Similarly, in a review of 39 studies, Kavale and Forness (1987) concluded that matching instruction to a student preference had little support and called for the model to be dismissed in favor of other evidence-based instructional methods.

Yet, despite those early refutational reviews, in the decades that followed, the concept of learning styles steadily gained influence and acceptance in educational circles and among the general public. The idea gained so much popularity that in 2008, the journal *Psychological Science in the Public Interest* commissioned a modern evaluation of the evidence. Thirty years after the initial reviews, the commissioned study concluded that there was (still) insufficient support for the matching hypothesis and the authors reported that many studies flatly contradicted the claim (Pashler et al., 2009). However, they also noted significant flaws in past research (namely that few studies actually included the necessary experimental methods to test the matching hypothesis) and called for further, more rigorous research.

Since then, other researchers have followed their guidelines, but the results have been the same. For example, Rogowsky et al. (2015) conducted a controlled study in which they examined the extent to which matching adults' learning style preferences (i.e., auditory, visual) to instructional modes predicted their comprehension and retention. They found no evidence for the matching hypothesis but, in contrast, reported that "visual learners" actually performed best across all the tests – which they suggested was evidence that teaching to preferred learning styles could actually be detrimental.

A review of relevant research completed *after* Pashler et al.'s (2009) critique found that empirical support for the matching hypothesis remained virtually nonexistent, while evidence contradicting it was much more prevalent (Cuevas, 2015). In sum, decades of research has overwhelmingly failed to support the idea that people have styles in which they learn best, or that catering to learning style preferences enhances learning. To be fair, over the years, there have been a handful of scattered studies reporting evidence of positive effects (Sternberg et al., 1999), but, again, methodological issues make those results tenuous and the overwhelming majority of controlled studies have shown that matching instruction with preferred learning style has no positive effect on learning (Cuevas, 2015; Kavale & Forness, 1987; Pashler et al., 2009; Rohrer & Pashler, 2012).

Understanding Beliefs

If there is so little credible scientific evidence that learning styles affect their learning, then why do so many people believe they do? And why has the belief persisted for so long? We think the popularity and persistence of the learning styles myth has several sources:

- The concept of learning styles is relatively simple, easy to understand and is consistent with pervasive beliefs about individual differences and individual uniqueness. People are different in many ways, and learning styles seem to be just another way people differ from one another. On the surface, learning styles provide a way to simultaneously recognize individuality, simplify learning, and promote inclusion.
- Learning "styles" are often conflated with other individual differences, such as interest and ability. People do differ in terms of their interests and abilities, which can and do impact their learning. But this is not the same as saying that high interest or ability in one area will enhance learning across all areas, or that they learn everything best in the same way. For instance, someone with strong visuo-spatial skills may show an advantage on visuo-spatial tasks (such as completing a maze, or replicating a drawing), but those same skills would not be advantageous for other tasks that require different skills (for instance, correctly recognizing the sound of a musical instrument, or balancing on a beam).

- Some people have learned about learning styles from a trusted source such as a teacher or friend and accepted it at face value.
- People believe in learning styles based on their personal experience. In other words, I may believe that I'm a visual learner because I have had experiences where I thought visual information helped me learn a new topic. But this type of evidence from personal experience is flawed in at least two ways. First, there are other plausible reasons for my learning. For example, suppose I have been reading about a topic and not learning much until I see a diagram in the text which makes it much clearer to me. I use this as evidence that I am a *visual learner*. But there are several alternative explanations. For example, the text could be poorly written and other students, regardless of their learning style would have difficulty with it too. The text could also include many new terms and concepts. Also, the visual diagram summarizes the verbal information clearly, and anyone regardless of their "learning style" would benefit from the visual information, not just visual learners. I cannot determine which of these is the best explanation because all I have to go on is my individual personal experience.
- A second limitation of relying on personal experience is our tendency to focus on information that confirms what we already believe. This is called confirmation bias (Nickerson, 1998). If I think I'm a visual learner, then I'm more likely to notice the times when a diagram, graphic, map or photo helped me learn. But I don't focus on or remember instances when I learned perfectly well from verbal information or from a combination of verbal and visual information. In addition, I may not remember other instances when visual information did not help me learn.
- People are simply not aware of the scientific evidence. Most people are unaware of any research on learning styles and therefore have no reason to disbelieve it. Moreover, much of the research is published in professional journals that are not of interest or accessible to most people.
- For those that *are* aware of research, many do not have the scientific literacy to critically evaluate research methodologies or interpret findings. For example, people may believe that self-report questionnaires provide evidence of learning effects. But as we discussed earlier, self-reports are inadequate ways to identify learning styles. Similarly, many people do not understand the necessity of the experimental methods we previously described for testing the learning styles matching hypothesis. Further, people often exhibit the burden of proof fallacy, whereby they assume that the burden of proof lies on researchers to *disprove* the learning styles claim, as opposed to the other way around. (This could also be called the "you can't prove it *doesn't* exist" fallacy.) But, in science and logic, the burden of proof always lies with the person(s) making the claim to provide confirmatory evidence; it is impossible to prove a negative.
- A final, reason that many people believe in learning styles is that a large number of businesses and publishers still sell the idea of learning styles.

What's the Harm?

To recap, even though the belief in learning styles is popular and looks good on the surface, researchers have been unable to scientifically justify the utility of assessing or accommodating learning style preferences. At best, one could argue that the belief in learning styles and efforts to accommodate them is merely unhelpful or ineffective. But, as others have argued, learning styles have the potential to be harmful in several ways.

First, learning styles encourage people to develop a fixed mindset about their abilities, which may limit their potential and hinder them from developing effective learning strategies (Dweck, 2008). Believing that you only learn one way may cause you to exert less effort or to give-up when content is presented in non-preferred ways, and may deter you from pursuing certain subjects or professions that appear to be dominated by other styles (Newton, 2015; Nancekivell et al., 2020; Scott 2010; Stahl, 1999). It could also lead to over-confidence and unrealistic expectations when information is presented in ways you *do* prefer.

Second, at an institutional level, learning styles have the potential to unnecessarily pigeon-hole students, and these labels can lead to self-fulfilling prophecies (Rosenthal & Jacobson, 1968). If educators believe that certain students can only learn in certain ways, they may lower their expectations, discourage students from pursuing certain subjects, and/or resort to using less effective teaching methods for the sake of catering to those perceived styles. Even if such accommodations are well-intended, all of those behaviors ultimately decrease the likelihood that students are successful in those areas and further reinforce the idea that abilities are fixed.

Third, assessing and catering to learning styles is a waste of valuable time and resources. On an individual level, students may focus on using study strategies they think are compatible with their learning style, at the expense of other strategies that could be more effective. In one study, about one third of students relied on strategies that coincided with their most dominant learning preference, *to no benefit*, and the most common strategies employed were actually some of the least effective (Husmann & O'Loughlin, 2019). Moreover, it is important for students to use a variety of approaches and learning styles to complete different kinds of tasks (Coffield et al., 2004a, 2004b). For instance, researchers found that the effectiveness of verbal vs. visual strategies varied depending on whether learners were being asked to recognize landmarks vs. being asked to judge relative directions (Kraemer et al., 2017).

Similarly, teachers may be wasting valuable time and resources in an effort to accommodate learning styles, when they could be implementing other evidence-based practices such as focusing on the best mode(s) for presenting the content, clarifying learning objectives, providing timely feedback, and making efforts to account for other individual differences such as background knowledge/experience (Hattie, 2008; Nuthall, 2007; Riener & Willingham, 2010). Additionally, given that students' learning style preferences may reflect perceived ability levels (e.g., a student may prefer auditory methods to compensate for poor reading skills), in attempting to cater to learners' preferences, teachers might actually be missing out on important opportunities to develop students' skills and abilities in other areas (Riener & Willingham, 2010; Stahl, 1999). A student might not *want* to learn through reading, but it is still an important skill that should be practiced and developed.

Lastly, instead of using in-class time to assess and discuss their students' learning style preferences, research suggests it would be far more valuable for teachers to initiate discussions of effective learning strategies (such as spaced practice, self-testing, and deep-processing techniques; Dunlosky et al., 2013). In other words, students would benefit from instruction aimed at developing skills and strategies that actually have the potential to benefit their learning, as opposed to instruction that propagates the falsehood of learning styles.

Summary and Conclusion

The learning styles myth is the belief that each person has a specific learning style, or a preferred way to learn new information, and that they learn best when new information is presented or studied in a format consistent with that style, for example, visual learners prefer and learn best from visual information. Surveys of the general public, educators, and students indicate that large majorities of people in many countries endorse learning styles, but the preponderance of empirical evidence refutes the theory. There is no good evidence that classifying or accommodating learning style preferences enhances learning, but it does have the potential to adversely affect our achievement and motivation for certain areas.

To be clear, the assertion that learning styles do not exist is NOT akin to saying that all people are the same, or will learn the same in any given situation. People differ in many ways that can and do impact their learning, such as their prior knowledge of content, strategies they use to learn, specific abilities relevant to what they are learning, interest, motivation, and socioeconomic background. As such, educators do need to use a variety of instructional methods to account for *those* differences. And multimodal instruction may benefit *all* students' learning to the extent that it offers increased repetition and practice, makes the learning experience more meaningful, and enhances learners' attention. For instance, research has shown that people learn better when verbal and visual information are well integrated rather than from visual or verbal information alone attention (Butcher, 2014; Moreno & Mayer, 2007). Likewise, students also need to develop learning strategies and habits to facilitate their learning across a variety of subject matter and skills and in a variety of situations. As one eminent psychologist, Daniel Willingham, suggested, "People should stop thinking of themselves as visual, verbal, or some other kind of learner … It's much better to think of everyone having a **toolbox** of ways to think, and think to yourself, which tool is best?" (as quoted by Khazan, 2018, emphasis added).

Note

1 We use the word "style" here for the sake of representing the views of learning styles proponents. But, as explained in the section on measurement issues, in most cases it would be more accurate to label them as learning style *preferences*, or modality preferences.

References

Arter, J. A., & Jenkins, J. A. (1979). Differential diagnosis. Prescriptive teaching: A critical appraisal. *Review of Educational Research, 49*(4), 517–555.

Butcher, K. R. (2014). The multimedia principle. In R. E. Mayer (Ed.), *The Cambridge handbook of multimedia learning* (pp. 174–205). The Cambridge University Press.

Cassidy, S. (2004). Learning styles: An overview of theories, models, and measures. *Educational Psychology, 24*(4), 419–444.

Coffield, F. (2012). Learning styles: Unreliable, invalid, and impractical and yet still widely used. In P. Adey & J. Dillon (Eds.), *Bad education: Debunking myths in education* (pp. 115–130). Open University Press.

Coffield, F., Moseley, D., Hall, E., & Ecclestone, K. (2004a). *Learning styles and pedagogy in post-16 learning. A systematic and critical review.* Learning and Skills Research Centre.

Coffield, F., Moseley, D., Hall, E., & Ecclestone, K. (2004b). *Should we be using learning styles? What research has to say to practice.* Learning and Skills Research Centre.

Cuevas, J. (2015). Is learning styles-based instruction effective? A comprehensive analysis of recent research on learning styles. *Theory and Research in Education, 13*(3), 308–333.

Dandy, K. L., & Bendersky, K. (2014). Student and faculty beliefs about learning in higher education: Implications for teaching. *International Journal of Teaching and Learning in Higher Education, 26*(3), 358–380.

Dunlosky, J., Rawson, K. A., Marsh, E. J., Nathan, M. J., & Willingham, D. T. (2013). Improving students' learning with effective learning techniques: Promising directions from cognitive and educational psychology. *Psychological Science in the Public Interest, 14*(1), 4–58.

Dunn, R. & Dunn, K. (1992). *Teaching elementary students through their individual learning styles.* Allyn & Bacon.

Dunn, R., Griggs, S. A., Olson, J., Beasley, M., & Gorman, B. S. (1995). A meta-analytic validation of the Dunn and Dunn model of learning-style preferences. *The Journal of Educational Research, 88,* 353–362.

Dweck, C. S. (2008). *Mindset: The new psychology of success.* Random House.

Fleming, N. D. (2012, April). *The case against learning styles: "There is no evidence … "* VARK: A guide to learning preferences. https://vark-learn.com/wp-content/uploads/2014/08/The-Case-Against-Learning-Styles.pdf

Furey, W. (2020). The stubborn myth of "learning styles". *Education Next, 20*(3), 8–13.

Hattie, J. (2008). *Visible learning: A synthesis of over 800 meta-analyses relating to achievement.* Routledge.

Husmann, P. R., & O'Loughlin, V. D. (2019). Another nail in the coffin for learning styles? Disparities among undergraduate anatomy students' study strategies, class performance, and reported VARK learning styles. *Anatomical Sciences Education, 12*(1), 6–19.

Kampwirth, T. J., & Bates, M. (1980). Modality preference and teaching method: A review of research. *Academic Therapy, 15,* 597–605

Kavale, K. A., & Forness, S. R. (1987). Substance over style: Assessing the efficacy of modality testing and teaching. *Exceptional Children, 54,* 228–239.

Kavale, K. A., Hirshoren, A., & Forness, S. R. (1998). Meta-analytic validation of the Dunn and Dunn model of learning-style preferences: A critique of what was Dunn. *Learning Disabilities Research and Practice, 13,* 75–80.

Kavale, K. A., & LeFever, G. B. (2007). Dunn and Dunn model of learning-style preferences: Critique of Lovelace meta-analysis. *The Journal of Educational Research, 101,* 94–97.

Khazan, O. (2018, April 11). The myth of learning styles. *The Atlantic.* https://www.theatlantic.com/science/archive/2018/04/the-myth-of-learning-styles/557687/

Kraemer, D. J., Schinazi, V. R., Cawkwell, P. B., Tekriwal, A., Epstein, R. A., & Thompson-Schill, S. L. (2017). Verbalizing, visualizing, and navigating: The effect of strategies on encoding a large-scale virtual environment. *Journal of Experimental Psychology: Learning, Memory, and Cognition, 43*(4), 611.

Lovelace, M. K. (2005). Meta-analysis of experimental research based on the Dunn and Dunn model. *The Journal of Educational Research, 98,* 176–183.

Macdonald, K., Germine, L., Anderson, A., Christodoulou, J., & McGrath, L. M. (2017). Dispelling the myth: Training in education or neuroscience decreases but does not eliminate beliefs in neuromyths. *Frontiers in Psychology, 8,* 1314.

Moreno, R., & Mayer, R. (2007). Interactive multimodal learning environments. *Educational Psychology Review, 19*(3), 309–326.

Nancekivell, S. E., Shah, P., & Gelman, S. A. (2020). Maybe they're born with it, or maybe it's experience: Toward a deeper understanding of the learning style myth. *Journal of Educational Psychology, 112*(2), 221–235.

Newton, P. M. (2015). The learning styles myth is thriving in higher education. *Frontiers in Psychology, 6,* 1908.

Newton, P. M., & Salvi, A. (2020, December). How common is belief in the learning styles neuromyth, and does it matter? A pragmatic systematic review. *Frontiers in Education, 5,* 602451.

Nickerson, R. (1998). Confirmation bias: A ubiquitous phenomenon in many guises. *Review of General Psychology, 2*(2), 175–220.

Nuthall, G. (2007). *The hidden lives of learners.* Nzcer Press.

Pashler, H., McDaniel, M., Rohrer, D., & Bjork, R. (2009). Learning styles: Concepts and evidence. *Psychological Science in the Public Interest, 9*(3), 105–119.

Pomerance, L., Greenberg, J., & Walsh, K. (2016). Learning about learning: What every new teacher needs to know. *National Council on Teacher Quality.* https://files.eric.ed.gov/fulltext/ED570861.pdf

Prithishkumar, I. J., & Michael, S. A. (2014). Understanding your student: Using the VARK model. *Journal of Postgraduate Medicine, 60*(2), 183–186

Riener, C., & Willingham, D. (2010). The myth of learning styles. *Change: The magazine of higher learning, 42*(5), 32–35.

Rogowsky, B. A., Calhoun, B. M., & Tallal, P. (2015). Matching learning style to instructional method: Effects on comprehension. *Journal of Educational Psychology, 107*(1), 64–78.

Rohrer, D., & Pashler, H. (2012). Learning styles: Where's the evidence? *Medical Education, 46*, 34–35.

Rosenthal, R., & Jacobson, L. (1968). *Pygmalion in the classroom: Teacher expectation and pupils' intellectual development.* Holt, Rinehart & Winston.

Scott, C. (2010). The enduring appeal of 'learning styles'. *Australian Journal of Education, 54*(1), 5–17.

Stahl, S. (1999). Different strokes for different folks? A critique of learning and thinking styles. *American Educator, 23*(2), 27–31.

Sternberg, R. J., Grigorenko, E. L., Ferrari, M., & Clinkenbeard, P. (1999). A triarchic analysis of an aptitude-treatment interaction. *European Journal of Psychological Assessment, 15*(1), 3–131.

Tarver, S. G., & Dawson, M. M. (1978). Modality preference and the teaching of reading: A review. *Journal of Learning Disabilities, 11*(1), 17–29.

Wininger, S. R., Redifer, J. L., Norman, A. D., & Ryle, M. K. (2019). Prevalence of learning styles in educational psychology and introduction to education textbooks: A content analysis. *Psychology Learning & Teaching, 18*(3), 221–243.

8 Brain Training and Intelligence

M. J. Schneider and Indre V. Viskontas

The brain training industry is now well-established, and most people are familiar with claims that brain fitness is akin to physical fitness – do these exercises daily and your mind will sharpen up! But is there evidence that supports these claims? Can we distinguish apps that work from those that do not? What criteria should we consider when evaluating the effectiveness of a brain training tool?

Brain training apps, games, and programs are marketed as tools to improve cognitive abilities for many but also to stave off cognitive decline associated with age and even degenerative conditions such as Alzheimer's disease. These marketing claims assume that gains after training will transfer to cognitive function more generally. That is, training your mind on a game designed to help focus your attention will enable you to control your attentional focus in tasks outside of the game as well. This assumption is so pervasive that most people do not even consider whether skills trained using a given tool will transfer to real-world situations. But before we consider the evidence testing this assumption, it is helpful to distinguish tools designed to enhance function from those geared toward staving off decline.

Tools targeted at people who wish to improve existing abilities generally promise to improve cognitive functioning in school, work, or activities of daily living. In the education sector, some tools are marketed as fun games for kids, and promise a "leg-up" for school-readiness and future career success. Treatments marketed to working adults often highlight increased productivity and concentration as benefits of their programs. Some programs take a more wholistic approach to general brain health and market their product as a therapy to be used in conjunction with more traditional ways of maintaining health (i.e., balanced diet, exercise).

As mentioned earlier, brain training interventions may also be targeted at individuals wishing to prevent decline in cognitive functioning (e.g., memory) associated with age or degenerative conditions in which age is the greatest risk factor. These interventions target common fears people hold around aging – primarily that individuals will start forgetting things, slow down, and lose mental clarity. But some go a step further, and even suggest that they can mitigate, prevent, or even reverse cognitive impairment that accompanies neurodegenerative disorders.

Many companies marketing these products make strong claims about research-driven interventions and high success rates. They might claim that working memory is vital for various cognitive functions such as focus, reasoning, learning, and resisting distractions and that their tools are scientifically proven to improve working memory and attentional focus. But do these results translate into better cognitive function in tasks of daily living?

DOI: 10.4324/9781003107798-8

Examining the Claims

Although many companies themselves are highly confident in their products, most researchers are not in agreement about the efficacy and translatability of brain training techniques. Over time, psychologists and neuroscientists have conducted empirical studies, reviews, and meta-analyses to evaluate the marketing claims and the efficacy of brain training. After all, the potential applications of brain training are compelling. If brief, game-like interventions designed to improve abilities and prevent decline can lead to desirable, real-world outcomes, then these training programs could be a shortcut to improving people's lives. Additionally, they would serve a growing need, as our population grows older, and more and more people show signs of age-related neurodegenerative diseases. This chapter will examine the mechanisms of brain training exercises, evaluate the evidence of efficacy for several popular brain training options, and suggest directions for future research.

What Is Brain Training?

Brain training (or "cognitive training" or "mind training") refers to activities and interventions targeted at making individuals "smarter" or preventing cognitive decline via training specific components of cognition (Katz et al., 2018). As mentioned earlier, the goals of most brain training interventions are either to enhance one's cognitive abilities, and/or stave off the cognitive decline associated with age or age-related diseases. A person's cognitive abilities can generally be defined as the skills required to perform tasks related to learning, memory, reasoning, language, understanding, and other abilities that are associated with how our minds function (APA Dictionary of Psychology, n.d.).

Improving Abilities

We first examine brain training programs that aim to improve existing abilities. When one engages in brain training exercises, they are intended to improve different components of a person's cognitive abilities such as executive function, attention, and working memory. Executive function is an umbrella term that describes an individual's "higher level" cognitive abilities such as planning, problem solving, and decision making that require logical and abstract thinking (*APA Dictionary of Psychology*, n.d.; Diamond, 2012). Many brain training programs coach one aspect of executive functioning in an attempt to improve cognitive abilities more generally. For example, a participant might train their attention by practicing a series of attention tasks for several weeks, then to test improvement, and complete a novel series of attention tasks. To test whether cognitive ability improves more generally, a participant may complete a battery of tests assessing working memory, attention, problem solving, and other executive function skills. This battery assesses whether training in one domain transfers to other domains of cognition and generates overall improvement.

Why do most interventions target these areas of cognition specifically? Katz et al. (2018) noted the reasons why brain training might target executive function, working memory, and attention. They suggest that these abilities are necessary for higher level, complex behaviors and they are strongly correlated with valued outcomes such as higher intelligence, academic success, and positive life outcomes. So naturally, if better attention, working memory, and executive abilities lead to a plethora of desirable traits and life outcomes, people want to boost performance in these areas. When interventions attempt to train these abilities, we are asking a fundamental question about the abilities themselves: are they changeable? Will our abilities, and subsequently our life outcomes improve as a result of input and training, or are they set in stone? In a sense, these interventions tap into our desire for the fountain of youth and our drive to continue to improve our minds.

Staving Off Cognitive Decline

Stereotypes about older adults often include portrayals of inevitable and undesirable cognitive decline (Barber, 2017; Hummert et al., 1994). That perception, however, was called into question when a longitudinal study out of the University of Minnesota identified the perfect cohort of individuals for studying cognitive decline – Catholic nuns who were members of the same order – the School Sisters of Notre Dame. The nun study is a longitudinal study from which dozens of empirical articles have been published, contributing to our understanding of cognitive decline, and methods for prevention. In 1986, psychologists began this project with 678 nuns, and they followed their cognitive and neurological health over several years (Snowdon et al., 1996). The nuns served as perfect subjects because the conditions they lived in were as close as one can get to a laboratory setting in the real world, given that the rules of the order made their lives similar in a number of important ways. The nun cohort allowed the researchers to control for several potential confounding variables: none of them had a history of drug of alcohol use, there were no pregnancies, and their daily actions were routine and easily documented.

One finding that was published early in the study was particularly relevant to brain training practices (Snowdon et al., 1996). Researchers coded autobiographies written by the nuns when they were around 22 years of age to quantify overall linguistic ability. Then, an average of 58 years later, the same nuns were given a battery of cognitive tests to determine the relationship between early adulthood linguistic ability, and later cognitive decline. Results revealed a strong relationship between early life cognitive ability (quantified as linguistic ability) and cognitive function later in life (quantified by performance on cognitive tests and presence of neurodegenerative diseases). Nuns with higher abilities earlier in life fared better later in life. They also found that some nuns who maintained excellent cognitive functioning later in life had signs of Alzheimer's disease pathology post-mortem. These findings were interpreted as suggestive of the fact that nuns who remained mentally active could stave off the symptoms of age-related pathology. This interpretation provided strong motivation for promoting brain health and to keep our minds active as we age.

Brain Training Products and Media Perception

As the nun study gained prominence and media coverage, there was an explosion of brain training products in the early 2000s, and research examining their efficacy soon followed. There are now dozens of different brain training products available in the market, with many of the biggest companies providing computer-based brain training tasks. While some companies have published a notable amount of research on their interventions, others remain untested. Many popular brands have failed to produce any peer reviewed evidence in support of their interventions (Simons et al., 2016). Yet these interventions are still readily marketed and widely purchased.

As a result, many brain training programs marketed at preventing decline include game-like training activities, along with educational videos and tips; however, many also include assessments of one's current brain health and trajectory to allow for "personalized care." Most companies highlight multiple articles showing their product works on their websites and in other marketing materials.

The relationship between empirical evidence and what is marketed has been examined by some governmental agencies. In 2016, the U.S. Federal Trade Commission charged *Lumosity*, a brain training company, with deceptive advertising; they reached a settlement with *Lumosity* and the company agreed to pay $2 million (*Lumosity to Pay $2 Million*, 2016). The FTC also required the company that owns *Lumosity* to produce empirical research before making similar claims in the future. *Lumosity* markets online brain training games and their website indicates they have since published around 20 peer reviewed publications with thousands of participants showcasing the efficacy of their product. For example, according to one study mentioned on their site, after 10 weeks of their program, participants improved on several cognitive variables (Hardy et al., 2015).

The *Lumosity* case posed seemingly simple questions that can be asked about all brain training products – do brain training games work, and how can we test their efficacy? To help answer this question, Simons et al. (2016) provided a comprehensive meta-analysis of the evidence related to brain-training programs. Overall, the authors of this meta-analysis summed up the available research literature by concluding that they found

> extensive evidence that brain-training interventions improve performance on the trained tasks, less evidence that such interventions improve performance on closely related tasks, and little evidence that training enhances performance on distantly related tasks or that training improves everyday cognitive performance. (p. 103)

Outlets such as *The Atlantic* highlighted this prominent meta-analysis, and several outlets weighed in (Aamodt & Wang, 2007; Howard, 2016; Yong, 2016). Companies selling the products critiqued the paper by focusing on the possible biases of the authors, while other researchers noted the value of the major review for informing future studies (Yong, 2016). CNN also published an article noting the release of Simons et al.'s (2016) paper and its impacts on the scientific community (Howard, 2016).

While the two articles covered some similar points – the lack of compelling evidence, and the volume of studies included in this review – the CNN article also focused on a separate review that highlighted the potential for placebo effects (Foroughi et al., 2016; Howard, 2016). Foroughi et al. (2016) found that participants who responded to a flyer advertising cognitive training improved 5–10 IQ points after only one session of training, whereas those responding to a neutral flyer showed no improvement. Thus, they argued that due to a lack of understanding surrounding the mechanism of cognitive training, researchers cannot rule out placebo effects as a reason for the effects of cognitive training. The publication of these articles, letters from both sides of the debate, and the growing market for brain training products have pushed this discourse into the mainstream.

Brain Training Research

Limitations for Consideration

Generalizability. Many reviews of brain training literature note important limitations to our current understanding. The first limitation is that there are simply too many interventions, and not enough studies conducted on all of them. While each study may be able to address whether a particular intervention is somewhat effective, this information should not be generalized to all brain training. Katz et al. (2018) draw a helpful analogy here by comparing brain training research to that of medicine. If doctors asked the general question "does medicine work?" and then tested this by running trials on specific kinds of medication, they would fail to answer the primary question in earnest. The same thing is happening in brain training research. We can answer the question "what is the effect of this particular intervention on certain outcomes?" but we have not yet answered the question, "does brain training work?"

Near vs. Far Transfer. It is known with some certainty that brain training in a specific area (e.g., attention) can be successful in improving one's ability in that same area, but the benefits of training do not always transfer to other domains of executive function (Diamond, 2012; Katz et al., 2018; Owen et al., 2010; Simons et al., 2016; Uddin & Reyes, 2021). So, if one completes an intervention targeted at improving attention, it's likely that one's performance on attention tasks will improve, but performance on tests of other cognitive abilities, such as memory, might not. This inability for improvement in one cognitive area to lead to improvement in another area highlights an important concept in brain training known as transfer.

Transfer is generally categorized into two realms: near transfer and far transfer. Near transfer occurs when someone is trained in one skill successfully and their ability in that area is improved, and highly similar skills might also benefit. For example, learning to play the piano might improve fine motor coordination in the hands, which may transfer to similar skills such as typing. Far transfer occurs when someone is trained in a particular skill, and this training also improves their ability in a fairly different skill. For example, far transfer would explain why learning to play the piano might also benefit mathematical reasoning or vocabulary, skills that seem unrelated. Often brain training interventions are successful in accomplishing near transfer, but the evidence for far transfer is elusive (Melby-Lervåg et al., 2016; Melby-Lervåg & Hulme, 2013; Minear et al., 2016). Despite minimal evidence for far transfer in brain training interventions, many companies market their products broadly as programs designed to "keep you sharp" or are targeted at families who want to boost their child's academic and career success. These claims are largely unfounded.

Samples. In addition to the issue of generalizability, samples are often too small to conduct the complex analyses studies carry out. Most studies are limited in their ability to recruit participants, which often means the studies are underpowered. Individual demographic differences may also be contributing to the different outcomes seen across studies. Interventions may be significant for individuals with cognitive impairments, but non-significant outside of clinical populations. The quality of data collection and intervention implementation in larger samples along with the minimal testing of "real life" applicable outcomes have also been scrutinized. Katz et al. (2018) note that most benefits of brain training are measured using standardized laboratory measures and few ecologically valid methods. Lastly, we note that brain training methods involve simple tasks performed in limited contexts (i.e., short computer games that involve minimal substantive knowledge) and yet companies commonly promote general benefits and cite testimonials from clients as evidence of these effects (Simons et al., 2016).

Active Control Groups. One of the most comprehensive reviews of brain training research to date was published by Simons et al. in 2016. This review examined evidence presented on behalf of, and in critique of brain training research by evaluating 132 trials. Of these studies, the article reported 71 that utilized random assignment in their design.

This is important, as those that fail to utilize random assignment cannot be considered true experiments, and while they may provide some insight, the limitations of this study design are ample.

Of the studies that use random assignment, 22 compared interventions to a passive control, and 49 compared interventions to an active control. Passive control groups are experimental groups that do not undergo any kind of intervention, whereas active controls engage in a program that is comparable to the experimental intervention, without the factor thought to drive the effect. Studies using passive controls found some effect for trained or similar tasks, but limitations of sample size and participant demographics make generalizing results unwise.

In addition, when you have a passive control group, you need to consider expectation effects: since the participants in the experimental group know that they are receiving some kind of intervention, they might try harder on the subsequent tests, or have more self-confidence, or there might be other factors that explain superior performance. That is why an active control group is critical in studies evaluating brain training tools.

Unfortunately, the active control studies provided little evidence for improvement outside of speed of processing tasks, in related and unrelated domains. Additionally, effect sizes were often small, meaning even when results were statistically significant, they may be of little practical significance.

Physical Exercise. While brain training activities do seem to have some promising effects, physical exercise has also been known to improve cognitive functioning, wellbeing, and prevent neurodegeneration, and there is ample research in this area (Mandolesi et al., 2018). The evidence in support of the positive effects of exercise is quite robust, and physical exercise produces many of the results sought after by brain training programs. It can promote neuroplasticity and improve performance in behavioral tasks (Mandolesi et al., 2018). Whereas brain training programs may be more of a gamble, physical exercise is a promising intervention for those looking to enhance or prevent decline in cognitive performance. This evidence begs the question, compared to exercise, is brain training an effective intervention?

Questions to Consider

One major critique of brain training research is that, while researchers can observe that brain training is influencing cognition, they do not understand much about how or why this happens. Very few interventions have generated general cognitive improvement that transfers to desirable real-world outcomes. Theories about the nature of skill transfer generally fall into two overarching frameworks: the first is formal discipline theory, and the second is the theory of transfer by identical elements (Simons et al., 2016). The formal discipline framework posits that the mind consists of various abilities that we can improve with practice, and so it follows that with training, one can theoretically improve the mind. Formal discipline theory was challenged by Edward Thorndike who proposed the theory of transfer by identical elements, which proposed that skills acquired in training are closely linked to the stimuli and tasks required during learning. This theory highlighted the importance of context for transfer. That is, when conditions of training mimics the conditions or context in which those skills will be used, transfer is more likely. Modern views of transfer often include considerations of context and skill malleability when considering how training/learning will manifest in different domains (Simons et al., 2016). Brain training interventions have put these theories to the test to see what abilities we can improve, and if this improvement transfers to multiple domains.

There seems to be consensus about the role of transfer in brain training, that near, or "superficial" transfer may occur, but the evidence for far transfer is minimal at best (Katz et al., 2018). For example, working memory could be improved by training, but working memory training does not lead to improvements in other domains (Melby-Lervåg et al., 2016; Melby-Lervåg & Hulme, 2013; Minear et al., 2016). An issue that arises here is the possibility that participants are not actually improving their working memory but are instead learning superficial strategies that help them improve their performance on specific tests of working memory. Thus, we are left wondering, is there a true test of near transfer, or is it currently indistinguishable from the acquisition of superficial strategies that lead to performance improvements? Meta-analyses by Owen et al. (2010) and Simons et al. (2016) came to the same conclusion about near vs. far transfer and asked: what is the true difference between near and far transfer? How do we make distinctions between related "near transfer" tasks and non-related "far transfer" tasks in a way that is not subjective or arbitrary? (Owen et al., 2010; Simons et al., 2016).

Past research on brain training has focused heavily on the question of *if* brain training works, and this has yielded important findings. Some studies and meta-analyses have concluded that brain training may be effective for people with cognitive impairments (Bonnechère et al., 2020; Hill et al., 2017; Lawrence et al., 2017; Leung et al., 2015); however, many reviewers remain skeptical and most believe more research is necessary to reach consensus (Gates et al., 2019; Nguyen et al., 2021). Effects in specific samples are easier to identify, but when we attempt to generalize these findings across all demographics, some gaps in knowledge appear.

Summary and Conclusion

There is likely little harm in engaging in brain training exercises, but the benefits are not entirely clear, and if time or energy are at a premium, older adults or those at risk of developing mild cognitive impairment might be better served spending it engaging in physical exercise or in social interactions. We can conclude evidence of near transfer exists, and many interventions can improve abilities in a particular domain, but what are the implications for practical, real-world outcomes? Brain training remains a highly debated topic in academic and mainstream discourse, with one point most sides can agree on – more data are necessary. Limitations of sample, design, and generalizability make it difficult to generate larger claims about efficacy. Often there is a stark contrast between evidence for brain training, and what is being marketed to the public. Yet, the brain training industry continues to grow, and new tools are entering the market regularly. In order to make informed decisions, consumers need to understand transfer, the importance of active control groups, and the effectiveness of other interventions, including physical exercise and a social support network.

References

Aamodt, S., & Wang, S. (2007, November 8). Opinion | Exercise on the brain. *The New York Times.* https://www.nytimes.com/2007/11/08/opinion/08aamodt.html

APA Dictionary of Psychology. (n.d.). Retrieved September 27, 2021, from https://dictionary.apa.org/cognitive-ability

Barber S. J. (2017). An examination of age-based stereotype threat about cognitive decline: Implications for stereotype-threat research and theory development. Perspectives on Psychological Science, 12(1), 62–90.

Berger, E. M., Fehr, E., Hermes, H., Schunk, D., & Winkel, K. (2020). The impact of working memory training on children's cognitive and noncognitive skills (SSRN scholarly paper ID 3622337). Social Science Research Network. https://papers.ssrn.com/abstract=3622337

Bonnechère, B., Langley, C., & Sahakian, B. J. (2020). The use of commercial computerised cognitive games in older adults: A meta-analysis. *Scientific Reports, 10*(1), 15276. doi:10.1038/s41598-020-72281-3

Diamond, A. (2012). Activities and programs that improve children's executive functions. *Current Directions in Psychological Science, 21*(5), 335–341. doi:10.1177/0963721412453722

Foroughi, C. K., Monfort, S. S., Paczynski, M., McKnight, P. E., & Greenwood, P. M. (2016). Placebo effects in cognitive training. *Proceedings of the National Academy of Sciences, 113*(27), 7470–7474. doi:10.1073/pnas.1601243113

Gates, N. J., Vernooij, R. W., Di Nisio, M., Karim, S., March, E., Martínez, G., & Rutjes, A. W. (2019). Computerised cognitive training for preventing dementia in people with mild cognitive impairment. *The Cochrane Database of Systematic Reviews, 3*, CD012279. doi:10.1002/14651858.CD012279.pub2

Hardy, J. L., Nelson, R. A., Thomason, M. E., Sternberg, D. A., Katovich, K., Farzin, F., & Scanlon, M. (2015). Enhancing cognitive abilities with comprehensive training: A large, online, randomized, active-controlled trial. *PLoS One, 10*(9), e0134467. doi:10.1371/journal.pone.0134467

Hill, N. T. M., Mowszowski, L., Naismith, S. L., Chadwick, V. L., Valenzuela, M., & Lampit, A. (2017). Computerized cognitive training in older adults with mild cognitive impairment or dementia: A systematic review and meta-analysis. *The American Journal of Psychiatry, 174*(4), 329–340. doi:10.1176/appi.ajp.2016.16030360

Howard, B. J. (2016). Do brain-training exercises really work? CNN. https://www.cnn.com/2016/10/20/health/brain-training-exercises/index.html

Hummert, M. L., Garstka, T. A., Shaner, J. L., & Strahm, S. (1994). Stereotypes of the elderly held by young, middle-aged, and elderly adults. *Journal of Gerontology, 49*(5), P240–P249. doi:10.1093/geronj/49.5.p240

Katz, B., Shah, P., & Meyer, D. E. (2018). How to play 20 questions with nature and lose: Reflections on 100 years of brain-training research. *Proceedings of the National Academy of Sciences, 115*(40), 9897–9904. doi:10.1073/pnas.1617102114

Lawrence, B. J., Gasson, N., Bucks, R. S., Troeung, L., & Loftus, A. M. (2017). Cognitive training and noninvasive brain stimulation for cognition in Parkinson's disease: A meta-analysis. *Neurorehabilitation and Neural Repair, 31*(7), 597–608. doi:10.1177/1545968317712468

Leung, I. H. K., Walton, C. C., Hallock, H., Lewis, S. J. G., Valenzuela, M., & Lampit, A. (2015). Cognitive training in Parkinson disease: A systematic review and meta-analysis. *Neurology, 85*(21), 1843–1851. doi:10.1212/WNL.0000000000002145

Lumosity to Pay $2 Million to Settle FTC Deceptive Advertising Charges for Its "Brain Training" Program. (2016). Federal Trade Commission. https://www.ftc.gov/news-events/press-releases/2016/01/lumosity-pay-2-million-settle-ftc-deceptive-advertising-charges

Mandolesi, L., Polverino, A., Montuori, S., Foti, F., Ferraioli, G., Sorrentino, P., & Sorrentino, G. (2018). Effects of physical exercise on cognitive functioning and wellbeing: Biological and psychological benefits. *Frontiers in Psychology, 9*, 509. doi:10.3389/fpsyg.2018.00509

Melby-Lervåg, M., & Hulme, C. (2013). Is working memory training effective? A meta-analytic review. *Developmental Psychology, 49*(2), 270–291. doi:10.1037/a0028228

Melby-Lervåg, M., Redick, T. S., & Hulme, C. (2016). Working memory training does not improve performance on measures of intelligence or other measures of "far transfer": Evidence from a meta-analytic review. *Perspectives on Psychological Science, 11*(4), 512–534. doi:10.1177/1745691616635612

Minear, M., Brasher, F., Guerrero, C. B., Brasher, M., Moore, A., & Sukeena, J. (2016). A simultaneous examination of two forms of working memory training: Evidence for near transfer only. *Memory & Cognition, 44*(7), 1014–1037. doi:10.3758/s13421-016-0616-9

Nguyen, L., Murphy, K., & Andrews, G. (2021). A game a day keeps cognitive decline away? A systematic review and meta-analysis of commercially-available brain training programs in healthy and cognitively impaired older adults. *Neuropsychology Review*. doi: 10.1007/s11065-021-09515-2

Owen, A. M., Hampshire, A., Grahn, J. A., Stenton, R., Dajani, S., Burns, A. S., Howard, R. J., & Ballard, C. G. (2010). Putting brain training to the test. *Nature, 465*(7299), 775–778. doi: 10.1038/nature09042

Simons, D. J., Boot, W. R., Charness, N., Gathercole, S. E., Chabris, C. F., Hambrick, D. Z., & Stine-Morrow, E. A. L. (2016). Do "brain-training" programs work? *Psychological Science in the Public Interest, 17*(3), 103–186. doi: 10.1177/1529100616661983

Snowdon, D. A., Kemper, S. J., Mortimer, J. A., Greiner, L. H., Wekstein, D. R., & Markesbery, W. R. (1996). Linguistic ability in early life and cognitive function and Alzheimer's disease in late life. Findings from the Nun Study. *JAMA, 275*(7), 528–532.

Uddin, L. Q., & Reyes, A. D. L. (2021). Cultivating allyship through casual mentoring to promote diversity. *Trends in Cognitive Sciences, 25*(10), 813–815. doi: 10.1016/j.tics.2021.07.014

Yong, E. (2016, October 3). The weak evidence behind brain-training games. *The Atlantic*. https://www.theatlantic.com/science/archive/2016/10/the-weak-evidence-behind-brain-training-games/502559/

9 Psychosexual Stages and Development

Michael I. Axelrod and Christine C. Vriesema

Few, if any, in psychology's history have garnered more attention from scholars, pundits, and the general public than Sigmund Freud. His influence on Western culture is widely acknowledged and, although coming into the public's view well over a century ago, Freud's legacy remains significant. His contributions to medicine, mental illness, personality theory, and developmental theory greatly influenced the field of psychiatry and the practice of psychotherapy. He merged ideas and observations to describe a unifying theory of human behavior and establish a framework for treating psychological problems. This chapter focuses on one element of Freud's theory – the relationship between psychosexual stages of development and personality. This chapter begins with a discussion of Freud's primary claim that virtually all areas of one's personality are influenced by successes or failures navigating related developmental challenges before the onset of puberty as well as related claims involving the relationship between early childhood experiences and psychopathology. This chapter then describes where Freud's claim is referenced within psychology and popular culture and provides evidence for the continued belief in this idea. Commentary on the evidence supporting and refuting Freud's theory will be presented.

Examining the Claims

An account of Freud's psychosexual theory of development begins with his *Three Essays on the Theory of Sexuality*, initially published in 1905 (Freud, 1962). In this seminal work, Freud suggested sexual experiences held an important place in an individual's psychological functioning and that infantile sexuality prodigiously influenced human development (Fancher & Rutherford, 2016). This was an entirely novel perspective from which to view infancy. Previously, infancy and childhood were considered periods of innocence, void of sexuality, and that biological factors, not experience, shaped human development (Goodwin, 2015; Marion, 2016). Freud also posited babies were born capable of experiencing sensual pleasure from the stimulation of body parts and that "over the course of normal development, certain parts of the body become erogenous zones, specific areas of intense satisfaction and sensual pleasure" (Fancher & Rutherford, 2016, p. 418). It was with *Three Essays* that Freud famously introduced five psychosexual stages: oral, anal, phallic, latency, and genital. See Table 9.1 for an overview.

Freud indicated that children moved sequentially through these psychosexual stages, claiming virtually all areas of one's personality were influenced by successes or failures navigating developmental challenges related to each stage (Kalat, 2013). According to Freud, all normal and abnormal behavior was a result of early experiences forming the

DOI: 10.4324/9781003107798-9

Table 9.1 Sigmund Freud's five psychosexual stages

Stage	Age Range	Behavior Exhibited
Oral	Birth–1 year	The mouth or oral zone was associated with infants' natural instinct to nurse.
Anal	1–3 years	Toilet training begins, and children start discovering pleasure in the voluntary control of defecation and urination.
Phallic	3–5 years	Children discover the significance of their genitals and the pleasure experienced in that erogenous zone.
Latency	5 years–puberty	Sexual drives are repressed or forgotten until adulthood.
Genital	Adolescence	Teenagers balance basic sexual urges with the need to conform to societal norms.

foundation of the personality (Miller, 1983). The corresponding erogenous areas associated with the oral, anal, and phallic stages generated sexual tensions that required stimulation or relief. Unhealthy levels of stimulation (i.e., too little or too much) at any one of these stages caused the child to be fixated, or stuck, resulting in the development of personality types associated with the specific stage (Greenwood, 2015). Infants receiving too much oral pleasure inevitably grew up to compulsively eat or smoke. Adults fixated at the anal stage were likely to become obsessively clean or rigidly rely on schedules or routines, developing what many call an "anal personality." During the phallic stage, children became sexually attracted to their opposite-sex parent and developed a rivalry with the same-sex parent. Oedipal or Electra complexes appear during this stage when children are unable to resolve associated conflicts.

Freud contended that the phallic stage was most important for understanding normal and abnormal adult personalities and made the Oedipal complex the foundation of his theory (Greenwood, 2015). The Oedipal complex is generated during the phallic stage when male children are said to develop strong sexual feelings for their mother and establish a rivalry with their father for their mother's attention. Male children experience castration anxiety because of the fear they have for their more powerful father. This anxiety develops specifically during the phallic stage because of its association with the genital area. The conflict and resulting anxiety that emerges is resolved only when the male child identifies with his father and figuratively gains access to his mother (Salkind, 2004). Freud contended that identification with the opposite-sex parent was responsible for the development of the *superego*, which involved the internalization of the moral values of that parent. For Freud, this, in part, connected his theories of psychosexual development and personality, and offered him an avenue to conceptually link conflicts occurring in early childhood to later problems with anxiety and neuroticism (Greenwood, 2015).

According to Freud, the anxieties people experienced were partially responsible for feelings related to instinctual drives of the *id* and socially inappropriate ways people satisfy those drives. He conceived the concept of defense mechanisms to explain how people avoided these anxieties (Miller, 1983). Defense mechanisms, such as repression or projection, are deployed unconsciously by the *ego* to relieve tension caused by anxiety. Freud used defense mechanisms to explain both normal and abnormal behavior. For Freud's time, this was a unique theoretical position. Greenwood (2015) highlighted this point by suggesting Freud's meta-theory included "all aspects of human life, from the most bizarre dreams to the mundane choices of everyday life" (p. 511) and that current experiences, whether typical or pathological, were expressed as a function of sexual experiences and memories of early childhood. Freud's theory implies that infant and childhood experiences with feeding or toileting are associated with later personality features and psychopathology. Not surprisingly, many pop psychology claims related to the conceptualization and treatment of feeding and toileting problems have their origins with Freud's assertion that a child's failure to successfully navigate psychosexual stages serves as the backdrop for noteworthy clinical problems. For example, many accounts of toilet training have roots with Freud. The theory was taken to suggest that a child's experiences with toilet training would profoundly impact personality and serve as a foundation for later psychological problems (Hunt, 1979). Anna Freud used her father's theory to assert that overly harsh and regimented toilet training required the child to deploy defense mechanisms (e.g., repression) that later manifested into symptoms of obsessive-compulsive disorder (e.g., aversion to germs, extremes in regularity and routine; Young-Bruehl, 2008). This perspective also implies that problems with toileting, such as nocturnal enuresis (i.e., bedwetting) and fecal incontinence, are symptoms of underlying emotional disturbances rooted in abnormal psychosexual development (Mishne, 1993). Psychodynamic formulations have suggested bedwetting is a function of displaced aggression against parents, poorly expressed emotional distress, or conflict between child and mother resulting in the child demanding their mother's affection through urination (Axelrod & Deegan, 2019). Regarding fecal incontinence, early psychodynamic theorists suggested a relationship between soiling and aggression, anal sexuality, and jealousy of one or both parents (Morichaw-Beauchant, 1922).

Pop Psychology, Pop Culture, and Public Perception

Freud introduced ideas that were bold for his time. His developmental and theoretical frameworks, for example, emphasized sexuality and eroticism, topics that were taboo during the late 19th and early 20th centuries. He promoted psychoanalysis as an effective alternative to the medical treatment of mental illness, which only served to elevate his stature among his physician colleagues and the public (Crews, 2017). Following his 1909 lectures at Clark University in Massachusetts, Freud's first time speaking in America, interest in Freud exploded (Goodwin, 2015). Yet, American psychologists found his work to be unscientific (Matthews, 1967). According to historian C. James Goodwin (2015), Freud's theoretical position "might not have played well within academia, but it had a strong impact on the medical practice of psychiatry, and it caught the imagination of the general public" (p. 362). Naturally, Freud's work on psychoanalysis was most popular. Approximately 170 articles were published about the topic in American medical journals and nearly 50 articles about psychoanalysis appeared in popular magazines such as *McClure's*, *Ladies Home Journal*, and *The Nation* between 1912 and 1918 (Green & Rieber, 1980). Freud's ideas, especially his theory of psychosocial development, influenced modern psychiatry, psychology, and popular culture (Walsh et al., 2014).

Freudian concepts related to psychosexual development show up in abundance in pop psychology and have been used to sell books and to defend prejudice. For example, during World War II, Freud's theory was used by allied propogandists to suggest Japanese mothers' toilet training practices were responsible for Japanese personality characteristics. Academics attributed Japanese mothers' overly sterile and rigid toilet training practices to the Japanese propensity toward brutality in war, blaming their presumed viciousness on repressed rage (Axelrod & Deegan, 2019). At approximately the same time, American anthropologist Ruth Benedict claimed the Japanese inclination toward cleanliness was a result of negative toilet training experiences, and Weston Le Barre, another American anthropologist, associated unusually harsh toilet training practices to explain why, in his opinion, Japanese people were "the most compulsive in the world" (Barnouw, 1963, p. 122). These assertions were based primarily on Freud's idea that early childhood experiences profoundly impacted adult personality and Anna Freud's later assumption that overly strict toilet training practices led to children repressing their negative emotional experiences resulting in later personality problems.

The self-help literature also references Freud's theory of psychosexual development to explain phenomena and borrow frameworks. Thomas A. Harris, in his 1967 popular self-help book *I'm OK – You're OK*, theorized that the typical person is impaired during childhood and engages in life via a paranoid, self-pitying lens (Harris, 1967). This perspective was intended to assist people in designing plans for better living with the primary assumption being most people are not okay but rather psychologically damaged because of early experiences. Another self-help author M. Scott Peck, in his series of *The Road Less Traveled* books, attributed many of his key concepts to Freud (Salerno, 2005). Peck (1978) suggested that people passed sequentially through a series of spiritual stages, much like Freud's stages of psychosexual development, and that people's problems were a result of some spiritual fixation at one specific stage. Also like Freud, Peck's hypothesis rested on the assumption that development happens in distinct stages and failure to successfully navigate challenges at any one stage causes current problems.

Freud's theory has also influenced modern psychology and psychotherapy. He described several defense mechanisms (e.g., denial, projection, repression) used by people to bury the experiences of anxiety that were a result of unresolved conflicts occurring during the anal, oral, and phallic stages of development. Freud believed that a purpose of psychotherapy was to bring unconscious thoughts and feelings to the conscious mind by confronting these defense mechanisms. Although little evidence exists for this as a theory, the notion of defense mechanisms as a psychotherapeutic concept remains a popular theme. A search of PsychInfo using the terms "defense mechanisms" and "psychotherapy/therapy/counseling" found 364 books and 2,182 articles in academic journals were published between 2001 and 2021.

Since first introduced in the early 20th century, Freud's theory of psychosexual development has been used by musicians, writers, and filmmakers to grab audiences' attention. Freudian themes of unresolved parent-child conflict, personality flaws supposedly brought on by problems in infancy and early childhood, and exposed defense mechanisms are frequently mentioned in popular culture. Writers from Shakespeare (e.g., *Hamlet*) to Eugene O'Neill (e.g., *Long Day's Journey into Night*) have illustrated the Oedipus complex and its resulting tragedy through characters that loved their mothers and despised their fathers. Themes related to the Oedipal complex have also been played out on the big screen, most famously in *Psycho*. Finally, Tony Soprano and his psychiatrist Dr. Melfi spend much of their time in therapy talking about Tony's childhood and, more specifically, his relationship with his mother. According to Gabbard (2002), writers for *The Sopranos* highlighted Tony's psychopathy through a psychological lens tinted by Freud's Oedipal complex and, more broadly, the consequences of unresolved challenges of the early psychosexual developmental stages.

Freud's theory remains somewhat popular in psychology and has become, in many ways, implanted in our culture. Certain aspects of his theory of psychosexual development, including some discussed earlier, are widely considered true by various segments of the population. Evidence for this exists in the research examining beliefs about myths in psychology. Studies conducted with college students, parents, pre-professionals, and the public have found certain myths rooted in Freud's theory of psychosexual development are held by many as true. For example, several empirical investigations have found that people tend to believe the notion that bedwetting is a sign of a child's underlying emotional problems – a decidedly Freudian concept. Fruit et al. (2019) reported that one-third of pre-professional nurses and speech-language pathologists surveyed endorsed the myth that children who frequently wet the bed typically have underlying emotional issues. Hupp et al. (2017) found that almost half of college students and parents surveyed believed the same mythical statement.

Surprisingly, Freud's theory of psychosexual development can be found on many national professional licensure exams. Published study materials for the Examination of Professional Practice in Psychology (EPPP) and the National Counselor Exam (NCE) include information specific to the psychosexual stages of development (Association for Advanced Training in the Behavioral Sciences, 2020; National Counseling Exam, n.d.). While it might be a stretch to suggest this indicates widespread belief in Freud's theory among these professionals, test developers in these professional fields appear to view Freud's theory as relevant to practice. The presence of psychosexual development on these examinations also suggests some professional training programs at least reference Freud in their curricula.

The Evidence

Freud's theory of psychosexual development remains popular. Within a research context, the perspective influenced the field of psychology by calling attention to the importance of early childhood experiences, the role of the unconscious mind in shaping behavior, and the need to understand developmental trends over time (Papalia et al., 2008). These contributions inspired research across numerous topics such as personality and attachment. Despite Freud's influence on public and scientific thinking, however, the psychosexual developmental theory itself lacks strong evidence. For example, critical components of stages such as the Oedipal complex are now considered to be obsolete (Papalia et al., 2008). Related phenomena, such as repression, are also inherently difficult – if not impossible – to study in relation to the experiences that Freud described (Papalia et al., 2008). Yet, the ability to test the tenets of a theory and to falsify claims is necessary criteria for strong and effective theories (Morling, 2021).

Overall, Freud represented his theory of psychosexual development as scientific, although he has been criticized for presenting fictional case studies to support his claims, misinterpreting data, rejecting or ignoring alternative explanation and theories, and failing to offer his ideas to rigorous experimental testing (Goodwin, 2015; Greenwood, 2015). However, researchers and applied psychodynamic practitioners have attempted to use scientific methods to support Freud's psychosexual developmental theory and, more specifically, the relationship between psychosexual development and personality. This section briefly reviews that literature and provides evidence against Freud's theory in favor of alternative perspectives.

One potential reason why the psychosexual developmental theory endures despite its limitations may be that researchers continue to observe aspects of Freud's legacy in other areas of psychology (Westen, 1998). For example, the unconscious mind was central to Freud's theory, and psychotherapy aimed to uncover these unconscious thoughts.

Westen (1998) argued that evidence for the unconscious mind can be found across many psychological processes, such as memory, emotion, and implicit bias. Studies in these areas suggest that people engage in behaviors based on thoughts and feelings that exist outside effortful cognitive processing. Similarly, another major theme in Freud's theory was the importance of early childhood experiences in shaping subsequent development. These themes can also be observed in attachment research that examines the relationship between early parent-child interactions and the ways that children later engage in relationships with others as adults (Bretherton, 1990). However, even though Freudian themes can be found in other areas of psychological research, there are important caveats to note that distinguish the psychosexual developmental theory from the other psychological perspectives mentioned in this section.

One caveat is that there is minimal evidence demonstrating how individual psychosexual stages in the early years shape personality, development, and psychopathology (Silverman, 2017). Freud presented a theory of attachment that begins in the oral stage, arguing that mothers and infants create bonds during the feeding process (Fitton, 2012). However, the theory raised questions that Freud did not address empirically (e.g., questions about separation anxiety, how specific social behaviors influenced personality development). Subsequent attachment research differed from early psychoanalytic perspectives in that the later attachment work systematically addressed these unanswered questions (Fitton, 2012).

A second caveat is that the unconscious processes described in Freud's theory are largely unsubstantiated, particularly those claiming that human behavior reflects an attempt to disguise one's sexual and violent feelings (Baumesiter et al., 1998). These unsubstantiated claims are in direct contrast to the extensive empirical research showing evidence of unconscious processes in other areas of psychology (e.g., implicit bias, decision-making processes, and priming). Moreover, the unconscious urges described in Freud's theory tend to focus on early sexual experiences. However, there is little research investigating children's sexual behavior, thereby making it difficult to assess the importance of sexuality in the normative development of children and its positive or negative consequences (Joseph, 2015).

Beyond the broad themes in Freud's psychosexual developmental theory, there has also been a focus on exploring the connection between the different developmental stages and the emergence of specific personality traits. For example, Freud initially characterized an "anal personality" as one that is obsessively focused on cleanliness and morality. Other researchers later expanded on Freud's description to include additional traits, such as orderliness and perfectionism (Haslam, 2011). To examine these characteristics more systematically, Grygier (1961) created *The Dynamic Personality Inventory*, a survey that measured traits like rigidity, attention to detail, and submissiveness to authority, among others (Haslam, 2011). Kline and Storey (1978) tested the validity of this survey and found that the anal traits largely correlated with one another, suggesting that the characteristics might reflect the personality type that Freud described. More recently, Haslam (2011) argued that anal personality traits can be observed across other psychological disorders and constructs as well, such as obsessive-compulsive personality disorder, perfectionism, authoritarianism, and orderliness.

Despite the modest findings connecting Freud's theory and personality traits, however, there are drawbacks to this research as well as empirical evidence that points to alternative explanations. First, there is no evidence for a causal link between the emergence of anal characteristics (e.g., rigidity, cleanliness) and children's toilet training experiences. This includes the timing of toilet training, the severity of the training, and the tactics that parents used to train their children (Haslam, 2011). Second, motivation research highlights alternative explanations for the potential connection between toilet training experiences and the emergence of anal characteristics. For example, strict toilet training practices might reflect high parental standards more broadly. These high expectations in the home might have encouraged children to similarly adopt high standards for themselves and to pursue a personal need for achievement (McClelland & Pilon, 1983). Thus, it is less about the toilet training experiences that Freud described and more about children's socialization experiences in general.

Overall, while some argue that Freudian themes persist in more contemporary psychological research areas (Haslam, 2011; Westen, 1998), there are key limitations and alternative explanations that ultimately provide evidence against Freud's theory. Namely, strong empirical evidence supporting Freud's theory is limited, as the existing literature is plagued by methodological shortcomings, questionable interpretations of results, and nonsignificant findings. Moreover, considerable scientific data have been produced that refute much of what Freud proposed since he first introduced his theory (Silverman, 2017).

Understanding Beliefs

The limitations of Freud's theory raise questions as to why the perspective continues to appear in academic work and popular media. Although there are likely many reasons for the pervasiveness of Freud's theory, several possible explanations include its presence in academic classes and textbooks, a tendency for people to seek out information that aligns with their preexisting beliefs (i.e., confirmation bias), and the ability to easily recall themes associated with the theory (i.e., the availability heuristic). This section briefly describes each explanation and then outlines how these pervasive beliefs can do harm.

Freud's stages of psychosexual development are still taught in a range of disciplines. In college classrooms, Freud's stages of development are commonly part of human development courses and textbooks, yet the information is not always presented critically. Although some texts (Papalia et al., 2008) balance describing Freud's theory with key critiques, other texts (Berger, 2016) provide extensive descriptions of Freudian principles in each stage of human development without ever explicitly introducing any critiques. Therefore, one reason why people might continue to endorse Freud's perspective is that they continue to learn about the theory while not always having access to critical reviews.

For individuals who observe Freud outside of their academic classes, confirmation bias also may play a role. Confirmation bias is the tendency for people to seek out or interpret information in ways that align with their preexisting beliefs (Nickerson, 1998). For example, researchers familiar with Freudian themes might argue that key principles can be observed in other psychological domains related to personality, unconscious thoughts, and early childhood experiences (Haslam, 2011; Westen, 1998). Despite research that provides alternative explanations and highlights limitations of Freud's theory, confirmation bias might continue to support people's belief in his perspective. Moreover, confirmation bias tends to amplify other biases (Gilovich & Ross, 2015) that might similarly work to reinforce one's preexisting beliefs.

One such bias is the availability heuristic. This heuristic suggests that people believe a phenomenon to be more pervasive the quicker they can recall examples of it (Tversky & Kahneman, 1974). In the context of Freud, popular examples of the theory abound, thus serving to strengthen the ease with which people can recall themes associated with the theory.

The presence of Freud in popular media as well as academic writing likely support the general public's belief that Freudian themes have merit. As one example, an online magazine author (Petter, 2017) provided an overview of a non-peer reviewed empirical study that found a link between the eye color of participants' romantic partners and the eye color of the participants' other-sex parent (DeBruine et al., 2017). Popular media like this supports the ease with which people can recall instances associated with the theory and provide additional evidence for confirmation bias (in this case, failing to consider the non-peer reviewed status of the study).

Overall, the pervasiveness of Freud's theory in academic and popular spaces likely lends itself to supporting people's belief in the psychosexual developmental theory. While this may provide evidence that Freud did in fact catch "the imagination of the general public" (Goodwin, 2015, p. 326), there are costs associated with its popularity. Namely, the theory may have contributed to the use of assessments and clinical techniques that are not supported by empirical evidence as well as to public skepticism of psychology.

Mental health professionals have access to a multitude of psychological assessments that research has supported as reliable and valid (Lilienfeld et al., 2006). However, there are a few assessments that remain popular despite their limited validity. These include the Rorschach Inkblot Test, the Thematic Apperception Test, and the Draw-A-Person test – all tests rely on *projection* to capture people's unconscious thoughts and motives (Lilienfeld et al., 2006). Thus, while some professionals might use assessments like these to measure psychological outcomes, there is little evidence that the tests can reliably support clinical diagnoses across most contexts (Lilienfeld et al., 2006). Professionals who continue to rely on Freudian-based assessments like these may ultimately fail to support the individuals with whom they are working if they are unable to reliably diagnose or determine the underlying causes of clients' concerns.

Critiques of psychology permeate society, with some people questioning the utility of the field. The use of unsubstantiated assessments and clinical practices like those mentioned above may in part contribute to this public doubt of psychology (Lilienfeld, 2012). Part of the challenges associated with the doubt is that the public may not be as knowledgeable about specific fields and subfields of psychology (Furnham et al., 1990). Yet, at the same time, people across age ranges generally feel like psychological phenomena are "easier" to explain than information in other scientific fields (Lilienfeld, 2012). It is possible that the availability heuristic plays a role in this context, too. Specifically, because Freudian themes permeate popular culture, these ideas may feel more familiar. The ease of recalling these ideas may encourage the public to feel more knowledgeable about psychology than they actually are and to think of elements of Freud's theory when considering psychology more broadly.

Summary and Conclusion

This chapter highlighted Freud's psychosexual theory of development and the related claim that nearly all areas of one's personality are influenced by successes and failures navigating developmental challenges in the oral, anal, and phallic stages of infancy and early childhood. Related ideas grew out of Freud's theory including the Oedipal complex, defense mechanisms, repressed memories, and a model of treating mental illness and psychological disorders (i.e., psychoanalysis). However, the scientific evidence supporting the collection of Freud's claims is limited, and there is sufficient research in favor of alternative perspectives. Even so, Freud's stages of psychosexual development and related claims endure in psychology and in popular culture. The consequences are troublesome, given the implications of these claims for unsupported theoretical stances, misguided conceptualizations of psychopathology, unsupported treatments, and public doubt about psychology. Moving forward, researchers, practitioners, and educators will need to find an appropriate balance between acknowledging Freud's contributions to psychology and providing a well-rounded critique of his work.

References

American Board of Pediatrics. (n.d.). *Content outline: Developmental-behavioral pediatrics*. Retrieved from https://www.abp.org/sites/abp/files/pdf/developmental_behavioral_content_outline.pdf

Association for Advanced Training in the Behavioral Sciences. (2020, September 25). The top 10 theories and concepts in the growth and lifespan development section of the EPPP [Web log post]. Retrieved from https://aatbs.com/blog/post/the-top-10-theories-and-concepts-in-the-growth-and-lifespan-development-section-of-the-eppp

Axelrod, M. I., & Deegan, J. P. (2019). Toileting. In S. Hupp (Ed.), *Pseudoscience in child and adolescent psychotherapy: A skeptical field guide* (pp. 225–242). Cambridge University Press.

Barnouw, V. (1963). *Culture and personality*. Dorsey Press.

Baumesiter, R. F., Dale, K., & Sommer, K. L. (1998). Freudian defense mechanisms and empirical findings in modern social psychology: Reaction formation, projection, displacement, undoing, isolation, sublimation, and denial. *Journal of Personality, 66*(6), 1081–1124.

Berger, K. S. (2016). *Invitation to the Life Span* (3rd edition). Macmillan Learning.

Billings, D. M. (2009). *Lippincott's content review for NCLEX-RN*. Lippincott.

Boag, S. (2006). Freudian repression, the common view, and pathological science. *Review of General Psychology, 10*, 74–86.

Bretherton, I. (1990). Communication patterns, internal working models, and the intergenerational transmission of attachment relationships. *Infant Mental Health Journal, 11*(3), 237–252.

Crews, F. (2017). *Freud: The making of an illusion*. Metropolitan Books.

DeBruine, L. M., Jones, B. C., & Little, A. C. (2017). *Positive sexual imprinting for human eye color*. bioRxiv.

Fancher, R. E., & Rutherford, A. (2016). *Pioneers of psychology: A history*. W.W. Norton.

Fitton, V. A. (2012). Attachment theory: History, research, and practice. *Psychoanalytic Social Work, 19*, 121–143.

Fong-Torres, B. (2006). *The Doors*. Hyperion Books.

Freud, S. (1962). *Three essays on the theory of sexuality*. Basic Book. [Reprint of the 1905 edition].

Fruit, N. A., Jorgensen, K. J., Helwig, E. C., George, K. J., Schmidt, C. K., & Axelrod, M. I. (2019, August). *Fact or fiction: Pre-professionals' beliefs about child psychology myths*. Poster session presented at the meeting of the American Psychological Association, Chicago, IL.

Furnham, A., & Wardley, Z. (1990). Lay theories of psychotherapy I: Attitudes toward, and beliefs about, psychotherapy and therapists. *Journal of clinical Psychology, 46*(6), 878–890.

Gabbard, G. O. (2002). *The psychology of The Sopranos: Love, death, desire and betrayal in America's favorite gangster family*. Basic Books.

Gilovich, T., & Ross, L. (2015). *The wisest one in the room: How you can benefit from social psychology's most powerful insights* (First Free Press hardcover edition). Free Press.

Godoi, D. O., & Fiamenghi, G. A. (2018). Effect of a rupture in psychosexual development: A theoretical case study on sexual abuse. *Open Science Journal of Psychology, 5*, 24–27.

Goodwin, C. J. (2015). *A history of modern psychology* (5th edition). Wiley.

Graybow, S. (2015). *Understanding failure: Social workers reflect on their licensing examination experience* (unpublished doctoral dissertation). City University of New York.

Green, M., & Rieber, R. W. (1980). The assimilation of psychoanalysis in America. In R. W. Rieber & K. Salzinger (Eds.), *Psychology: Theoretical-historical perspectives* (pp. 263–304). Academic Press.

Greenwood, J. D. (2015). *A conceptual history of psychology: Exploring the tangled web* (2nd edition). Cambridge University Press.

Grygier, T. G. (1961). The dynamic personality inventory. NFER.

Harris, T. A. (1967). *I'm ok – you're okay*. Harper and Row.

Haslam, N. (2011). The return of the anal character. *Review of General Psychology, 15*(4), 351–360.

Hunt, J. M. (1979). Psychological development: Early experiences. *Annual Review of Psychology, 30*, 103–143.

Hupp, S., Stary, A., & Jewell, J. (2017). Science vs. silliness for parents: Debunking the myths of child psychology. *Skeptical Inquirer, 41*(1). Retrieved from https://www.csicop.org/si/show/science_vs._silliness_for_parents_debunking_the_myths_of_child_psychology

Josephs, L. (2015). How children learn about sex: A crossspecies and cross-cultural analysis. *Analysis of Sexual Behaviour, 44*, 1059–1069.

Kalat, J. W. (2013). Introduction to psychology. Tenth Edition. Wadsworth.

Kline, P., & Storey, R. (1978). The dynamic personality inventory: What does it measure? *British Journal of Psychology, 69*, 375–383.

Lilienfeld, S. O. (2012). Public skepticism of psychology: Why many people perceive the study of human behavior as unscientific. *American Psychologist, 67*(2), 111–129.

Lilienfeld, S. O., Wood, J. M., & Garb, H. N. (2006) Why questionable psychological tests remain popular. *The Scientific Review of Alternative Medicine, 10*, 6–15.

Marion, P. (2016). Infantile sexuality and Freud's legacy. *The International Journal of Psychoanalysis, 97*, 641–664.

Matthews, F. H. (1967). The Americanization of Sigmund Freud: Adaptations of psychoanalysis before 1917. *Journal of American Studies, 1*, 39–62.

McClelland, D. C., & Pilon, D. A. (1983). Sources of adult motives in patterns of parent behavior in early childhood. *Journal of Personality and Social Psychology, 44*, 564–574.

Miller, P. H. (1983). *Theories of developmental psychology.* W.H. Freeman.

Mishne, J. M. (1993). Primary nocturnal enuresis: A psychodynamic clinical perspective. *Child and Adolescent Social Work Journal, 10*, 469–495.

Morichaw-Beauchant, R. (1922). False incontinence in children. *Paris Medical, 12*, 83.

Morling, B. (2021). *Research methods in psychology* (4th edition). W. W. Norton & Co.

Nash, R. A., Wade, K. A., Garry, M., Loftus, E. F., & Ost, J. (2017). Misrepresentations and flawed logic about the prevalence of false memories. *Applied Cognitive Psychology, 31*, 31–33.

National Counseling Exam. (n.d.). *NCE exam prep: Audio study material.* https://nationalcounselingexam.com/audio-study-material

Nickerson, R. S. (1998). Confirmation bias: A ubiquitous phenomenon in many guises. *Review of General Psychology, 2*(2), 175–220.

Papalia, D., Olds, S., & Feldman, R. (2008). *Human development* (11th edition). McGraw-Hill Education.

Peck, M. S. (1978). *The road less travelled: A new psychology of love, traditional values and spiritual growth.* Touchstone.

Petter, O. (2017, October 28). We seek romantic partners who look like our parents, finds study: Freud would say 'I told you so.' *Independent.* https://www.independent.co.uk/life-style/dating-romantic-partners-parents-look-study-relationships-attraction-a8022521.html

Salerno, S. (2005). *Sham: How the self-help movement made America helpless.* Random House.

Salkind, H. J. (2004). *An introduction to theories of human development.* Sage.

Silverman, D. K. (2017). Psychosexual stages of development (Frued). In: Zeigler-Hill, V., & Shackelford, T. (Eds.), Encyclopedia of personality and individual differences. Springer.

Swami, V., Tran, U., Thorn, L., Nader, I. W., von Nordheim, L., Pietschnig, J., ... Voracek, M. (2015). Are the scope and nature of psychology properly understood? An examination of belief in myths of popular psychology among university students. *Advances in Psychology Research*, 3–29. Retrieved from https://www.researchgate.net/publication/303723081_Are_the_scope_and_nature_of_psychology_properly_understood_An_examination_of_belief_in_myths_of_popular_psychology_among_university_students

Tversky, A., & Kahneman, D. (1974). Judgment under uncertainty: Heuristics and biases. *Science*, *185*(4157), 1124–1131.

Walsh, R. T. G., Teo, T., & Baydala, A. (2014). *A critical history and philosophy of psychology*. Cambridge University Press.

Westen, D. (1998). The scientific legacy of Sigmund Freud: Toward a psychodynamically informed psychological science. *Psychological Bulletin*, *124*(3), 333–371.

Wong, J. L. (1994). Lay theories of psychotherapy and perceptions of therapists: A replication and extension of Furnham and Wardley. *Journal of Clinical Psychology*, *50*(4), 624–632.

Young-Bruehl, E. (2008). *Anna Freud: A biography* (2nd edition). Yale University Press.

10 Horoscopes and Emotion

Zachary C. LaBrot, Chelsea Johnson, and Emily Maxime

Belief in larger, unexplainable cosmic forces that dictate the order of the universe is relatively commonplace (Lyons, 2005; Moore, 2005; Pew Research Center, 2018). Indeed, despite the advancements in natural, physical, and social sciences that help humans understand the world around them, there remains a plethora of phenomena that science cannot yet explain. While this is a reality that scientists across all disciplines must accept, it also serves as motivation for the continued pursuit of the scientific explanation of the universe, with particular emphasis on how it influences humankind and other life on Earth. Although there is much more that science has yet to explain, the application of the scientific process over thousands of years has allowed us to understand many phenomena that were previously misunderstood.

One such phenomenon is astrology. Astrology is the practice of studying the effects that the position of cosmic bodies in space can have on human emotion, behavior, and life events. This practice can be traced back to its origin in Babylonian, Greek, and Egyptian civilizations. Thought to be originally derived by the Babylonians in 700 B.C., 12 constellations studied via eclipses, clouds, and the relative positions of planetary bodies resulted in the 12 Zodiac signs we know today (i.e., Aquarius, Pisces, Aries, Taurus, Gemini, Cancer, Leo, Virgo, Libra, Scorpio, Sagittarius, and Capricorn; see Image 10.1). In essence, ancient civilizations appear to have believed that astrology was a means of communicating with heavenly powers and deities (Van der Waerden, 1952). The Babylonian's interpretation of the Zodiac involved making predictions about their population, such as battle outcomes or harvest output. However, ancient Greeks were responsible for utilizing the Zodiac to understand and make predictions about individuals, which is most closely aligned with how the Zodiac is used in modern times (Van der Waerden, 1952). These predictions were made via horoscopes, which are diagrams of the cosmic bodies' positions in space and Zodiac signs at the specific time and location of an individual's birth.

Astrologists claim that the exact time and location a person is born directly affects an individual's development of emotions, personality, and subsequent behavioral proclivities. Although many astrologists recognize that the human genome is responsible for internal biological processes, they believe that a purely biological orientation leaves out the effects of the cosmic environment's immediate impact on humans. Purportedly, the position of various cosmic bodies, such as planets and star constellations, at the time and place an individual is born influences how that individual's genome interacts with the cosmic and physical environment (Kelly & Saklofske, 2021). In astrology, this

DOI: 10.4324/9781003107798-10

Image 10.1 Zodiac Signs [credit: Shutterstock].

notion is referred to as, "as above, so below," meaning that the effects that cosmic bodies have in space essentially "trickle" down to earth and can thus influence humans. As such, astrologers commonly believe that human emotion and behavior can be understood in the context of an individual's horoscope (Kelly & Saklofske, 2021).

This notion has clearly stood the test of time, as millions of people across the globe use their daily horoscopes to understand aspects of themselves that have not readily been explained by other sources (Allum, 2011; Campion, 2004; National Science Board, 2000; Pew Research Center, 2018). For example, people use their horoscopes to understand their emotions, personality traits, hidden talents, and other complex aspects of their own nature. Furthermore, the information gleaned from horoscopes can purportedly help people improve confidence, choose well-suited friendships and romantic relationships, and even make wise career and financial decisions (Kelly & Saklofske, 2021). These are powerful claims and offer a straightforward, yet gripping, understanding of how people can better understand themselves and subsequently make important life decisions.

However, if these claims are to be understood and ultimately accepted (or denied), they must first be critically analyzed to determine the extent of their validity. The purpose of this chapter is to explore the validity of the claims that horoscopes provide useful information about people's emotions and other unique characteristics, and that this understanding can aid in making life decisions. Furthermore, empirical explanations for people's beliefs in the validity of horoscopes and the effects horoscopes have on individuals are described.

Examining the Claims

Pop Psychology, Pop Culture, and Public Perception

Across the globe, many people will inevitably read their horoscopes at some point. Initially, daily horoscopes could be, and still are, found in magazines and newspapers. However, in this remarkable age of access to technology and information, horoscopes of all varieties can be found on the Internet including on social media platforms (McKoy, 2019; Namaste, 2019). Indeed, it is challenging to use social media without ever seeing a link that leads to a horoscope (McKoy, 2019; Namaste, 2019). This level of access makes it almost too easy to find out what the cosmic bodies can predict on a given day.

A couple decades ago, nearly half of the American population read their horoscopes (Allum, 2011; National Science Board, 2000). More recently, and given the easy access to horoscopes through the Internet and social media, approximately 25–70% of people continue to read their horoscopes (Campion, 2004; Pew Research Center, 2018; Stierwalt, 2020), with approximately 30% of Americans holding a firm belief in the validity of astrology (Gelman, 2020). Given its widespread consumption by the public, it's fair to say that horoscopes have been well-integrated into pop culture.

A possible explanation for the widespread consumption of horoscopes is due to its psychological implications. Indeed, early psychological research on horoscopes did so in the context of personality assessment (Fichten & Sunerton, 1983; Forer, 1949). In fact, probably the most iconic use of horoscopes has been to understand individuals' emotions and related personality type and traits (Wu & Chen, 2021). This makes sense, given that a fundamental assumption of horoscopes is that they impact an individual's traits based on the specific position of various cosmic bodies at time of birth (Kelly & Saklofske, 2021).

Each Zodiac sign, and corresponding horoscope, contains inherent "good" and "bad" emotions and personality traits. For example, the signs of this chapter's authors are Scorpio, Aquarius, and Gemini, respectively. Scorpios are determined and intuitive but are also jealous and vindictive. Aquarius' are friendly and charitable but can be unemotional and indifferent. While Geminis are purportedly adaptive to new situations but can also be tense and nervous. Although a thorough description of the emotions and other personality traits of each Zodiac sign is beyond the scope of this chapter, what should be known is that each Zodiac sign's corresponding traits are used to determine exactly how an individual should behave in certain situations on certain days. This is how horoscopes allegedly make predictions; that is, an individual's described traits, according to their Zodiac sign, indicates how they should make life decisions (e.g., financial decisions, choosing friendships/ romantic partners). This is not completely unlike the study of personality in the field of psychology, in which certain personality characteristics are thought to be associated with certain talents and shortfalls (Judge et al., 1999; Pollock et al., 2016).

Because astrologists claim that astrology is useful for describing emotions and personality, it is no surprise that astrology has also been adopted and applied to address mental and behavioral health concerns. For example, some have attempted to apply astrology to diagnose various mental health conditions (Bhandary et al., 2018; Chauhan, 2015, 2016). Similarly, the use of astrology has been used as a therapeutic approach to address these mental health conditions (Chauhan, 2018; Pugh, 1983). Although astrology and horoscopes used in this manner are not as widespread as their use in describing traits and predicting behavior, there are significant implications for the wellbeing of others. Especially considering that effective and safe alternatives to addressing mental health concerns are widely available.

The Evidence

The scientific community has largely rejected or ignored horoscopes as a scientific method of predicting a person's emotions, personality, or behavior (McGrew & McFall, 1990). Nevertheless, many studies have actually evaluated the validity of horoscopes, with some studies yielding positive findings. For example, some research has found that astrologists can make accurate predictions by interpreting peoples' horoscopes (Clark, 1961, 1970; Joseph, 1975; Vidmar, 1979). Furthermore, research conducted by Mayo et al. (1978) and Smithers and Coopers (1978) consistently found that people born under "odd" astrological signs (i.e., Aries, Gemini, Leo, Libra, Sagittarius, and Aquarius) are more likely to exhibit extraversion, while those born under "water" signs (i.e., Cancer, Scorpio, and Pisces) are more likely to exhibit neuroticism (Kelly, 1979). However, methodological issues, such as small sample sizes and lack of participant blinding, in addition to difficulties replicating these results, have prevented researchers from providing unbiased evidence for the validity of horoscopes (Kelly, 1979; McGrew & McFall, 1990). More contemporary research has evaluated the validity of horoscopes for more practical and applied purposes, such as marketing. Kizgin (2013), for example, found that the Aquarius, Libra, Cancer, and Taurus signs were far more likely to purchase "luxurious products," as reflected by consumption trends.

Regardless, a large number of empirical studies have clearly demonstrated that horoscopes are not valid predictors of emotions, personality, or behavior. In fact, Dean et al. (2021) conducted a comprehensive review of horoscope research in which every possible relationship between astrological phenomena and human outcomes were evaluated. Ultimately, Dean et al. (2021) concluded that empirical research examining horoscopes, and astrology in general, is largely based on opinions and assumptions, rather than scientific evidence. More specifically, research clearly demonstrates that horoscopes have not been found to (1) determine that astrologically compatible couples are at lower risk for divorce (Helgertz & Scott, 2020), (2) improve interpersonal relationships (Blackmore & Seebold, 2001), or (3) predict an individual's personality traits (Kelly, 1979; Rogers & Glendon, 2010; Tyson, 1984; Wyman & Vyse, 2008). Given the extensive history of empirical research that finds that horoscopes are no more accurate than chance, the question that remains pertains to why some studies still find that horoscopes impact human behavior and perception.

Fortunately, research has provided explanations for why horoscope studies report positive findings. van Rooij (1994) found that people are more likely to engage in sign-related behaviors if they are aware of their astrological sign, which may be attributed to the self-attribution bias. That is, individuals attribute their behaviors (successes and failures) to forces outside of their control; in this case, the effects of a cosmic body's position in space relative to a person's time and location of birth (van Rooij, 1994). Furthermore, Munro and Munro (2000) found that people are more likely to report that recent events closely align with predictions presented with their astrological sign. Similarly, Colbert et al. (2016) found that people are more likely to interpret ambiguous stimuli (e.g., picture of hand grasping a wallet) positively or negatively based on the wording of a made-up horoscope. That is, when participants read a negatively worded horoscope, they were more likely to interpret ambiguous stimuli negatively, while those who read a positively worded horoscope interpreted the same ambiguous stimuli positively (Colbert et al., 2016). These studies suggest that people's knowledge of their astrological sign and what those signs entail is enough to influence their behavior and perceptions about the validity of horoscopes. Conversely, those who are unaware of their astrological sign are less likely to endorse that their behaviors and perceptions are commensurate with a horoscope's predictions (Munro & Munro, 2000; van Rooij, 1994). In sum, many research studies have demonstrated that horoscopes do not provide reliable, valid, or factual information. However, horoscopes can be meaningful to individuals who read and believe in them (Kelly & Saklofske, 2021).

Understanding Beliefs

Astrologists and consumers of horoscopes continue to claim that horoscopes indeed work based on the position of cosmic bodies, and many people believe these claims due to personal biases, fallacies, and various other motivations (Colbert et al., 2016; Munro & Munro, 2000; Kelly & Saklofske, 2021; van Rooij, 1994). One well-established explanation for people's belief in the validity of horoscopes is called the *Barnum effect.*

The Barnum effect, also known as the Forer effect, was named after the renowned circus entrepreneur, P. T. Barnum, who famously claimed that his circus had something for everyone to enjoy (Dickson & Kelly, 1985). The Barnum effect is the tendency for people to accept vague and ambiguous statements as accurate descriptions of their own emotions, personality, and behavior (Dickson & Kelly, 1985; Forer, 1949). Barnum statements, then, are those vague, ambiguous, and often positively phrased statements that people read and tend to accept as true about themselves (Beins, 2010). For example, some Barnum statements may include, "you have a great need for other people to like and admire you," and "you have a tendency to be critical of yourself," and "at times you are extroverted, sociable, while at other times you are introverted, wary, reserved" (The Barnum Effect, n.d.). Statements such as these may seem unique to an individual, however, if carefully considered, it becomes clear that these types of statements are generally true of most people at least some of the time. Much like P. T. Barnum's famed circus enterprise, Barnum statements have a little something for everyone. Several scientific studies have cited the Barnum effect as the primary reason that people accept horoscopes' predictions as valid and true descriptions of their emotions, personality, and behavior. That is, horoscopes' predictions and descriptions are so vague and ambiguous, people are likely to accept them to be true of themselves because, at least some of the time, they are true.

Forer (1949) conducted the seminal experiment that demonstrated how easily college students could be influenced by Barnum statements. In this study, 39 college students in an introductory psychology course took a personality test. Instead of receiving the actual individualized results in a narrative format, each student received the same 13 Barnum statements as the "result" of the personality test. Upon receiving the results, the students rated an average of 10.2 of the 13 statements to be true of themselves, suggesting that they believed most of the Barnum statements were unique to their own personalities.

While this experiment first brought the Barnum effect's impact on validity of personality assessment into the light of the scientific community, it inadvertently shed light on another matter. That is, the 13 Barnum statements used were randomly derived from a newsstand astrology book. That is, the Barnum statements were horoscopes (Forer, 1949). This consequently led to a line of scientific research that tested the Barnum effect as a reason people tend to believe in their horoscopes.

Since that seminal experiment, many other experiments have found that the Barnum effect is indeed the key factor responsible for people's belief in the validity of the descriptions and predictions of horoscopes. That is, horoscopes' descriptions of people's emotions, personality, and behavior are vague and ambiguous enough that they are generally true of most people, and thus individuals are likely to accept them as factual (Fichten & Sunerton, 1983; Glick et al., 1989; Rogers & Soule, 2009; Wyman & Vyse, 2008). People's belief in horoscopes, as mediated by the Barnum effect, is thought to be the result of a few different underlying psychological processes.

First, the Barnum effect is thought to enact upon the self-serving bias, such that people tend to accept positive statements and reject negative statements. Second, the Barnum effect also involves the confirmation bias, in which people tend to search for and accept statements that support their belief while rejecting alternative explanations. Finally, selective memory for instances in which Barnum statements were highly accurate and diminished attention and concern for instances in which Barnum statements were inaccurate enhances the Barnum effect (Beins, 2010). Now, when considered from the perspective of horoscopes as mere Barnum statements, it becomes clear that horoscopes indeed can be best explained by these well-documented psychological processes (MacLeod & Mathews, 2004; Nickerson, 1998; Rapee et al., 1994; Shepperd et al., 2008).

Regardless, people continue to believe in the supernatural aspect of horoscopes' abilities to make accurate descriptions and predications about one's life (Lyons, 2005; Moore, 2005; Pew Research Center, 2018). This can certainly be fun at times; indeed, even the authors of this chapter admit to reading their horoscopes from time to time. However, without knowledge of the scientific validity (or lack thereof) and reasons people believe in horoscopes, certain harms may be inherent. First, some people may make risky or poor decisions (e.g., high stake or low stake) based on horoscopes that could have unexpected and unwelcome outcomes. For example, a daily reading of a horoscope may say, "financial stability is inherent in the near future if you are willing to take a risk," which may result in some individuals prematurely leaving a well-established job. Second, people can invest money into things like a monthly subscription to daily horoscopes and readings that do not provide unique or helpful information when they could have invested in services or various professionals that have higher likelihoods of successful outcomes. Similarly, some people may invest in psychological astrology and rely on astrology and horoscopes for diagnoses and types of therapy that are not effective. As such, people may not only lose money but may continue to suffer from various mental health conditions that can be diagnosed and effectively treated through scientifically supported means.

Summary and Conclusion

Initially, horoscopes appear to be somewhat logical in explaining human emotions, personality, and behavior. Indeed, the notion of, "as above, so below" closely resembles the natural, physical, and social sciences' notion of how one's environment interacts with their genome (i.e., nature vs. nurture). However, after nearly a century, many scientific studies have clearly demonstrated that the descriptions and predictions made by horoscopes are no greater than chance and are greatly influenced by biased assumptions as opposed to objectively observable truths (Dean, 2021; Kelly & Saklofske, 2021). Specifically, psychological research examining the Barnum Effect has clearly demonstrated that the descriptions and predictions made by horoscopes are so vague and ambiguous that people tend to accept them because they generally describe most people at least some of the time (Fichten & Sunerton, 1983; Glick et al., 1989; Rogers & Soule,

2009; Wyman & Vyse, 2008). Nevertheless, horoscopes are still widely prevalent in newspapers, magazines, and the internet via many social media platforms (Allum, 2011; Campion, 2004; McKoy, 2019; Namaste, 2019; National Science Board, 2000).

As such, we offer the following recommendations and cautions based on the scientific evidence of horoscopes. First, we do not recommend that people should necessarily avoid reading their horoscopes at all costs. Reading horoscopes can be fun and great conversation starters. However, given that horoscopes' predictions are no greater than chance (Dean et al., 2021; Kelly & Saklofske, 2021), we strongly encourage those who read horoscopes refrain from using them to make important life choices (e.g., choosing a romantic partner, quitting a job, investing money, etc.), as these could have unwanted, and unnecessary, negative outcomes. Instead, we recommend consulting with relevant professionals and trusted individuals when making important life decisions. Second, we strongly caution against mental health diagnostic and therapeutic services based on astrology, as these could lead to unnecessary loss of finances and worsening mental health conditions when scientifically sound and safe alternatives are readily available. Finally, research suggests that horoscopes indeed impact individual's behaviors if they have belief in their validity (Colbert et al., 2016; Munro & Munro, 2000; van Rooij, 1994). As such, we strongly encourage people to remember the powerful role the Barnum effect plays in acceptance of horoscopes. Barnum statements can be quite influential, and in the form of horoscopes, can be quite convincing (Fichten & Sunerton, 1983; Glick et al., 1989; Rogers & Soule, 2009; Wyman & Vyse, 2008). As such, it is important to remember that regardless of how highly accurate a horoscope's prediction appears one should maintain a strong sense of skepticism.

References

Allum, N. (2011). What makes some people think astrology is scientific? *Science Communication, 33*(3), 341–366.

Astrological Zodiac Personality Traits. (n.d.). *Astrological zodiac traits/sun sign personalities*. Retrieved November 28, 2021, from http://nuclear.ucdavis.edu/~rpicha/personal/astrology/

Beins, B. S. (2010). Barnum effect. In I. B. Weiner & W. E. Craighead (Eds.), *The Corsini encyclopedia of psychology*. doi:10.1002/9780470479216.corpsy0108

Bhandary, R. P., Sharma, P. S. V. N., & Tharoor, H. (2018). Prediction of mental illness using Indian astrology: Cross-sectional findings from a prospective study. *Journal of Scientific Exploration, 32*(3), 555–578.

Blackmore, S., & Seebold, M. (2001). The effect of horoscopes on women's relationships. *Correlation, 19*(2), 17–32.

Campion, N. (2004). *The book of world horoscopes*. Wessex Astrologer.

Chauhan, A. (2015). Co-relating the sexual behavior and abnormal sexual orientation (psychological disorder) to astrology. *Journal of Psychotherapy & Psychological Disorders, 3*(1), 1–4.

Chauhan, A. (2016). Evaluating depression and its causes by astrology. *International Journal of Mental Health & Psychiatry, 2*(1), 1–5.

Chauhan, A. (2018). Alternate remedies for depression based on the principles of red book astrology. *Journal of Psychiatry and Cognitive Behavior, 1*, 1.

Clark, V. (1961). Experimental astrology. *In Search, 4*, 102–112.

Clark, V. (1970). An investigation of the validity and reliability of the astrological technique. *Aquarian Agent, 1*, 2–3.

Colbert, M., Van Cappellan, P., Bourdon, M., & Cohen, A. B. (2016). Good day for Leos: Horoscope's influence on perception, cognitive performances, and creativity. *Personality and Individual Differences, 101*, 348–355.

Dean, G. A., Mather, Nias, D. & Smit, R. (2021) *Understanding astrology: A critical review of a thousand empirical studies 1900–2020*. Amsterdam: Aino Publications. A critical overview of one-thousand studies on astrology (a large number conducted by astrologers). Is open access available for free download from www. astrology-and-science.com

Dickson, D. H., & Kelly, I. W. (1985). The "Barnum Effect" in personality assessment: A review of the literature. *Psychological Reports*, 57(2), 367–382.

Fichten, C. S., & Sunerton, B. (1983). Popular horoscopes and the "Barnum Effect." *The Journal of Psychology*, 114(1), 123–134.

Forer, B. R. (1949). The fallacy of personal validation: A classroom demonstration of gullibility. *The Journal of Abnormal and Social Psychology*, 44(1), 118–123.

Gelman, A. (2020, April). *Statistical modeling, causal inference, and social science*. Statistical Modeling Causal Inference, and Social Science. Retrieved November 20, 2021, from https://statmodeling.stat.columbia.edu/2020/04/11/42552/

Glick, P., Gottesman, D., & Jolton, J. (1989). The fault is not in the starts: Susceptibility of skeptics and believers in astrology to the Barnum Effect. *Personality and Social Psychology Bulletin*, 15(4), 572–583.

Helgertz, J., & Scott, K. (2020). The validity of astrological predictions on marriage and divorce: A longitudinal analysis of Swedish register data. *Genus*, 76(1), 1–18.

Joseph, R. A. (1975). A Vernon Clark model experiment distinguishing exceptionally gifted high performance from profoundly retarded low performance children. *Journal of Geocosmic Research*, 1, 55–72.

Judge, T. A., Higgins, C. A., Thoresen, C. J., & Barrick, M. R. (1999). The big five personality traits, general mental ability, and career success across the life span. *Personnel Psychology*, 52(3), 621–652.

Kelly, I. W. (1979). Astrology and science: A critical examination. *Psychological Reports*, 44, 1231–1240.

Kelly, I. W., & Saklofske, D. H. (2021). Contemporary western astrology: A philosophical critique 2021. Preprint retrieved from https://philpapers.org/rec/KELCWA-3. DOI: 10.13140/RG.2.2.34658.81605

Kizgin, Y. (2013). Is there any impact of horoscopes on luxury consumption trends? *Business Management Dynamics*, 3(2), 69–83.

Lyons, L. (2005, November). *Paranormal beliefs come (super)naturally to some*. Gallup. https://news.gallup.com/poll/19558/Paranormal-Beliefs-Come-SuperNaturally-Some.aspx

MacLeod, C., & Mathews, A. (2004). Selective memory effects in anxiety disorders: An overview of research finding and their implications. In D. Reisberg & P. Hertel (Eds.), *Memory and Emotion* (pp. 155–185). Oxford University Press.

Mayo, J., White, O., & Eysenck, H. J. (1978). An empirical study of the relation between astrological factors and personality. *The Journal of Social Psychology*, 105(2), 229–236.

McGrew, J. H., & McFall, R. M. (1990). A scientific inquiry into the validity of astrology. *Journal of Scientific Exploration*, 4(1), 75–83.

McKoy, K. (2019). *Astrology in the social media age*. The Stony Brook Press. http://sbpress.com/2019/05/astrology-in-the-social-media-age/

Moore, D. W. (2005, June). *Three in four Americans believe in paranormal*. Gallup. https://news.gallup.com/poll/16915/Three-Four-Americans-Believe-Paranormal.aspx

Munro, G. D., & Munro, J. E. (2000). Using daily horoscopes to demonstrate expectancy confirmation. *Teaching of Psychology*, 27(2), 114–116.

Namaste, J. (2019). *The internet changed astrology. Then came the memes*. WIRED. https://www.wired.com/story/astrology-and-the-internet/

National Science Board. (2000). *Science and engineering indicators: 2000*. Arlington, VA.

Nickerson, R. S. (1998). Confirmation bias: A ubiquitous phenomenon in many guises. *Review of General Psychology*, 2(2), 175–220.

Pew Research Center. (2018, October). 'New age' beliefs common among both religious and nonreligious Americans. https://www.pewresearch.org/fact-tank/2018/10/01/new-age-beliefs-common-among-both-religious-and-nonreligious-americans/

Pollock, N. C., McCabe, G. A., Southard, A. C., & Zeigler-Hill, V. (2016). Pathological personality traits and emotion regulation difficulties. *Personality and Individual Differences*, 95, 168–177.

Pugh, J. F. (1983). Astrological counseling in contemporary India. *Culture, Medicine and Psychiatry*, 7(3), 279–299.

Rapee, R. M., McCallum, S. L., Melville, L. F., Ravenscroft, H., & Rodney, J. M. (1994). Memory bias in social phobia. *Behaviour Research and Therapy*, 32(1), 89–99.

Rogers, M. E., & Glendon, A. I. (2010). Personality and birthdate: Taurus, year of the ox, or complete bull? In *Personality and Individual Differences: Current Directions*.

Rogers, P., & Soule, J. (2009). Cross-cultural difference in the acceptance of Barnum profiles supposedly derived from western versus Chinese astrology. *Journal of Cross-Cultural Psychology*, 40(3), 381–399.

Shepperd, J., Malone, W., & Sweeny, K. (2008). Exploring causes of the self-serving bias. *Social and Personality Psychology Compass*, 2(2), 895–908.

Smithers, A. G., & Coopers, H. J. (1978). Personality and season of birth. *The Journal of Social Psychology*, 105(2), 237–241.

Snyder, C. R. (1974). Why horoscopes are true: The effects of specificity on acceptance of astrological interpretations. *Journal of Clinical Psychology*, 30(4), 577–580.

Stierwalt, E. E. S. (2020, June). *Is astrology real? Here's what science says*. Scientific American. Retrieved November 26, 2021, from https://www.scientificamerican.com/article/is-astrology-real-heres-what-science-says/

The Barnum Demonstration. (n.d.). The Barnum effect. Retrieved November 24, 2021, from https://psych.fullerton.edu/mbirnbaum/psych101/barnum_demo.htm

Tyson, G. (1984). An empirical test of the astrological theory of personality. *Personality and Individual Differences*, 5(2), 247–250.

Van der Waerden, B. L. (1952). History of the zodiac. *Archiv für Orientforschung*, 216–230. doi:131.95.109.31

van Rooij, J. J. F. (1994). Introversion-extraversion: Astrology versus psychology. *Personality and Individual Differences*, 16(6), 985–988.

Vidmar, J. E. (1979). *Astrological discrimination between authentic and spurious birthdates*. University of Northern Colorado.

Wu, Y., & Chen, Z. Z. (2021). The attraction of horoscopes: A consensual qualitative research on astrological personality description. In *Computational Social Science* (pp. 202–209). CRC Press.

Wyman, A. J., & Vyse, S. (2008). Science versus the stars: A double-blind test of the validity of the NEO Five-Factor Inventory and computer-generated astrological natal charts. *The Journal of General Psychology*, 135(3), 287–300.

11 Spectrophilia and Sexuality

Karen Stollznow

Hercules is one of the most famous Greco-Roman heroes. He is best known as the strongest of all mortals, who was even stronger than many gods. There was a reason for his superhuman strength; he was a demi-god. Hercules had a complicated family tree. According to classical mythology, Hercules was the son of Zeus, the ruler of all gods on Mount Olympus and all the mortals on earth. His mother was the beautiful and virtuous Alcmeme, a mortal princess. The conception occurred when Zeus disguised himself as Alcmeme's husband Amphitryon, and then seduced her. Zeus had a reputation for impregnating mortal and immortal women, much to the chagrin of his long-suffering wife, Hera, and sometimes he did so in the guise of a swan or a bull. Ancient Greeks who believed in their religion literally also believed that Zeus could produce offspring with human women in the real world. For example, Alexander the Great's mother Olympias claimed that he was the son of Zeus (and apparently not Philip II of Macedon). Ancient sources tell us that Alexander actually believed this himself, because it was confirmed by none other than the Oracle of Zeus-Ammon at Siwa in Egypt (Fox, 2004). As strange as this sounds, a belief in relationships between humans and gods or other mythological beings is not an aberration in folklore, popular culture, or even contemporary accounts.

Spectrophilia is the name often given to the alleged phenomenon of sexual encounters between humans and ghosts (ghosts are sometimes referred to as "specters") (Di Lorenzo et al., 2018). In mythology, folklore, and popular culture, there are many stories of humans engaging in sex with ghosts, and also gods, demons, angels, spirits, aliens, or other supernatural entities. This chapter will discuss the mythology, folklore, contemporary encounters, and critical thinking about spectrophilia.

Examining the Claims

Mythology and Folklore

Claims of romantic encounters with otherworldly beings date back to Mesopotamian mythology, in which a *lilu* was said to be a demon that disturbed sleeping women. In the ancient text the Sumerian King List, Lilu, is named as the father of Gilgamesh, the hero-king of Uruk (Raphael, 1964). *Lilitu* is the demon's female counterpart, a Babylonian goddess who visits men in their sleep and begets children from them. She is also the basis for Lilith, the demonic figure of Jewish folklore.

In the early Jewish and Christian traditions, stories of "inter-being" sex can be found in the ancient Hebrew text *The Book of Enoch*, in which angels or "Watchers" are dispatched to Earth to watch over humankind. They soon begin to lust after human women and to

DOI: 10.4324/9781003107798-11

procreate with them. The offspring of these illicit unions were the Nephilim, a race of giants. *The Book of Genesis* also makes reference to these mysterious beings; "The Nephilim were on the earth in those days – and also afterward – when the sons of God went in to the daughters of humans, who bore children to them" (Genesis 6:4). Eventually, God allowed the Great Flood to eradicate the Nephilim, meanwhile preserving the human race.

In his book *The City of God* (*De civitate Dei contra paganos*), 5th-century theologian and philosopher Augustine of Hippo reported the phenomenon of demons that assume a corporal form to seduce human victims. Translated from the original Latin, he wrote,

> Many persons affirm that they have had the experience, or have heard from such as have experienced it, that the Satyrs and Fauns, whom the common folk call incubi, have often presented themselves before women, and have sought and procured intercourse with them.

Incubus is a 13th-century term that is derived from the Latin *incubare*, which means "to lie upon, or weigh upon" (Harper, 2021). By the 14th century, the term *succubus* emerged, from Late Latin *succuba* ("strumpet"), to describe demons that assume the form of women to steal the seed of men (Ibid.). Not even holy men were spared the temptations of these female demons. In the legend of St. Hippolytus, a nude woman once visited a priest, but when he threw his vestments over her to cover her nakedness, she turned back into what she really was; a corpse that the devil had animated to seduce him (Huysmans & King, 2011).

The belief in supernatural lovers is a cross-cultural phenomenon. Augustine compares incubi to Celtic demons, "whom the Gauls name Dusii, and are relentlessly committed to this defilement, attempting and achieving so many things of such a kind that to deny it would seem brazen" (Augustine of Hippo, 15.23). According to Arabian mythology, some types of *jinn* could impregnate women or lure men to fornicate with them, birthing hybrid children (Ghanim, 2018). In Hungary, a *lidérc* can shape shift into three different guises: a featherless chicken, a fiery light that hovers over a household where someone will soon die, or a demon that manifests as a long-lost lover or a deceased spouse (Mack, 1999). The vampiric Yukki-onna of Japanese lore tempts men into having sexual intercourse, draining them of their life-force as they do so, pleasuring them until they die (Bane, 2012). The half-human, half-goat satyrs of Greek mythology were the gods of lust who enjoyed sex with humans, while artists often portrayed male satyrs with exaggerated erections.

Many historical works of art reveal a fascination with this provocative topic. Medieval illustrations depicted demons swooping in on an entwined couple to assume the husband's form and impregnate the wife, producing demon spawn, or imps visiting an infant to swap it with a fairy child. In early Arthurian legend chronicled by Geoffrey of Monmouth and Robert de Boron, it was told that an incubus sired Merlin the magician. Many illuminated manuscripts depict the night of conception, showing a demon preying upon a virtuous sleeping woman.

Other artworks represented more consensual demonic trysts, such as a 16th-century Italian woodcut of a witch giving the ritual kiss to Satan's rear end. Infamously, belief in intimate relations between humans (especially women) and demons featured prominently in the witch trials of Early Modern Europe and Colonial America. During this time, an estimated 35,000–100,000 people were executed for accusations of witchcraft. Many alleged witches made confessions, usually under torture, of cavorting with the devil and were burned at the stake for it. Much of this demonology was inspired by the works of Saint Augustine and his 13th-century adherent, the philosopher Saint Thomas Aquinas. Their theories influenced the 15th-century handbook *The Malleus Malificarum* ("Hammer of Witches"). This infamous witch hunter manual has a preoccupation with women who supposedly copulate with devils, citing Aquinas' hypotheses about demon sex, including his belief that witches and wizards were the product of dalliances between mortals and incubi or succubi.

Popular Culture

Centuries later, the notion of relations between humans and otherworldly spirits is still around. In Western pop culture, the concept of sexual spirits has provided rich fodder for romance and fantasy in books, films, and television. Fictional portrayals of ghostly relationships are of varying degrees of explicitness. In *The Ghost and Mrs. Muir*, the classic movie and TV series based on the 1945 novel by R. A. Dick, widow Mrs. Muir has an unconventional romance with a spirit haunting her seaside cottage, the ghost of the deceased former owner seaman Captain Gregg. In the 1990 movie *Ghost*, the characters played by Demi Moore and Patrick Swayze are lovers in this world, and the next, after he dies unexpectedly. In one of the final scenes, Whoopi Goldberg, playing a psychic medium, channels Swayze's character so that he and his sweetheart can enjoy one final night of romance. Paranormal erotica is also a popular genre of fiction, while there are online communities of amateur authors dedicated to writing steamy stories about spirits.

The idea of spiritual lovers supplies rich material for humor too. In the 1984 supernatural comedy *Ghostbusters*, Dan Aykroyd's character Dr. Raymond Stanz is a parapsychologist who starts a ghost catching business in New York City. In one scene, he falls asleep and dreams about a beautiful ghost woman who has been dead for 100 years. Invisible hands unzip his jeans and it's implied that the female specter pleases him, leaving him cross-eyed. In the film *Ghost Team One* (2013), two roommates fall in love with a woman who believes their home is haunted because a murder had taken place there decades ago. She believes that she once had a sexual encounter with a poltergeist. In their efforts to woo her, the pair decides to shoot a documentary about the history of the house, but they are surprised to actually capture evidence of supernatural activity. In a scene reminiscent of *Ghostbusters*, one of the characters has an intimate encounter with a ghost.

Sexual intercourse with supernatural beings is a popular subject in the horror genre as well. Two examples include the macabre 1960s movie *Rosemary's Baby* and the 1980s movie *The Entity*. *The Entity* is based on novel of the same title that purportedly was inspired by a true-life case.

Modern Accounts of Spectrophilia

Stories of sexual relations between humans and ghosts are not just found in mythology or modern works of fiction, but there are also a surprising amount of alleged real life examples. In an advice column in *Slate* an anonymous writer reported that her friend was engaging in sex with the ghost of "John," a man who had lived in her New York City apartment during the 1920s. The woman contemplated reigniting an old flame, but feared making her phantom lover jealous (Juzwiak, 2020). Unsurprisingly, these stories appear occasionally in tabloids. In 2018, a British psychic reportedly fell in love with a spirit during a trip to Australia. The pair even consummated the relationship on the flight back home. They became engaged, although the psychic later called off the nuptials because her ghostly fiancé "kept disappearing" and started "doing drugs and partying too much" (O'Neill, 2020). Spiritual marriages are not uncommon in other religions and cultures. In particular, such unions are a popular Voodoo custom, in which the living are paired with a spiritual spouse to bring good luck, provide protection from misfortune, and ease financial woes (Stollznow, 2013).

Several celebrities have reported experiences with ghostly sexual partners. In a racy 2004 interview with men's magazine *FHM*, the model and actor Anna Nicole Smith was asked, "What's the kinkiest sex you've had?" She reportedly replied, "A ghost would crawl up my leg and have sex with me at an apartment a long time ago in Texas." Reportedly adding, "I was freaked out about it, but then I was, like, 'Well, you know what? He's never hurt me and he just gave me some amazing sex, so I have no problem'" (FHM, 2004). The singer Kesha reportedly revealed that her 2012 song "Supernatural" was written about her "experiences with the supernatural … but in a sexy way" (Rahman, 2012). She later reported on the talk show *Jimmy Kimmel Live!* that her vagina was now "haunted" as a result of the encounters. .

Personal encounters are also reported by men. Singer Bobby Brown once reportedly lived in a "haunted" mansion in Atlanta, Georgia in which he had an experience with an amorous spirit. "One memorable night, one of the ghosts descended from the ceiling and had sex with me," Brown claimed (Brown, 2017, p. 78). Dan Aykroyd's fictional sexual encounter with a ghost in the movie *Ghostbusters* was allegedly preceded by a real experience. In a 2019 podcast interview, Aykroyd revealed that he had slept with a "seduction ghost" (Rogan, 2020).

Seduction ghosts are also a popular subject on ghost hunting television shows. In a Valentine's Day episode of *Ghost Adventures*, the team investigates claims surrounding an inn. It is said that a female spirit haunts Room 9 of the inn, initiating intimate encounters with the men who spend a night there. A ghost hunter on the show says, "I had an experience I'll never forget. It was a different feeling; that environment was ecstasy. I just felt very loved." In the Travel Channel documentary *Ghostly Lovers*, several women are interviewed about their trysts with unseen forces.

Natural Explanations for Supernatural Claims

As we can see, there is much anecdotal evidence for spectrophilia. So, what is really going on here? From the variation in claims and experiences, there is no single explanation that accounts for all of the cases. In accordance with the principles of Occam's Razor, the simplest explanation is usually the right one. That is, we ought to seek natural explanations before looking to paranormal explanations. Barring fantasies, delusions, and publicity stunts, and aside from obvious suggestions such as nocturnal emissions (i.e., wet dreams), some cases may have a psychological cause. Our biggest clue is that in many of these cases the victim was in bed or asleep at the time of the occurrence. Therefore, many stories of ghostly sex might be attributed to hallucinations, and specifically, a condition known as sleep paralysis. This is a kind of parasomnia, which refers to unusual experiences that happen while falling asleep, sleeping, or waking from sleep. Sleep paralysis occurs when a person's brain is awake, but their body isn't, leaving the person trapped in a state between wakefulness and sleep. This often causes a temporary inability to speak or move, known as atonia. Sleep paralysis is an interruption of the REM stage of sleep. It typically takes place when a person is falling asleep (hypnogogic hallucinations) or while they're waking up (hypnopompic hallucinations) (Cheyne et al., 1999). Sleep paralysis is a relatively common sleep condition in the general population and generally not serious (Sharpless & Barber, 2011). It can be caused by factors including sleep deprivation, jet lag, or stress, and it is linked to sleep disorders such as narcolepsy or sleep apnea.

An episode of sleep paralysis can present a wide range of visual, auditory, and tactile hallucinations, in which people may see, sense, or feel things that don't exist, such as the perception of a malevolent presence in the room. These "intruder hallucinations" may logically explain many alleged paranormal encounters, from shadow people and vampires to alien abductions. (The accounts of "contactees," those people who claim to have contact with extraterrestrials, are often a modern-day version of demon lovers, including stories of sexual encounters, some allegedly resulting in alien-human hybrid children.) Whether people envision a witch, werewolf, or a demon, they seem to conjure up a creature that is in line with their religious, spiritual, or cultural beliefs.

Pleasurable or blissful hallucinations are in the minority, while most episodes are distressing. Assaults are common hallucination themes. Chest pressure hallucinations comprise a feeling of pressure on the chest, breathing difficulties, and pain. These are tellingly labeled "incubus hallucinations," in which an incubus or succubus is occasionally a feature, causing the victim to believe that a demon was holding them down (Oliver & Lewis, 1996, p. 218). Sleep paralysis is occasionally known as Old Hag Syndrome, taken from the superstitious belief that an "old hag" or "night hag" sits or rides on top of her victims' chests while they sleep. The hag renders them immobile and breathless, and indeed many sufferers experience a sense of suffocation. The French writer Guy de Maupassant appears to describe such a visitation in his short story *La Horla*.

> I sleep—for a while—two or three hours—then a dream—no—a nightmare seizes me in its grip, I know full well that I am lying down and that I am asleep … . I sense it and I know it … and I am also aware that somebody is coming up to me, looking at me, running his fingers over me, climbing on to my bed, kneeling on my chest, taking me by the throat and squeezing … squeezing … with all its might, trying to strangle me. I struggle, but I am tied down by that dreadful feeling of helplessness which paralyzes us in our dreams. I want to cry out—but I can't. I want to move—I can't do it. I try, making terrible, strenuous efforts, gasping for breath, to turn on my side, to throw off this creature who is crushing me and choking me—but I can't! Then, suddenly, I wake up, panic-stricken, covered in sweat. I light a candle. I am alone.
>
> (Maupassant, 1887, p. 33)

Sleep paralysis is often a terrifying experience, for which reason it can also be referred to as a "waking nightmare." Experiencers are often unable to discern nightmare from reality. As discussed above, *incubus* comes from the Latin term meaning, "to lie upon, or weigh upon," reminiscent of the incubus hallucination. Interestingly, the Latin *incubo* also has the additional sense of "nightmare" (Harper, 2021). We might be tempted to think that nightmares are a recent explanation for demon sex, but this theory has been around for a while. The Swiss-English artist John Henry Fuseli painted *The Nightmare* (1781), depicting a sleeping woman draped across a disheveled bed while a goblin crouches on her chest. The figure is often interpreted as an incubus and the painting thought to be a depiction of sleep paralysis (French & Santomauro, 2007). This iconic painting is arguably Fuseli's most famous, and due to its popularity, he painted several versions of the artwork.

Hallucinations are consistent with paranormal narratives identified in numerous contemporary examples and also historical accounts. While superstitious beliefs may explain many claims of visitations from ghosts and demons in the past, other accounts may have a more worldly explanation. Before the days of modern science, the devil might be blamed for pediatric difficulties, including disease or developmental disabilities, a child's death, or one who grew to be evil or strangely gifted. In times of sexual taboos and repression, the devil could be blamed for all kinds of indiscretions, from forbidden sexual intercourse and pregnancies out to wedlock to the birth of a child who did not resemble his father. The devil was also a scapegoat for mortal lust and desire. Especially clever incubi were thought to be able to make themselves appear in the form of real people, such as a husband, neighbor, or even a member of the clergy. To make sensual encounters sound less appealing, the Church spread the rumor that the devil's semen and phallus was either ice cold or burning hot, made of iron, or double-pronged. "The devil made me do it" was also an excuse for bad behavior.

Similar historical cases support the theory of sleep paralysis as an explanation. During the Salem Witch Trials of the 17th century, tavern owner Bridget Bishop was accused of being a witch. A number of victims came forward with their terrifying stories of her haunting them in their sleep. Sometime "between waking and sleeping," Bishop appeared in Samuel Gray's bedroom (Lucas, 2018, p. 119). She reappeared several months later wearing "the same Garb and Clothes," her visitation causing his child to have seizures and die. In another story, while in bed with his wife, Richard Coman saw "the curtains at the end of the bed open" and Bishop laid on his "breast or body and so oppressed him that he could not speak nor stir no not so much as to wake his wife." The following evening she reappeared and "took hold of him by the throat and almost hauled him out of the bed." On the basis of this testimony, and that supplied by several other upright married men of the Puritan community, Bishop was found guilty of witchcraft. On June 10, 1692, she was hanged on Gallows Hill.

Summary and Conclusion

There is nothing wrong with enjoying paranormal romance and fantasy in books, movies, and television. There is little harm if a person experiences a sexual daydream and happily believes that they have had an intimate encounter with a spirit or ghost; although this is not the most logical explanation for these experiences. But there can be real-world consequences for these claims. There is glaring danger in historical cases where people (especially women) have been abused, raped, or even murdered for their alleged sexual relations with demons. There is also danger in modern beliefs that sex with imaginary demons can lead to gynecological disorders, as promulgated by some modern day leaders. Both past and present there is a clear misogyny underpinning these beliefs. From old hags and succubi to witches, women are either accused of bewitching innocent men or they become the victims of attacks.

Why do people believe in seductive spirits? There is no single reason why people believe in these claims. Just like potential scientific explanations for these phenomena, there are as many reasons that people believe as there are alleged incidents. Historically, when religion held more ground than science, a belief in angels, demons, and spirits fit the popular theology and worldview of the time. Attacks by these monsters were a way to explain what was not yet understood, when people lived in fear of their souls. To a lesser extent, that fear is still around, and grounded in modern religious and spiritual beliefs. Modern psychology has afforded us plausible explanations for the idea of amorous spirits, in the form of hallucinations and various sleep phenomena. However, for those who haven't had exposure to these explanations, their experiences can still seem like a mystery.

The belief in spectrophilia has existed for thousands of years. Accounts of these phenomena are not some curio of history, but form the basis of many contemporary worldviews. From ancient mythology to modern spiritual beliefs, these stories vary across time and culture. Seductive creatures take the form of benign beings such as spirits and ghosts, to more malevolent entities, such as demons or even Satan himself. Whether the creature is an angel or an alien, the experiences appear to follow the beliefs of the era. But with our modern understanding of psychology there is no need to live in fear of attacks from demons and evil monsters. Natural explanations, including dreams, hallucinations, and sleep paralysis, provide rational explanations for these supernatural claims.

References

Bane, T. (2012). *Encyclopedia of demons in the world religions and cultures*. McFarland & Company.

Brown, B., & Chiles, N. (2017). *Every little step: My story*. Dey Street Books.

Cheyne, J. A., Rueffer, S. D., & Newby-Clark, I. R. (1999). Hypnagogic and hypnopompic hallucinations during sleep paralysis: Neurological and cultural construction of the night-mare. *Consciousness and Cognition, 8*(3), 319–337.

Di Lorenzo, G., Gorea, F., Longo, L., & Ribolsi, M. (2018). Paraphilia and paraphilic disorders. In E. Jannini & A. Siracusano (Eds.), *Sexual dysfunctions in mentally ill patients*. Trends in Andrology and Sexual Medicine. Springer.

FHM (2004). Anna Nicole Smith interview. Issue 46 (July).

Fox, R. L. (2004). *Alexander the great*. Penguin.

French, C., & Santomauro, J. (2007). Something wicked this way comes: Causes and interpretations of sleep paralysis. In S. D. Sala (Ed.), *Tall tales about the mind & brain*. Oxford University Press.

Ghanim, D. (2018). *The sexual world of the Arabian nights*. Cambridge University Press.

Harper, D. (2021). Online etymology dictionary. Retrieved from https://www.etymonline.com

Huysmans, J. K., & King, B. (2011). *La-Bas: A journey into the self*. Dedalus Books.

Juzwiak, R. (2020). My friend thinks she's having sex with a ghost. Retrieved from https://slate.com/human-interest/2020/07/sex-ghost-quarantine-advice.html

Lucas, W. (2018). Damned by a red paragon bodice: Witchcraft and the power of cloth and clothing in puritan society. *Massachusetts Historical Review, 20*, 119–149.

Mack C. K., & Mack, D. (1999). *A field guide to demons, fairies, fallen angels and other subversive spirits*. Henry Holt and Company.

Maupassant, G. (1887). *The horla and others. guy de maupassant's best weird fiction and ghost stories: Tales of mystery, murder, fantasy & horror*. Melville House.

Oliver E. D., & Lewis, J. R. (1996). *Angels A to Z, Incubi and Succubi*. Visible Ink Press.

O'Neill, N. (2020). Woman calls off wedding with ghost after he 'kept disappearing.' Retrieved from https://nypost.com/2020/10/14/woman-calls-off-wedding-with-ghost-after-he-kept-disappearing/

Rahman, R. (2012). *Ke$ha: I had sex with a ghost*. Retrieved from https://ew.com/article/2012/09/27/kesha-sex-with-ghost/

Raphael, P. (1964). Lilith. *The Journal of American Folklore, 77*(306, Oct.–Dec.), 295.

Rogan, J. (2020). Dan Aykroyd. The Joe Rogan experience. Episode #1351.

Saint Augustine of Hippo. (1887). (426 AD) *City of God*. Image Classics.

Sharpless, B. A., & Barber, J. P. (2011). Lifetime prevalence rates of sleep paralysis: A systematic review. *Sleep Medicine Reviews, 15*(5), 311–315.

Stollznow, K. (2013). *God Bless America*. Pitchstone Press.

12 Alternative Medicine and Health

Steven Novella

As a practicing physician, I am often asked what I think about alternative medicine, either for a specific condition or in general. Often patients are looking for more options and have heard alternative medicine could be beneficial. Generally speaking, alternative medicine can be described as a range of treatments that aren't already considered part of science-based medicine. Thus, they provide alternatives to mainstream medicine, especially when mainstream medicine doesn't provide the solution they are hoping for. Some examples of alternative medicine include homeopathy (Ernst, 2010; Novella, 2020), naturopathy (Gavura, 2014; Hermes, 2018), reflexology (Ernst et al., 2011; Hall, 2018), and acupuncture (Colquhoun & Novella, 2013; Gorski, 2020). These approaches are commonly used for medical conditions, and they are also commonly used for treating mental disorders, often serving as core components to pop psychology treatments for depression, anxiety, and pain, among other conditions. Given the large number of alternative medicine techniques and the large number of conditions that alternative medicine is used to treat, there have been countless claims made about these approaches to treatment. This chapter will address the broad claim that alternative medicine is effective, and by doing so will address some more specific claims as well.

Examining the Claims

What is alternative medicine? The problem with asking about "alternative medicine" is that it's the wrong question. A concise or even meaningful answer is elusive, because first you have to figure out what alternative medicine is. I am not just referring to the shifting branding of so-called alternative medicine, which evolved into complementary medicine, then complementary and alternative medicine (CAM), and then integrative medicine (Gorski, 2015; Gorski & Novella, 2014). There are also spin-offs and other labels including natural medicine (Hall, 2021), holistic medicine (Royal, 2018), ancient/traditional medicine (Ramey, 2010), and functional medicine (Gorski, 2016).

The core problem is that alternative medicine (the term I will use throughout this chapter for convenience) is an artificial category. It is functionally a brand, deliberately vague (the vagueness is a feature not a bug), used primarily for marketing purposes. But it lacks any scientific definition or coherent philosophy of medicine.

I have been studying alternative medicine in all its forms for decades, and as far as I can tell the only real definition of alternative medicine is this – anything goes. That's it. It is, in practice, the absence of a science-based standard of care. There is no positive standard of care that defines alternative medicine or that its practitioners adhere to. They are simply unconstrained by logic or scientific evidence.

DOI: 10.4324/9781003107798-12

Before the rebranding as alternative medicine sometime around the 1970s, the popular practices now considered "alternative" were called health fraud, or more colloquially, "quackery." Rebranding these dubious treatments as legitimate alternatives to scientific medicine is perhaps the greatest triumph of marketing over common sense in the last century.

Popular definitions include the notion that alternative treatments are "natural" or "holistic," and serve as alternatives to drugs and surgery. The definitions tend to leverage ancient wisdom or are spiritual in nature. It is easy to demonstrate, however, that none of these definitions are consistent, true, or in some cases even meaningful. Saying that alternative treatments are holistic, for example, does nothing to solve the vague definition problem – it just introduces another vague term.

One line of evidence that alternative medicine is fundamentally about a lack of a standard of care is the legal battles used to promote its practitioners. Many states in the United States now have so-called "health care freedom laws." These are presented as giving patients the right to choose their treatments, but they are really about the right of practitioners to sell their medical products and services without being held to any standard. These laws explicitly create a double standard. The wording varies from state to state, but they all are formulated in a similar way – a health care practitioner cannot have their license to practice taken away or acted against for practicing unscientific methods or below the accepted standard of care if what they are doing is deemed "alternative." This is where the vague definition is an advantage. These laws are essentially get-out-of-jail free cards for practicing substandard care.

Natural Medicine

Let's take a look at some of the concepts that are frequently used to define alternative medicine, starting with "natural" (Bellamy, 2016). The term natural as a marketing term has been around for centuries, and is therefore nothing new. The marketing goal is to create a health halo around any product labeled natural, to reassure the consumer and to short-circuit any thoughtful analysis of the claims being made. But what does it mean?

When scientists talk about a definition they are often referring to what is called an "operational definition." This means we can apply a set of criteria to definitively include everything that belongs in a category and exclude everything that does not. If, for example, your blood pressure is 140/90 mmHg or greater on three separate measurements, you have hypertension. That is a clear definition, but what, therefore, is the operational definition of the term "natural"?

We might suggest that "natural" means "occurring in nature," as opposed to something that never existed in nature until it was synthesized by people. But what if the substance itself was synthesized in a factory even though it actually already does exist in nature? Is the bioidentical chemically synthesized vitamin C the same as the vitamin C that's derived from an orange? The scientific answer, by the way, is yes, by definition.

What if we take something from nature and tweak it? If I take the leaf of a plant, dry it, then crush it up into a powder, is that natural? How much processing crosses the line to no longer being natural? What if I separate out some of the constituents – are all the constituents of the leaf natural? What if the plant is cooked, which chemically alters its composition? What if I combine several naturally derived substances together so that they undergo a chemical reaction to alter their molecular structure?

The far more important question than where to draw the line between natural and artificial is: why should we care? There is no law of nature, no principle of biology or chemistry, that dictates that substances that occur in nature are more likely to be safe and effective than synthesized substances. If anything, the opposite is true. Plants evolve chemicals specifically to be toxic to animals, to keep animals from eating them. More than 99% of the toxins and pesticides you will consume in your life are made within the plants you eat, not added by farmers.

In fact, almost all of the food consumed by humans has been extensively cultivated to significantly reduce their natural toxins. I would not suggest going into the woods and consuming a random plant. The deadliest poisons we know are all naturally occurring.

Being "natural" is a poor proxy for being safe and effective. That's what we really want, for anything we consume or any treatment we receive to be more likely to help us than to harm us, to have medical benefits in excess of the risks or side effects. "Natural" is a marketing term intended to make the consumer assume that the product is safe and healthful, but it means nothing of the sort.

If we want to know that a treatment is safe and effective, why not just determine that directly? That is what science does. The real question is: how do we know the potential risks and benefits of any treatment? We have a few centuries of experience here – the overwhelmingly clear answer is science.

This is not to suggest that using science to determine best practices in medicine is easy or always works out. Quite the contrary – the science of medicine is extremely challenging, and our institutions of science and medicine are problematic. But they are the best we have, and they are always improving. If we are going to have any chance of predicting the results of a treatment, it's by using the best science available. Substituting a comforting marketing term for science is, to be blunt, a scam.

It also bears stating that not all treatments that are considered alternative can also be reasonably considered natural. Alternative treatments include drugs, invasive procedures, and sometimes extreme physical conditions that are decidedly unnatural.

Holistic Medicine

What about "holistic," that seems unimpeachable, right? Again, there is a problem of the vagueness of the definition, but more to the point most alternative treatments are decidedly not holistic, while many medical treatments are.

The notion of holistic care is that it considers the whole person, mind, body, and spirit (Royal, 2018). For "spirit" we can also include social and cultural factors and not necessarily endorse or require any specific religious belief. This concept is not new within mainstream medicine. We just use different terminology, often referring to this approach as the "biopsychosocial" model of medicine, which explicitly considers the patient as a whole person in all their various contexts.

But scientific medicine is also reductionist, which means it endeavors to understand the underlying mechanisms of health, disease, wellness, and disorders. There is tremendous power in reductionism. Understanding that an autoimmune reaction against the Beta cells in the pancreas, the ones that produce insulin, causes Type I diabetes revolutionized our ability to treat this disease, and dramatically improved the lives of those who suffer from this condition. Reductionist science and medicine should not be denigrated or minimized.

But it's not the whole picture, and doctors generally understand this. I treat migraines, for example, and when I do I consider the patient's diet, lifestyle factors, sleep, caffeine intake, hormonal status, and family history. I also use medication to prevent and treat migraine attacks, and these medications are increasingly based on a basic science understanding of what migraines are and what is happening during a migraine attack. It is the best of holistic and reductionist medicine.

This is why it is particularly galling when proponents of alternative medicine pretend they invented the idea and that a holistic approach distinguishes the brand. It doesn't. Most alternative treatments are decidedly not holistic (or reductionist, they are the worst of both worlds). How, for example, is acupuncture holistic? Medical acupuncture is based on sticking needles into alleged acupuncture points to treat just about everything. It is based on the notion that all disease is caused by the same mechanism, problems with the flow of chi through meridians. None of this is based in reality, but further it is a maximally narrow approach to health. How is that holistic?

The same is true of straight chiropractic, homeopathy, energy medicine, or reflexology. These are all based on the notion that there is one cause of all disease (and interestingly are often mutually exclusive). We have a saying in medicine, if your only tool is a hammer then every problem looks like a nail. Alternative treatments are typically one-tool approaches to healthcare.

Ancient Medicine

Being ancient should also be of no comfort (Ramey, 2010). Ancient practitioners did not have a better understanding of health and disease than modern doctors. They basically had no idea what was going on. They did not even have a concept of disease. They did not know what the organs did, knew almost nothing of human anatomy (which wasn't even studied until the 16th century), and did not understand genetics, biochemistry, or physiology. Neuroscience was a black box. They were stumbling around in the dark.

What every single culture did was invent superstitions and mythology to give them the illusion that they could control nature. These superstitions are mutually incoherent, and have no relation to what was later discovered to be reality. At best many cultures did figure out some basics through trial and error, such as the pharmacological effects of plants in their environment (at least the obvious effects). Many figured out some practical aspects of doing simple surgery or facilitating child birth.

But this practical knowledge was heavily mixed with superstition and nonsense. Physicians in Western cultures believed you could diagnose anything by examining the precise color and hue of the urine. They believed illness was caused by imbalances of the four humors, which made blood-letting a popular (and harmful) intervention. They thought puss was a sign that a wound was healing, rather than a sign that the wound is dangerously infected, because they had no idea about microbiology and infections.

These ideas are all silly, even though they thrived for thousands of years. They are no more silly than the notions that thrived in other parts of the world, like the fact that mysterious energy flows through our bodies in a pattern that matches the astrological signs in the sky. But the superstitions of another part of the world can seem exotic, and can be marketed as ancient wisdom.

The Example of Homeopathy

Let's take a quick look at a specific modality that is considered one of the mainstays of alternative medicine – homeopathy. Most of the public does not know what homeopathy is and believe it is herbal or natural treatments. But this is not true.

Homeopathy was invented by Samuel Christian Hahnemann (1755–1843), a German physician practicing at a time before the real advent of scientific medicine. Using anecdotal observation and questionable reasoning, he developed several laws of homeopathic medicine. First, he believed in the notional that "like cures like" – that a small dose of a substance will cure symptoms caused by that substance. This is a form of sympathetic magic, with no basis in reality. So, for example, if onions make you tear, then a small amount of extract of onion will cure a disease that causes tearing, such as the flu.

Hahnemann further came to believe that the more a substance is diluted the more powerful it becomes. Common homeopathic dilutions include a 1:100 dilution carried out 30 times (abbreviated 30C). That is so dilute that no original substance remains in the preparation, something Hahnemann knew. But he believed that the magical essence of the substance would remain. So, if you want to go to sleep, you could take a preparation of caffeine, but don't worry, there likely won't be any actual caffeine in the homeopathic product.

Hahnemann also believed that his treatments needed to be activated, usually by shaking them ten times in each plane. Why? Again, there is no scientific reason. His methods of preparation have more in common with witchcraft than science.

All of this is the essence of homeopathy to this day – homeopathic products contain fanciful ingredients based on dubious logic and diluted out of existence. So basically you are paying for sugar pills on which a drop of pure water has been placed. The scientific plausibility that any such treatment can have any physiological effect, let alone treat a symptom or disease, is essentially zero.

Even still there have been thousands of clinical studies looking at whether or not homeopathic treatments work. After more than a hundred years of such studies, we can conclusively state that homeopathy works for nothing. There isn't a single indication for which a homeopathic treatment has been shown to work under rigorous scientific conditions. Multiple systematic reviews of the research (Ernst, 2002) have reached this conclusion – homeopathy simply does not work, and there is no reason to think that it should.

Placing the label of "natural" or "holistic" onto a homeopathic product does not change this fundamental reality. Bashing science-based medicine, or even pointing out legitimate short-comings, does not make homeopathic products work either.

Summary and Conclusion

Alternative medicine is defined more by what *it is not* than what it really is. That is, alternative medicine is a collection of physical health and mental health practices that are not otherwise considered part of science-based medicine. Thus, by definition, alternative medicine practices do not have empirical support. Practitioners of alternative medicine often make it sound safe and effective by using terms like "natural" and "holistic," and they may also claim that their techniques are steeped in ancient traditions. However, claims like these are not valid. In fact, natural substances can be dangerous, and the claim that a technique is effective because it is ancient also uses weak logic.

To be fair, it's always possible for a treatment be considered ineffective for some time before well-done research is able to finally support the effectiveness of the treatment. This happens all the time in science. Unfortunately, the problem for alternative medicine proponents is that when a treatment does have enough research to be considered science-based, then the treatment is no longer consider alternative. Thus, by definition, alternative medicine is forever going to be stuck on the fringe sidelines of the health fields, and proponents will be stuck emphasizing marketing instead of results.

That is the essence of alternative medicine – all marketing, no reality.

References

Bellamy, J. (2016). What (if anything) does "natural" mean? Retrieved from https://sciencebasedmedicine. org/what-if-anything-does-natural-mean/

Colquhoun, D., & Novella, S. P. (2013). Acupuncture is theatrical placebo. *Anesthesia & Analgesia*, *116*(6), 1360–1363.

Ernst, E. (2002). A systematic review of systematic reviews of homeopathy. *British Journal of Clinical Pharmacology*, *54*(6), 577–582.

Ernst, E. (2010). Homeopathy: what does the "best" evidence tell us? *Medical Journal of Australia*, *192*(8), 458–460.

Ernst, E., Posadzki, P., & Lee, M. S. (2011). Reflexology: An update of a systematic review of randomised clinical trials. *Maturitas*, *68*(2), 116–120.

Gavura (2014). Naturopathy vs. science: Autism. Retrieved from https://sciencebasedmedicine.org/ naturopathy-vs-science-autism/

Gorski, D. (2015). NCCIH and the true evolution of integrative medicine. Retrieved from https:// sciencebasedmedicine.org/true-evolution-integrative-medicine/

Gorski, D. (2016). Functional medicine: The ultimate misnomer in the world of integrative medicine. Retrieved from https://sciencebasedmedicine.org/functional-medicine-the-ultimate-misnomer-in-the-world-of-integrative-medicine/

Gorski, D. (2020). More evidence that acupuncture doesn't work for chronic pain. Retrieved from https://sciencebasedmedicine.org/more-evidence-that-acupuncture-doesnt-work-for-chronic-pain/

Gorski, D. H., & Novella, S. P. (2014). Clinical trials of integrative medicine: Testing whether magic works?. *Trends in Molecular Medicine*, *20*(9), 473–476.

Hall, H. (2018). Modern reflexology: Still as bogus as pre-modern reflexology. Retrieved from https:// sciencebasedmedicine.org/modern-reflexology-still-as-bogus-as-pre-modern-reflexology/

Hall, H. (2021). The natural medicine handbook. Retrieved from https://sciencebasedmedicine.org/ the-natural-medicine-handbook/

Hermes, B. M. (2018). An inside look at naturopathic medicine: A whistleblower's deconstruction and its core principles. In A. B. Kaufman and J. C. Kaufman (Eds.), *The pseudoscience: The conspiracy against science* (pp. 137–169). The MIT Press.

Novella, S. (2020). Homeopathy is worthless and not always harmless. Retrieved from https:// sciencebasedmedicine.org/homeopathy-is-worthless-and-not-always-harmless/

Ramey, D. (2010). Acupuncture and history: The "ancient" therapy that's been around for several decades. Retrieved from

Royal, D. (2018). I used to be a holistic nutritionist. Retrieved from https://sciencebasedmedicine. org/i-used-to-be-a-holistic-nutritionist/

13 Selling Flimflam and Social Influences

Anthony R. Pratkanis

As the chapters in this book make clear, the selling of pseudoscience, fringe science, and other questionable claims – or what I call *flimflam* – is ubiquitous in our daily lives. In this chapter, instead of evaluating claims about a specific type of flimflam, I will address the question: how do we come to believe in and purchase such things as unsupported medicine and treatments traditionally termed quackery, horoscopes, demon possession, energy healing, and the like? In answering this question, I will approach it as an experimental social psychologist by using the core research findings on persuasion and social influence to reveal the social forces that can lead us to accept questionable claims.

Examining the Claims

One common belief is that people who accept questionable claims have something wrong with them – they are gullible, stupid, naïve, foolish, or lacking in some other characteristic. In other words, only foolish people do foolish things. One problem with this belief is that it is not supported by research. For example, in our work on who is victimized by fraud crimes, we find that anyone can be robbed in a fraud. In one study, known fraud victims were given a battery of questions in attempt to identify a victim profile (AARP, 1996). No profile emerged from the results. In another study, we contacted known victims of lottery and investment frauds along with a random control group and asked them questions designed to measure a range of personality characteristics such as locus of control, trust, propensity to confess, need for cognition, hypnotic susceptibility, and so on. None of these scales predicted victimization (AARP, 2003). We did find that some variables did predict specific fraud vulnerability such that lottery victims tended to not trust others and to feel the world controlled them, whereas investment fraud victims felt they controlled the world. Our results were replicated in another survey conducted by the UK Office of Fair Trading (2006) which concluded:

> Our research dispels the myth that only the vulnerable, elderly or naïve are taken in by scams. Anyone can be taken in because scams are customised to fit the profile of the people being targeted. There really is a scam for everyone.

The belief that only foolish people do foolish things is an example of the fundamental attribution error or a tendency to overestimate the roles of personality and dispositional factors compared to the roles of situational and environmental factors in terms of explaining social behavior causes (Ross, 1977). In other words, when we see someone believing in

DOI: 10.4324/9781003107798-13

flimflam, we have a tendency to jump at the conclusion that there is something wrong with "them," and ignore the social forces that might lead to that belief and action.

In analyzing how we come to believe in and purchase flimflam, the social psychologist begins with the proposition: people who do foolish things are not necessarily foolish (Aronson, 1992). In other words, to understand why someone (including ourselves) might believe and do a foolish thing we must begin by understanding the power of the situation and the social world the person lives in (Ross & Nisbett, 1991). We do that by identifying the social influences in that situation – in this case, the social influence tactics used to sell flimflam. A good understanding of these social influence tactics will help us better examine claims made about any topic. Below I will describe some of the more common tactics.

Phantom Dreams

The basis of most flimflams is a phantom alternative – an option that looks real, is typically superior to other choices, but is unavailable (Pratkanis & Farquhar, 1992). The key to selling a flimflam is to sell the phantom as real and possible and something that can be obtained with the right belief, effort, and, of course, money, but, in reality, it is a false dream.

The sale of a phantom begins by creating ostensible solutions to satisfy our most basic needs and desires. As such, phantoms often purport to provide things such as:

- Health (quack cures, diets, "healing" rituals, mental health pseudoscience, psychic surgery, faith healing).
- Wealth (get-rich-quick schemes, lucky lottery numbers, investment fraud).
- Social popularity (weight loss regimes, love potions, dating and romance fraud, becoming an "expert" with "secret" knowledge about UFOs, the Loch Ness Monster, and the moon landing).
- Fear of death and the end of our existence (séances, life-after-death claims).
- Reduction in the anxiety of life's uncertainties (advice given by horoscopes, astrology, psychic mediums, and other means, phrenology, psychic detectives, conspiracy theories that "make sense" of the world and the desires and feelings of those who spread them).

It is relatively easy to create a phantom since it does not actually need to solve these needs, but just appear to do so. Compounding the problem, it's often difficult to spot the real from the fake course of action without the needed knowledge, expertise, and critical thinking skills.

Although a phantom dream is imaginary, its impact on our behavior is quite real in several ways. First, a phantom dream channels our thoughts. Television shows and YouTube videos about ancient astronauts, quack remedies, psychic detectives, and the like set an agenda – these topics become the focus of our attention and discussion. We share the stories, "debate" the topic, and, most importantly, subject ourselves to the influence tactics (described next) of those who sell the flimflam. Our attention is turned away from things that might actually make our lives better and more interesting such as learning about the remarkable discoveries in astronomy, taking steps to improve health by eating more fruits and vegetables or quitting smoking, and finding out how to actually solve a crime.

Second, a phantom motivates behavior through what can be termed phantom fixation. Once we come to believe that the attractive phantom is real, we are motivated to obtain it – spending money, time, and energy to make the dream come true. The ability to talk with a dead loved one or to fly like a yogi or bring about world peace with a yoga pose would be wonderful things if they were real and just that easy.

Finally, as attractive alternatives, phantoms tend to make us dissatisfied with everything else. Other real courses of action are seen as inferior and not worth doing. This contrasting of real alternatives strengthens the phantom trap. We become dissatisfied with the obtainable and what we can truly do to change our lives. As such, we miss out on actually living our lives – dealing with life's challenges and learning and growing as a person – in pursuit of a quick phantom fix that supposedly would allow us to live happily ever after.

Story-Telling: The Invented Ruse

In his book, *Swindling and Selling*, Arthur Allen Leff (1976) makes the cogent point that in carrying out a fraud or offering a deal, the con and the seller need to provide a reason (justification) for why the opportunity is possible and available to the target. In other words, why is it possible for a phantom – say, to speak to the dead, to obtain triple returns on an investment, to cure cancer with a low intensity laser – to suddenly be available to meet our most pressing needs? After all, such things have never been seen before, and we are right to be suspicious.

To allay our concerns, the seller of flimflam invents a ruse or story to make the fake look real (Bell & Whaley, 1991; Clark & Mitchell, 2019). For example, early séances as a means to talk with the dead were justified by the discovery of spiritualism, supposed "scientific" tests of psychic phenomena, and the portrayal of the medium as a "sensitive" with special occult powers. In the original Ponzi scheme, Charles Ponzi justified his claim of producing remarkable returns on investment by proclaiming he had figured out a way to take advantage of the International Postal Reply Coupon market. Similarly, Bernie Madoff justified his investment fraud by claiming he had a secret, proprietary trading scheme. Robert "Larry" Lytle, who pleaded guilty to defrauding consumers because he was selling the "QLaser System" (a light-emitting device) as a treatment for over 200 conditions, explained how his device worked in terms of Einstein's theory of relativity and the bio-stimulation of different wave lengths of light and energy (Lytle, 2004). In her remarkable autobiography, patent medicine pitch woman Violet McNeal describes how quackery was sold to Americans during the early 20th century (McNeal, 1947). According to her account, the sellers of patent medicine generally faked one of three identities: Native American, a healer from the mysterious East, or a Quaker. Claiming the cure-all was discovered by Native Americans or from the "Far East" reinforced the story that it was an esoteric, traditional, and all-natural remedy unknown to modern Western man or woman. The Quaker pitch emphasized the purity of the tonic.

A good narrative helps to guide our thoughts (e.g., the cure is natural and traditional), determines the credibility of information (e.g., as a natural cure, this makes sense), and ultimately directs evaluation and choice (e.g., it works for Native Americans and Quakers, why not me?). As such, stories cement information in our mind and tend to persist even in the face of strong, discrediting information (Anderson et al., 1980; see Pratkanis (2007) for the use of stories in influence).

Tailored Pitches

In our research on economic fraud crimes, we found that con criminals profile their victims to craft the most effective message (Pratkanis & Shadel, 2005). They engage in tactics such as: (a) purchasing victim lists from each other and list brokers which describe potential targets in terms of age, interests, dreams and needs, financial data, family patterns, among other information; (b) "interviewing" the target of the fraud to find out relevant information for a pitch; and (c) pitching a target repeatedly to find out what works and does not. One of the most valuable assets of con criminals is their victim list, which contains the names and personal details on those they will attempt to rob with their schemes. Such lists can be used to construct the pitch. For example, if a con knows you are sick with cancer or facing financial difficulties or want to save endangered wolves, then a phantom can quickly be created to meet your desires. Personal information can be used to establish an instant connection with the target. As one of the con criminals we interviewed put it: if the target says they are a veteran of WWII, then he says he is a veteran of Desert Storm.

Similar techniques can be found in psychic and other flimflams. In his confession on how he worked the psychic flimflam, Lamar Keene (1997) describes how he would keep index cards containing information he gathered on a person during a psychic reading. This information would be used later or shared with other "psychics" in his network to produce astonishing readings. Keene operated in the pre-Internet/pre-social media days and thus his information was gathered slowly over time. Of course, today similar information can be obtained with a quick Google of the target and a visit to her or his Facebook page. Social media can also be used as a tool to gather such information through such things as fun surveys (e.g., to find out what Disney princess you are) and posts asking everyone to put the name of their first pet (and possible password or security code answer) in the comments.

Fake healers can use the technique of pre-show to gather needed information. For example, before the healing event, attendees can fill out prayer cards with their healing requests and other information. During the service, the fake healer can call out names and appear, by purported divine intervention, to know the person's illness and personal life story. Typically, the fake healer will "cure" shills (plants who fake illnesses) and those with painful health problems such as arthritis for which the pain can be overlooked in the excitement of the moment. The prayer cards (along with Googling and social media) provide the needed information.

In our research on economic fraud crimes, we find that anyone can become the victim of a fraud crime – it's a matter of the con hitting on the right phantom and hitting us at the most opportune time (AARP, 2003; UK Office of Fair Trading, 2006). However, we also found one variable that makes us more susceptible to fraud – when we are facing life stresses (NASD IEF, 2006). This makes sense. When we are facing life's difficulties – financial troubles, loss of a loved one, romantic regrets, health issues – it is easy for the purveyor of flimflam to construct the needed phantom at a time when our cognitive capacity is directed toward other concerns and not with refuting a pitch. In a similar vein, those who are distressed and looking for meaning in life are most susceptible to cultic influence (Singer, 1995), the experience of stressful life events is correlated with believe in conspiracy theories (Swami et al., 2016), and relative deprivation or a feeling that one should be getting more out of life is a major predictor of accepting extremist and racist propaganda (Pratkanis, 2009; Pratkanis & Turner, 1999). For example, in carrying out a finance and loan fraud, con criminals look for "DM" or desperate men (and women) who are in dire need of money because, for example, he or she cannot obtain a legitimate loan to make an investment or pay off a debt (Greene, 1981; Howard, 2017). Life distresses can even predict the acceptance of superstitious belief in a nation. In their study of Germany from 1918 to 1940, Padgett and Jorgenson (1982) found that when economic threat (as measured by real wages, unemployment, and productivity) was high, interest in astrology and mysticism increased (compared to when economic threat was low).

Source Credibility and Authority

Two of the most robust research findings in social psychology are as follows: (a) we tend to listen to those who are credible (expert and trustworthy) sources (Hovland et al., 1953); (b) we tend to obey authorities (Milgram, 1974). The merchant of flimflam leverages these two basic human tendencies by creating a persona as a credible authority and then using that persona to hawk a phantom.

To build a perception of a credible authority, flimflam sellers engage in a variety of techniques. Those who sell quackery create fake degrees often from fake (or diploma mill) universities and hand-out brochures full of testimonials to the effectiveness of their abilities. Sellers will claim specialized knowledge and training in such things as hypnosis, energy healing, native and traditional healing, and low-energy lasers. Advocates of UFO or Bigfoot or Nessie sightings often become directors of made-up "research centers." "Psychic detectives" come with long "resumes" of purported police service. Psychics tout successes (and ignore their many misses). Credibility is easier to manufacture than we might normally think as illustrated by the Carlos hoax created by Randi and Alvarez (2009). In this hoax, Randi and Alvarez created a fake psychic named Carlos complete with a fake resume. TV news shows eagerly featured Carlos and his "amazing" powers.

Once a fake credibility is established, it can be used to sell flimflam in at least two ways. First, we often do not have the time or resources to investigate and evaluate every claim that appears on TV, on social media, or even in our personal lives. In such cases, the presence of a "credible" source can lead one to quickly infer that the message has merit and should be accepted. Second, once the "authority" of the flimflam supplier is firmly established, then it can be used to command us in a manner similar to what Stanley Milgram observed in his obedience to authority research (Milgram, 1974). In other words, much like with other authorities, we accept the quack's "prescription" of unproven remedies and follow the psychic fraud's command to pay money to keep the evil spirits away.

It often makes sense to listen to those with expertise and authority. However, it makes little sense to follow someone who knows next to nothing. This is especially the case when the fake health, wellness, or financial guru attacks the medical establishment and sound investment advice – in other words, attacks real knowledge and expertise (see the projection tactic below). How does it come to pass that we listen to those with little to no real knowledge? In a recent study, Sheehan (2022) answered this question by looking at how those who are chronically unemployed and cannot obtain work end up becoming paid advisers to others on how to get a job. He finds that they do this by (a) sharing their clients' sense of immorality at the hiring process; (b) gaining trust by being similar to their clients (Cialdini, 1984) and empathizing with the pain of job loss; and (c) offering themselves as a role model for changing their lives. In other words, they tell people down on their luck what they want to hear – it is a bad system – as opposed to providing information (that might be disagreeable) on how to obtain a job. The likability of the employment guru replaces expertise.

Social Consensus and Social Identity

The flimflam merchant will also use our social relationships with others to sell their phantoms by employing the influence tactics of social consensus and social identity.

When we see other people doing something, we are more likely to do the same through the conformity created by social consensus – if everyone is doing it, it must be the right thing to do. Social consensus engages two psychological processes that promote conformity (Deutsch & Gerard, 1955): (a) *information* or social proof ("if other people are doing it, it must be correct"; Cialdini, 1984) and (b) *normative* influences or social pressure to agree or go along with the group ("I don't want to be different from the group"; Asch, 1951).

The seller of flimflam will manufacture a false consensus (or take advantage of an apparent one). Quack remedies, astrological readings, unproven Covid treatments, get-rich-schemes often feature testimonials of people who speak to the "value" of the product. At a séance, the situation is constrained so that the sitters behave consistent with the desires of the medium, giving the impression that everyone is impressed with the psychic goings-on. Likes and posts/reposts on social media can be engineered to give the take-away that everyone agrees about the flimflam. Shills (confederates of the seller) are the first in line to buy or invest at seminars promoting unproven health regimes or phony investments. Con criminals tell their targets such things as, "Lots of people calling" and "Most investors coming in at $25–50k." At the height of his scheme, Charles Ponzi had people lined up around the block outside of his offices waiting to "invest." A steady stream of TV shows purporting to reveal the "truth" about ancient astronauts, Bigfoot, hidden sea creatures, and Nostradamus creates a false consensus that these things must be real.

Once we become engaged with a flimflam, it can provide us with a desired social identity or a sense of who we are based on our reference group memberships, whether they be real or aspirational (Abrams et al., 1990; Kelley & Volkart, 1952; Tajfel, 1981). Through flimflam, we can immediately become energy and nature healers, truth-seekers about 9/11 or the moon landing, someone who can see through the "lame-stream media," and "an expert" with more knowledge than those who have spent years of hard work studying a problem – all without actually having to heal anyone or developing real expertise. A social identity can be a powerful source of social influence in at least two ways. First, the social identity provides a simple rule to tell the individual what to do and believe; in other words, "I am a _____ [fill in the blank with an identity] and we do and believe _____ [fill in the blank with identity-related behavior and belief]." Second, some identities become important as a source of self-esteem. In such cases, influence is based on a desire to stay in the good graces of a positive group and avoid the pain of exclusion from a desired group and identity (Williams, 2001).

The power of a social identity to extract conformity can be seen in affinity frauds (scams that use a person's social group as the basis for the scheme) such as the Miracle Car scam (Phillips, 2005). Those instigating the fraud went to churches and played on the congregation members' belief in the prosperity gospel (or seed-faith) in which a small gift in God's name would bring a bigger reward. (The cons, of course, were careful not to draw any attention to the teachings found in Matthew 21:13.) The pitch asked believers to show their faith by giving a small amount of money ($100 to a couple of thousand dollars) in order to receive a new car. The perpetrators then enlisted pastors, deacons, and church leaders to promote the deal. As congregational members started to buy, it became the thing to do. In other words, "I am a member of this church, and we give so that we can receive a car." Members soon gained a positive identity as a smart, new car owner and blessed by God. Those who didn't give or who gave and wanted out were subjected to social pressures to be part of the church. The scam lasted seven years and sold 7,000 fake cars to 4,000 Christians for a take of over $21 million, before unraveling.

Scarcity

Another social influence tactic to make a flimflam look desirable is to make it look scarce (Cialdini, 1984). (Given that phantoms are generally rare, this is rather easily accomplished). As an effective social influence tactic, scarcity (a) plays on a rule in our head, "if it is rare, it must be valuable"; (b) creates a sense of urgency and panic that we need to act now and feeling of frustration (reactance) when we do not obtain the phantom; and (c) inflates our feelings of uniqueness and self-worth when we obtain something that is rare (Pratkanis, 2007).

Some examples of the use of scarcity to sell a phantom of a flimflam include the following: quack cures are described as "what doctors and the government don't want you to know"; crystals, magnets, and other such devices are pitched as rare and unique specimens; fraudulent investments in such things as "rare" coins, cryptocurrencies, and financial products are proclaimed as one-of-a-kind deals, available for a limited time only, and being offered only to you. Conspiracy theories, such as the goings-on at Area 51, the moon landing was faked, 9/11 was an inside job, are sold as secret, hidden information, and, when we seem to possess this insider knowledge, we can gain a self-esteem boost by projecting an image of someone who "has done their own research" and "can see through media lies."

Information Control: False Accusations, Projection, and Doubt Campaigns

The sellers of flimflam often encounter scientists, journalists, magicians, lawyers, informed citizens, and other "do-gooders and crusaders" who use evidence and reason to point out false claims made in selling the phantom. If left to stand, these criticisms can cut into sales and deflate the entire scheme. As such, the flimflam merchant needs to control the information environment and can do so using at least three techniques.

First, the peddler of a flimflam can falsely accuse the critics. For example, when magician Harry Houdini with his investigator Rose Mackenberg testified to Congress on the fakery of psychics, he in turn was called a liar and accused of slander by psychic mediums. In 14th century, Bishop Pierre d'Arcis, who contested the authenticity of the Shroud of Turin, was accused by shroud promoters as being motivated by jealousy and a desire to possess the shroud. One very common line of attack is to disparage prosecutors, plaintiffs' attorneys, and government regulators who attempt to hold those who make false claims and sell worthless products accountable with accusations such as they are taking away people's freedom, creating a nanny state, doing it only for the money, destroying the free market, engaging in government overreach, among other allegations. Such attacks can be effective because it can result in a negative impression of the target of attack, undermining their reputation (Wegner et al., 1981). In addition, such allegations set up a chilling, coercive effect as others may become fearful of speaking out.

A second information control tool for the flimflam merchant is a variant of the false accusation known as the projection tactic – accusing others of the misdeed you are doing

(Rucker & Pratkanis, 2001). In our research, we find that a projection attack (a) focused attention on the accused and away from the person making the accusation, (b) increased the blame placed on the target of projection, and (c) decreased the culpability of the accuser, making the accuser look good and moral for raising such issues. The effects of projection persisted despite attempts to raise suspicions about the motives of the accuser and providing evidence that the accuser was indeed guilty of the deeds.

Some examples of the use of the projection tactic include: Houdini was accused of planting a ruler on the psychic medium Margery; the ruler was used by Margery to create her fakery. John Brinkley, noted for profiting from such treatments as sewing goat testicles into male scrotums as a treatment for impotency, accused Morris Fishbein, an advocate for effective medical treatments, and the American Medical Association of being "grafters, crooks, & thieves." A common attack of evidence-based health care is to proclaim, "follow the money" and to look at the cost, while ignoring the over $30 billion spent in the United States per year on "alternative" treatment providers such as homeopaths, naturopaths, chelation therapists, mind-body experts, energy healing specialists, traditional healers, and purveyors of "natural" supplements (Bakalar, 2016). In economic and charity fraud, it is common for the criminal to accuse others of the misdeed – for example, John Duval Gluck, who operated a phony Santa Claus Association charity, accused other charities of spending all their money on overhead, and Oscar Hartzell, who ran the 1930s Drake Fortune scam, when accused of taking money from Mrs. Schied informed the police that it was indeed Mrs. Scheid who owed him money.

A third approach to controlling the information environment is through a doubt campaign (Michaels, 2008; Oreskes & Conway, 2010). The purpose of a doubt campaign is not to convince someone of something (say, the value of the flimflam) but instead to raise doubts and confusion about the facts with the goals of (a) making it difficult to know the truth, (b) creating the impression that there is a controversy (when there is little or none), and (c) forestalling any action until the "controversy" is resolved. The doubt campaign was pioneered in the 1950s and 1960s by tobacco companies seeking to dissuade consumers that their products were harmful, but now is used to create doubt and confusion on such issues as climate change, the efficacy of vaccines such as those preventing childhood illnesses and COVID-19, the value of masks for limiting the spread of COVID-19, and evidence against various conspiracy theories.

A doubt campaign consists of a variety of public relations tactics. Some to watch out for include: manufacture doubt by finding supposed flaws in any scientific study; create many fake "science" reports that purport to show the opposite of what scientists actually find; establish fake "science" and "research" organizations, which the media then covers as real; make up data and findings; promote the misreporting of scientific studies such that results opposite to those actually obtained are reported in the media and social media; find other causes for an effect (e.g., cancer caused by something other than smoking); use supposed contradictory findings to create a false issue to mislead and distract (e.g., why has lung cancer increased but not cancer of tongue/larynx?); and attack scientists and policy advocates with false accusations and projection.

Self-Generated Persuasion

One of the most effective means of influence is to have the target generate arguments in support of a position and thereby persuade her- or himself (Boninger et al., 1990; Lewin, 1947). Self-generated persuasion is effective because in essence it asks the target to think up good reasons for a proposition and to refute any counter argument. This self-generated message comes from a source that is considered credible, trustworthy, respected, and liked – ourselves.

There are a number of ways to sell flimflam using self-generated persuasion. One "nature" healer would ask customers, "Tell me how you are feeling better today?" along with social pressures to elicit a testimonial as to the positive effects of the quack product. Similarly, economic con criminals will ask questions such as, "Why do you trust me?" and "What do you think is going to happen to the price of silver as the U.S. Dollar continues to decline?" to elicit self-generated reasons for trust and for an investment in overpriced silver commodities. One extremely effective means of self-generated persuasion is the use of multi-level marketing (MLM) to turn the customer into a salesperson. In an MLM, a customer joins a sales force (often paying fees and purchasing inventory) and then sells the product, such as nutritional supplements, cryptocurrencies, healing magnets, and beauty supplies, to others. In the process of selling others, we persuade ourselves as to the value of the product. Social media companies are a dream comes true for those seeking to use self-generated persuasion to sell flimflam as we like, repost from, post about, comment on, pose with, and argue for any flimflam that might strike our fancy.

Commitment

In order to establish continued advocacy and use of a flimflam, the seller needs to secure a commitment, especially a public one, from the target. With a public commitment, a person is linked to a behavior or course of action – in this case, advocating for and using a flimflam. Breaking this binding produces a negative tension of not living up to one's promises and a concern that one will look inconsistent and untrustworthy (e.g., a need to save face). As such, securing a commitment increases the likelihood that the target will comply and perform that behavior (Brockner & Rubin, 1985; Salancik, 1977; Staw, 1976). Commitments are strongest when the behavior is public/visible, irreversible, and perceived to be freely chosen.

One method for securing a commitment is through the use of the foot-in-the-door tactic (Freedman & Fraser, 1966). It works this way: the seller starts with a small request, such as accepting a free energy-health audit or obtaining a free astrological reading. Then a larger request follows – purchasing an expensive vitamin regime or a full horoscope work-up. The first small request sets the commitment: why did I get the audit or consent to the reading if I didn't think it was worth it? As such, there is an increased likely of shelling out the cash for the vitamins and horoscope.

A series of small but increasing commitments can be strung together to result in escalating commitments to failing course of action. For example, a seller of quackery asks the target to keep an open mind about energy healing and obtain a free energy assessment. The next step might be an introductory priced energy healing session followed by the purchase of natural remedies, and then a series of energy healing sessions. Of course, it is important to delve deeper into the nature of energy flows in the body and that will require paying for a series of seminars and books on the topic. Now well versed in the energy healing arts, the customer turns into sales agent by advocating for the treatments and even joining an MLM organization to sell the flimflam to others (after paying fees and stocking an inventory, of course). As each step is taken, the public commitment becomes stronger. We justify our previous commitment by making even more commitments to the flimflam.

Flimflam is rampant on social media, and we can easily see why. Social media, with its emphasis on engagement (liking, reposting, posting, commenting, posing, arguing) provides many opportunities to make public, irreversible, and freely chosen commitments (as well as to allow those commitments to be used to create the appearance of social consensus as to the value of the flimflam). While making a commitment increases compliance, it also results in perhaps the most important ingredient in selling a flimflam: setting a rationalization trap.

The Rationalization Trap

Once a person is sold on a flimflam, and especially when he or she comes to purchase and publically advocate for the phantom option, it changes the way a person processes information. No longer is the goal "to find things out" but instead to defend and justify the beliefs and actions in what can be called a rationalization trap (Festinger, 1957; Pratkanis & Shadel, 2005; Tavris & Aronson, 2007). For example, consider a person who has just advocated in social media for a supposed cure for COVID-19 and there is every indication that the cure doesn't work and may cause unwanted side effects. This person is faced with two discrepant thoughts: "I am a good and capable person" but yet, "I just told everyone to use a worthless and potentially harmful remedy." When a person holds two discrepant thoughts, what social psychologists call *cognitive dissonance*, it results in an aversive tension state with painful implications for the self. In such a state, we are highly motivated to reduce the dissonance.

Of course, one way to reduce the dissonance is to admit a mistake – I was wrong about the cure – and to take responsibility for one's actions by alerting others and rejecting or, at least scrutinizing more carefully, the source of the disinformation about the quack COVID-19 treatment. While a mature response and what science requires (Feynman, 1985), it is often difficult to take this route to dissonance reduction, especially when we have made public commitments, self-generated arguments, and linked our social identities to the flimflam, in this case, the quack cure. Admitting a mistake often is taken to mean – to ourselves and to others – that we are not a good and capable person. After all, we were unable to see through the deception and then told others to do something that might damage their health.

Unfortunately, an all-too-often course of action is to dig in our heels further and to rationalize and justify our behavior. Some common ways to do this include: deny the evidence ("the data showing the ineffectiveness of the cure is made-up"), take some irrelevant aspect of the disagreeable research and pretend that it is damning ("the study was only done in New York"), derogate the source ("that's from the biased media and the doctors' union"), derogate others who expose the quackery ("nurses and doctors don't care about people"), perform a selective information search (search out and spread any study or claim no matter how unreliable that supports one's position), keep repeating discredit research as if it is true, bolster one's own self and one's intuition as a way of knowing ("I can see through the media; I did my research unlike those duped by big pharma"), derogate other forms of knowing, particularly science and reason ("science is a limited way of knowing unlike my intuition"), use whataboutism ("what about the time Fauci might have said something wrong"), seek external justification ("a cure that might work is better than having to wear a mask"), and, perhaps worst of all, self-censorship of putting ourselves in an information bubble where we only hear agreeable information and anything disagreeable is either not heard or ridiculed.

Obviously, a rationalization trap is a very effective means of selling a flimflam. Once we are in the trap, we will continue to buy the flimflam and advocate for the phantom option in an attempt to justify ourselves in the face of failing evidence.

Summary and Conclusion

In this chapter, we have found that the merchants of flimflam can use a variety of effective and common social influence tactics to hawk their wares. The sale begins with a phantom – an unavailable option made to look real – that ostensibly satisfies our needs and desires. A story is told by someone who appears to be credible to make the phantom look real. A pitch, often tailored to who we are, is given, which is backed by the power of apparent scarcity and social consensus and by appeals to our desired and real identities. We are induced to persuade ourselves and make commitments, which we then need to rationalize. Anyone who dares to debunk the flimflam tale is attacked, creating a one-side information bubble. The best way to deal with this onslaught of flimflam pitches is to understand the ways of persuasion and to ask questions that take as from being passive targets of social influence to active discoverers of the truth (as we describe in the postscript). A key component of being an active truth-finder is to have a plan for evaluating and making decisions about claims. When we do make a mistake, the honorable thing to do is to admit the error and take responsibility for our actions. The next part of this chapter will now be written by you, the reader, as you face the ubiquitous selling of flimflam in your daily life.

References

AARP. (1996). *Telemarketing fraud victimization of older Americans: An AARP survey*. Author.

AARP. (2003). *Off the hook: Reducing participation in telemarketing fraud*. Author.

Abrams, D., Wetherell, M., Cochrane, S., Hogg, M. A., & Turner, J. C. (1990). Knowing what to think by knowing who you are: Self-categorization and the nature of norm formation, conformity, and group polarization. *British Journal of Social Psychology, 29*, 97–119.

Anderson, C. A., Lepper, M. R., & Ross, L. (1980). Perseverance of social theories: The role of explanation in the persistence of discredited information. *Journal of Personality and Social Psychology, 39*, 1037–1049.

Aronson, E. (1992). *The social animal* (6th edition). W. H. Freeman.

Asch, S. E. (1951). Effects of group pressure upon modification and distortion of judgment. In H. Guetzkow (Ed.), *Groups, leadership and men* (pp. 177–190). Carnegie Press.

Bakalar, N. (2016, June 27). The alternative medical bill: $30.2 billion. Retrieved from https://www.nytimes.com/2016/06/28/health/alternative-complementary-medicine-costs.html#:~:text=Americans%20spend%20%2430.2%20billion%20a,4%20to%2017%20years%20old

Bell, J. B., & Whaley, B. (1991). *Cheating and deception*. Transaction Publishers.

Boninger, D. S., Brock, T. C., Cook, T. D., Gruder, C. L., & Romer, D. (1990). Discovery of reliable attitude change persistence resulting from a transmitter tuning set. *Psychological Science, 1*, 268–271.

Brockner, J., & Rubin, J. Z. (1985). *Entrapment in escalating conflicts*. Springer-Verlag.

Cialdini, R. B. (1984). *Influence: How and why people agree to things*. Morrow.

Clark, R. M., & Mitchell, W. L. (2019). *Deception: Counterdeception and counterintelligence*. Sage.

Deutsch, M., & Gerard, H. B. (1955). A study of the normative and informational social influences upon individual judgment. *Journal of Abnormal and Social Psychology, 51*, 629–636.

Festinger, L. (1957). *A theory of cognitive dissonance*. Stanford University Press.

Feynman, R. P. (1985). *Surely you're joking, Mr. Feynman*. Norton.

Freedman, J., & Fraser, S. (1966). Compliance without pressure: The foot-in-the-door technique. *Journal of Personality and Social Psychology, 4,* 195–202.

Greene, R. W. (1981). *The sting man: Inside ABSCAM.* Dutton.

Hovland, C. I., Janis, I. L., & Kelley, H. H. (1953). *Communication and persuasion: Psychological studies of opinion change.* Yale University Press.

Howard, D. (2017). *Chasing Phil: The adventures of two undercover agents with the world's most charming con man.* Broadway Books.

Keene, M. L. (1997). *The psychic mafia.* Prometheus Books.

Kelley, H. H., & Volkart, E. H. (1952). The resistance to change of group-anchored attitudes. *American Sociological Review, 17,* 453–465.

Leff, A. A. (1976). *Swindling and selling.* Free Press.

Lewin, K. (1947). Group decision and social change. In T. M. Newcomb & E. L. Hartley (Eds.), *Readings in social psychology* (pp. 330–344). Holt.

Lytle, L. (2004). *Healing light: Energy medicine of the future.* AuthorHouse.

McNeal, V. (1947). *Four white horses and a brass band.* Doubleday.

Michaels, D. (2008). *Doubt is their product: How industry's assault on science threatens your health.* Oxford University Press.

Milgram, S. (1974). *Obedience to authority.* Harper & Row.

NASD Investor Education Foundation. (2006, May 12). *Investor fraud study.* Author.

Office of Fair Trading. (2006, December). *Research on impact of mass marketed scams: A summary of research into the impact of scams on UK consumers.* Author.

Oreskes, N., & Conway, E. M. (2010). *Merchants of doubt: How a handful of scientists obscured the truth on issues from tobacco smoke to global warming.* Bloomsbury Press.

Padgett, V. R., & Jorgenson, D. O. (1982). Superstition and economic threat: Germany, 1918-1940. *Personality and Social Psychology Bulletin, 8*(4), 736–741.

Phillips, J. (2005). *God wants you to roll: The $21 million "miracle cars" scam – how two boys fleeced America's churchgoers.* Carroll & Graf Publishers.

Pratkanis, A. R. (2007). Social influence analysis: An index of tactics. In A. R. Pratkanis (Ed.), *The science of social influence: Advances and future progress* (pp. 17–82). Psychology Press.

Pratkanis, A. R. (2009). Public diplomacy in international conflicts: A social influence analysis. In N. Snow & P. M. Taylor (Eds.), *Handbook of public diplomacy* (pp. 111–153). Routledge.

Pratkanis, A. R., & Farquhar, P. H. (1992). A brief history of research on phantom alternatives: Evidence for seven empirical generalizations about phantoms. *Basic and Applied Social Psychology, 13,* 103–122.

Pratkanis, A. R., & Shadel, D. (2005). *Weapons of fraud.* AARP Washington.

Pratkanis, A. R. & Turner, M. E. (1999). The significance of affirmative action for the souls of white folk: Further implications of a helping model. *Journal of Social Issues, 55,* 787–815.

Randi, J. & Alvarez, J. (2009). *James Randi speaks: The Carlos hoax.* Retrieved from https://www.youtube.com/watch?v=y0hgP3ioAeA

Ross, L. (1977). The intuitive psychologist and his shortcomings: Distortions in the attribution process. In L. Berkowitz (Ed.), *Advances in experimental social psychology* (Vol. 10, pp. 173–220). Academic Press.

Ross, L., & Nisbett, R. E. (1991). *The person and the situation: Perspectives of social psychology.* McGraw Hill.

Rucker, D. D., & Pratkanis, A. R. (2001). Projection as an interpersonal influence tactic: The effects of the pot calling the kettle black. *Personality and Social Psychology Bulletin, 27,* 1494–1507.

Salancik, G. R. (1977, Summer). Commitment is too easy! *Organizational Dynamics, 6*(1), 62–80.

Sheehan, P. (2022). The paradox of self-help expertise: How unemployed workers become professional career coaches. *American Journal of Sociology, 127*(4), 1151–1182.

Singer, M. T. (1995). *Cults in our midst.* Jossey-Bass Publishers.

Staw, B. M. (1976). Knee-deep in the Big Muddy: A study of escalating commitment to a chosen course of action. *Organizational Behavior and Human Decision Process, 16,* 27–44.

Swami, V., Furnham, A., Smyth, N., Weis, L., Lay, A., & Clow, A. (2016). Putting the stress on conspiracy theories: Examining associations between psychological stress, anxiety, and belief in conspiracy theories. *Personality and Individual Differences, 99*, 72–76.

Tajfel, H. (1981). *Human groups and social categories*. Cambridge University Press.

Tavris, C., & Aronson, E. (2007). *Mistakes were made (but not by me): Why we justify foolish beliefs, bad decisions, and hurtful acts*. Harcourt.

Wegner, D. M., Wenzalaff, R., Kerker, R. M., & Beattie, A. E. (1981). Incrimination through innuendo: Can media questions become public answers? *Journal of Personality and Social Psychology, 40*, 822–832.

Williams, K. D. (2001). *Ostracism: The power of silence*. Guilford Press.

14 Projective Tests and Personality

Terence Hines

Projective tests are psychological assessments that are said to be able to reveal deep, unconscious aspects of a person's personality, hidden conflicts, and psychopathology. The test taker typically is asked to describe an ambiguous stimulus of some type or to produce a drawing. The basic idea of projective tests is that the test taker will "project" their unconscious feelings, desires, anxieties, and motivations onto the ambiguous stimulus they see or the drawings they create. By interpreting the test taker's responses, the psychologist, it is claimed, can uncover hidden aspects of the person's personality and any psychopathology. While there are dozens of projective tests, this chapter will cover the "big three" tests in the field; the Rorschach Ink Blot test, the Draw-a-Person (DAP) test, and the Thematic Apperception Test (TAT).

Examining the Claims

In order for any type of test to be used ethically, it must have two extremely important characteristics – reliability and validity. While these terms have everyday meanings, they have specific meanings in the field of testing. Reliability refers to the stability of a test result. Most psychological tests are designed to measure something that is relatively stable over time. For example, after adulthood, intelligence is quite stable over the years. That is, an intelligence test typically gives a person about the same result when taken at age 25 as at age 65. Another way to measure reliability is called inter-rater reliability. Using intelligence as an example again, if a person took an intelligence test that had a mean of 100 (and a standard deviation of 15) and one rater said the test indicated the person had an IQ of 125, another said the IQ was 44 and another that it was 167, that test would certainly not be reliable.

The second characteristic that a test must possess before it can be used ethically is validity. There are many ways to measure validity. To be valid, a test must actually measure what it claims to measure. Imagine that I have designed a test of skiing skill called the *Hines Test of Skiing Ability* (hereinafter, the HTSA). To see if the test is reliable, I could give it to a sample of 100 people and then give it again 6 months later. If there is a high correlation between test scores on the first and second administrations of the test, then the test is reliable. So far, so good. But just because a test is reliable does not in any way mean that it is valid. To determine validity of the HTSA it would be necessary to measure real-world skiing skill in some objective way and see if *that* measure correlated strongly with scores on the HTSA. One could do this by taking 100 people who had taken the HTSA, put them on a mountain and have an experienced skiing coach evaluate their performance. Then if, and only if, the coach's evaluations correlated highly

DOI: 10.4324/9781003107798-14

with HTSA scores could it be claimed that the test was valid. In this context, correlations that are high enough to establish reliability and validity typically have to be above 0.80.

A test can be reliable without being valid, but it cannot be valid if it is not reliable. This is because if a test isn't reliable, the results are bouncing around a lot. Since the variables that most tests claim to measure are quite stable over time (i.e., intelligence), if the results are not stable they will not correlate highly with the stable target variable. To make this point clear, consider a question I was asked on an exam when I was in graduate school taking a Tests and Measurements class: "Is your height in inches a reliable measure of your intelligence? Discuss." I got it wrong because I said something like "No – because there is no relationship between height and intelligence." In fact, height in inches is a perfectly *reliable* measure of a person's intelligence as an adult. An adult's height changes very little over time. I was 5 feet 11 inches tall when I was 20 and I'm 5 feet 11 inches tall now. Of course, it would be foolish to use height as a measure of intelligence because height is not correlated with intelligence. That is, it is not a *valid* measure of intelligence. My answer was wrong because I was saying that height in inches is not a valid measure of intelligence, which indeed it is not. But the question didn't ask about validity, it asked about reliability. This example may seem absurd but something very similar happened in one attempt to make scoring of a projective test reliable and valid, as will be discussed later.

Rorschach Ink Blot Test

Say "psychological test" to most people, especially undergraduate psychology majors, and what will probably pop into their mind is "that ink blot test," referring to the Rorschach Ink Blot Test developed by Hermann Rorschach in 1921 (Rorschach, 1927). In this test, an individual is shown a series of ink blots and asked to tell what they see (see Image 14.1). Their descriptions are then interpreted psychologically by a clinician, and these then are used to form a description of the individual's personality and any psychopathology. The best source for the history of and research on the Rorschach is the book *What's Wrong with the Rorschach* (Wood et al., 2003) from which I have drawn much of the information in this chapter. While the Rorschach was first published in 1921, it was not available in English until 1942. It didn't become popular among psychologists and psychiatrists until after WWII. However, even before its availability in English, the test had stirred enthusiasm among a small group in the United States. One member, Bruno Klopfer at New York City's Columbia University, rhapsodized that the test "does not reveal a behavioral picture, but rather shows – like an X-ray picture – the underlying structure which makes behavior understandable" (Klopfer, 1940, p. 26).

Unlike tests of intelligence (or skiing ability) mentioned earlier, the Rorschach does not generate just one or two scores. It doesn't directly generate scores at all. The test generates the person's narrative response to each of the ink blots. It is then up to the test giver, who has transcribed these (usually) verbal responses, to interpret them and, if they wish, to assign some sort of score to the responses. The scores are never anything like "Shelia got a 745 on the Rorschach." Usually different types of responses are counted and the types interpreted psychologically. So, one might get 15 white space responses (when the test taker comments on the white spaces on a Rorschach card) and 4 fire responses (where the test taker says that part of a blot reminds them of something related to fire). It is these sorts of responses that are then interpreted. There is a multitude of different scoring systems, each with its different methods of interpretation.

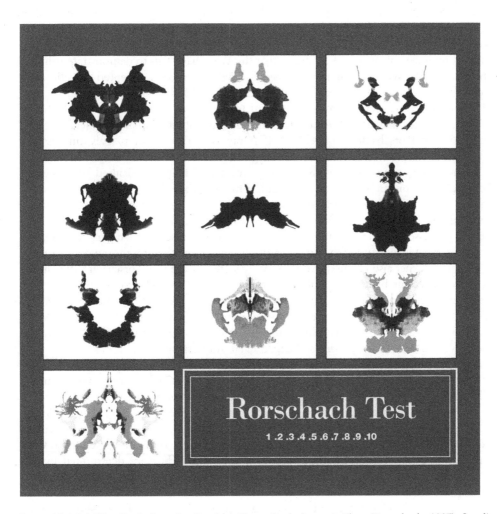

Image 14.1 Ink Blot Cards from the *Rorschach Test – Psychodiagnostic Plates* (Rorschach, 1927). [credit: Shutterstock].

As noted earlier, the first requirement for a useful psychological test is reliability. In regard to the Rorschach, reliability can be measured in two different ways. First, will the same person give the same or similar, responses to a given ink blot over time? In other words, if Betty sees a bird flying over a car in one ink blot, will she report the same impression when she sees the same blot sometime later? Second, will different clinicians interpret the response of a given person the same way? If Fred sees a large fish swimming in a pond in a blot, will different clinicians, experienced in using the Rorschach, come to the same conclusion about Fred? The answer to both questions is "no."

The heart of the Rorschach technique is the psychological interpretation of a person's responses. A good example of the sort of interpretations that users of the Rorschach indulge in comes from Piotrowski (1957, p. 429; cited in Wood et al., 2003, p. 121). In one card, a male patient saw two people ripping something apart but didn't specify the sex of either. According to Piotrowski, this "suggest[ed] homosexual tendencies" and showed that "the patient does not feel well in the biopsychological role of a man." For the test to be valid, it would have to be shown that gay men were significantly more likely than non-gay men to fail to specify the sex of people they see in the ink blots. The research reviewed by Wood et al. shows that the Rorschach fails to demonstrate validity. These sorts of psychological interpretations have never been accepted by clinicians and researchers who demand empirical evidence of reliability and validity. In the late 20th century, a major text on psychological testing stated that "The accumulation of published studies that have *failed* to demonstrate any validity for such projective techniques as the Rorschach and the D-A-P [Draw a Person Test] is truly impressive" (Anastasi, 1998, p. 621, emphasis in the original).

In the 1970s, a new scoring system was developed that was claimed to make the Rorschach not only reliable but also valid. This was Exner's (1974) "Comprehensive System." It did, in a particularly meaningless way, make the text reliable. If the rule is "every time anyone responds to blot number 7 by saying they see a fish out of water, label them as depressed" then the test is reliable in the same trivial sense that a person's height in inches is a reliable measure of their intelligence because their height is the same each time it is measured. Exner also claimed that his scoring system made the Rorschach valid and he supported this claim by citing unpublished studies from his research group. Over the years, these studies remained unpublished and were never made available for direct evaluation. Worse, when Exner described the same studies in his different published books, Wood et al. (2003, p. 220) argued that "his numbers sometimes changed inexplicably from one book to the next. They sometimes changed even in the same book."

Another important characteristic of any test is the process of creating norms for the test. Norms are vital and make it possible to understand what a score or scores mean. If I tell you that Jada got a score of 45.7 on the *Hines Alliterative Memory Test*, you have no idea what that represents because you don't know what the score of an average person would be. The 45.7 would be great if the average score is 30 (assuming that higher scores index better performance) or really poor if the average score is 87. Norms establish what constitutes normal vs. abnormal performance on a test. They are determined by administering the test to a group of individuals and calculating the average score and some measure of the variance of scores in the normal sample.

Exner claimed to have normed his scoring system on a sample of 700 people, but he consistently failed to provide the actual data from this norming sample to psychological scientists who requested it (Wood et al., 2003). Sharing such data is an ethical responsibility of any researcher. After much prodding it was revealed that the norming sample was not 700 people but 500 people. The data from 200 of these 500 had been entered into the statistics twice – an extremely serious error. Exner's scientific shortcomings should have scuttled his "comprehensive system" but it continues to be used to this day.

No research published since the 2003 review by Wood et al. has contradicted the conclusion that the Rorschach lacks reliability and validity as a clinical instrument. However, it can reveal some aspects of a person's cognition. Rorschach responses correlate roughly with a person's intelligence. This is because more intelligent individuals use a more varied and sophisticated vocabulary when describing the ink blots than less intelligent individuals. But this has nothing to do with the psychological factors, such as personality, that the test is said to reveal.

Another issue with the Rorschach is that it has what is termed negative validity. That is, it has a tendency to classify people with no mental health problems as psychologically disturbed, a characteristic called over-pathologizing. Proponents of the Rorschach might argue that these tests are catching problems that other tests miss. However, there are a few problems with this argument. First, part of test validation involves the examination of *convergent validity* (i.e., when two different tests reach the same conclusion). For projective tests, convergent validity is weak. Further, some critics have pointed out that the test will mis-classify as having some form of psychopathology about 75% of individuals who do not actually meet the diagnostic criteria for any mental health disorder (Wood et al., 2003, p. 259). In other words, the test has a 75% false alarm rate.

The consequences of over-pathologizing can be extremely serious. Mental health professionals unfamiliar with the problems with the Rorschach (as well as other projective tests) continue to use these tests to make very important and often life changing decisions. These include eligibility for parole, child custody judgments, and whether children are emotionally disturbed or have been sexually abused. Being wrong about such things can have disastrous consequences. Imagine a test for some serious disease, say lung cancer, that had a 75% false alarm rate. Such a test would not be in use very long!

Draw-a-Person Test

Another problem with projective tests in general, not just the Rorschach, is that of illusory correlations. This is best illustrated however by describing research done on another famous projective test, the Draw-a-Person (DAP) test. Introduced in 1926, the DAP is the oldest of the tests discussed here. It is simplicity itself. All the clinician needs is a piece of paper, a pencil, and a patient. The patient is instructed to draw a picture of a person and the clinician then interprets the drawing psychologically. Like the Rorschach, the idea is that the drawing will reflect the patient's personality, unconscious anxieties, feelings, conflicts, and the like. The clinician's job is to interpret the drawing to reveal these hidden psychological processes. In my introductory psychology classes, we have a lot of fun when I draw a person on the board (I'm a truly terrible artist) and have the students interpret the drawing psychologically. I tell them they can't insult me, and things can get pretty interesting.

Chapman and Chapman (1967, 1969) demonstrated the power of illusory correlations using the DAP. Individuals looked at drawings made by people with no psychopathology. Below each drawing were two "symptoms" that the viewers were told characterized the person who had done the drawing. The bogus symptoms were carefully associated with the drawings in such a way that there was no correlation between any characteristics of the drawings and any symptoms. In spite of this, the viewers reported seeing relationships between the symptoms and drawing characteristics. For example, one of the symptoms was "is worried about how manly he is." The viewers reported that this symptom was associated with emphasis on the shoulder areas of the drawings when, in fact there was no such association. They saw such an association because in Western culture, broad shoulders are associated with manliness. So, drawing on preexisting stereotypes, the viewers saw associations where they did not exist.

In the studies of Chapman and Chapman (1967, 1969), the viewers were undergraduate psychology students. Clinicians might object that students were not the right group to test and that trained clinical psychologists would not show an illusory correlation effect. This is a reasonable objection. Kurtz and Garfield (1978) showed that even trained clinicians see illusory correlations. Unfortunately, training and clinical experience do not eliminate the perception of illusory correlations.

It is extremely dangerous and deeply unethical to use unreliable and invalid tests to attempt to identify sexually abused children. The DAP has been promoted in just this way. Williams et al. (2005) noted that "art therapists are commonly asked to examine figure drawings for signs of sexual abuse, and to testify in court regarding their findings" but that "empirical backing for such claims remains absent" (p. 703). These authors reported a careful study of a DAP-like test that did not require children to draw and thus would not be confounded by artistic ability. They had children put together a person from plastic body parts – sort of a three-dimensional jigsaw puzzle. The results were clear – the test could not distinguish between children who had been abused and those who had not.

Expanding on the DAP idea, it has become popular among some psychologists to claim to be able to diagnose children's psychological state of mind and problems from their artwork. A prime example of this approach is the book *The Complete Guide to Children's Drawings. Accessing Children's Emotional World Through Their Artwork* (Wimmer, 2019). The book contains numerous reproductions of children's drawings with psychological meaning attributed to aspects of the drawing. For example, one shows a drawing of a tree, a bee (I think), and a flower. The caption reads "Shrunk elements indicating fear." Not only is it not clear which elements of the drawing are shrunk, the book cites little to no evidence to show that small images are more common in fearful than in non-fearful children. It is easy to imagine a study that would objectively determine if there is any relationship between shrinkage, or other aspects of children's drawings, and fearfulness. However, I could find no published study designed to determine if such a relationship exists. And yet the book simply asserts it. This is an example of when evidence from clinical experience appears to be taking priority over evidence from empirical research studies.

There have been studies of the content of children's drawings and whether they can be useful in discovering sexual abuse. Austin (2007) found that figure drawings could not distinguish between abused and non-abused children. Palmer et al. (2000) studied a "widely used diagnostic tool" (p. 169) called the House-Tree-Person test and found that these drawings could also not distinguish between non-abused children and children who have been sexually abused. In a systematic literature review, Veltman and Browne (2002) concluded that the evidence is "relatively inconclusive as to the value of children's drawings for the identification of possible maltreatment" (p. 19). No technique that is merely "inconclusive" should ever be used in making such an important decision as whether a child has been abused. The false alarm rate would be much too high.

Thematic Apperception Test

The last of the "big three" most popular projective tests is the Thematic Apperception Test (TAT) which was developed in the 1930s. This one consists of different pictures of people interacting in different ways. The pictures are shown to the test taker who is then asked to make up a story about what is happening in the picture. The content of the stories is then analyzed for motivation and other psychological variables thought to be stable characteristics of the individual. However, TAT responses are highly variable over time. A person taking the test who has watched a gory horror movie the night before will be likely to tell a different sort of story than someone who watched a feature length Disney cartoon. This effect was recognized early on. In a major book on the use of the TAT, Murstein (1963, p. 364) stated that the "TAT is extremely sensitive to environmental influences."

In an early study, Wildman and Wildman (1975) had experienced clinical psychologists try to differentiate the TAT responses of student nurses from those of patients in a psychiatric setting. Chance being 50%, the psychologists scored 57%, not statistically different from chance. In this study, the Rorschach was also used and the psychologists did better – 65% correct. While better than chance, the authors note that the result is "too low to be clinically useful" (p. 457).

Like the Rorschach, there are numerous scoring schemes for the TAT. Lilienfeld et al. (2000) summarized the research on these systems and found that there "is modest support for the construct validity of several TAT scoring schemes, particularly those assessing need for achievement and object relations" (p. 46). The latter term refers to how people relate to others. But problems persist such as lack of norms, low reliability, and the possibility that a scoring system may be biased against minority groups. As of this writing, the problems with the TAT persist, and it still lacks the basic characteristics needed to be valuable during assessment.

Why Do Projective Tests Continue to Be Used?

There are several reasons for the continued use of projective tests. One is simply tradition. These tests have been used for decades and so clinicians believe, incorrectly, that they must be reliable and valid. A second reason is selective memory, which is also known as confirmation bias. Imagine a therapist who has given a projective test to thousands of patients over her career. For some of those patients, the therapist has interpreted the test responses as showing that they had borderline personality disorder. Some percentage of these patients turn out to meet the criteria for this disorder, but most do not. The therapist will selectively remember those cases where her interpretation of the projective test responses was seemingly correct. She will be less likely to remember those instances where her interpretations were wrong. So, the projective test gets credit for being right but is not discounted for the more common mistakes and the therapist will claim that her "clinical experience" convinces her that the projective test is a valuable tool for detecting borderline personality disorder.

A closely related problem was pointed out by Wood et al. (2003, p. 149). Suppose our clinical psychologist has a practice where she specializes in treating borderline personality disorder. Thus, most of the patients she sees will show symptoms of this disorder. When she gives the projective test to her patients and sees signs of borderline personality disorder, she will conclude, erroneously, that the test is an excellent indicator of that condition. But since she only occasionally gives the Rorschach to individuals without borderline personality disorder, she won't see that they, too, would likely be misclassified by the test.

Simply sitting in a room and interacting with a patient, as one does when one administers a projective test, can give important information about the patient's personality and any psychopathology. A patient that suffers from some personality disorder, for example, is going to react differently in an interpersonal situation than one who does not. Those differences do not show up in projective test responses, but the clinician sitting and interacting with the individual will likely be able to gather information about what the problem may be. The projective test responses will then be credited with helping with the diagnosis. But it wasn't the projective test responses that led to the diagnosis, it was the patient's behavior.

Summary and Conclusion

Clinicians using projective tests will often argue that the tests are valid "based on my clinical experience." One should be suspicious of any such arguments. Clinical experience is a fine basis on which to form hypotheses about whether a procedure is reliable and valid. But those hypotheses must always be tested objectively. Clinical experience is the starting point in a search for truth, not the end of the search.

To be fair, some clinicians may use "projective" tests for purposes such as general information gathering. For example, a child psychologist might have a child draw their family, and this drawing might be a good springboard for discussion. If the whole family is smiling or frowning in the drawing, the therapist might inquire about why. This form of gathering information is not aimed at revealing hidden unconscious aspects of personality. Further, a psychologist might similarly use ink blots or the TAT as a way to get the patient to open up. The value of these tests for these purposes is unclear, and there are many other ways to achieve the same goals. In actuality, many therapists are not using projective tests for these benign purposes; instead, they are truly using them as a projective tool.

As a projective tool, projective tests have many concerning problems. In particular, the use of projective tests in legal proceedings is fraught with danger for the test taker. Projective tests almost certainly do not meet the legal standards, in the United States, to be considered evidence in court (Wood et al., 2003). Thus, clinicians who use such tests should not be permitted to testify in legal proceedings based on the results of such tests. It is worth quoting at some length the advice given by the late Robyn Dawes (1994, pp. 152–153) regarding projective tests:

> If a professional psychologist is "evaluating" you in a situation in which you are at risk and asks you for responses to ink blots … . or for a drawing of anything, walk out of that psychologist's office. Going through with such an examination creates the danger of having a serious decision made about you on totally invalid grounds. If your contact with the psychologist involves a legal matter, your civil liberties themselves may be at stake.

That warning still holds and should be extended to include anyone you are in charge of, as a parent or guardian, and even to more standard therapeutic situations. Clinicians using projective tests show themselves to be unfamiliar with the research literature and are acting unethically.

References

Austin, J. T. (2007). Using children's projective drawings to detect sexual abuse. *Dissertation Abstracts International, Section B, 67* (8B), 4698.

Anastasi, A. (1998). *Psychological testing.* (7th ed.). Pearson.

Chapman, L., & Chapman, J. (1967). Genesis of popular but erroneous psychodiagnostics observations. *Journal of Abnormal Psychology, 72*, 193–204.

Chapman, L., & Chapman, J. (1969). Illusory correlations as an obstacle to the use of valid psychodiagnostics signs. *Journal of Abnormal Psychology, 74*, 271–280.

Dawes, R. (1994). *House of cards: Psychology and psychotherapy based on myth.* Free Press.

Exner, J. E., Jr. (1974). *The Rorschach. A comprehensive system.* John Wiley.

Klopfer, B. (1940). Personality aspects revealed by the Rorschach method. *Rorschach Research Exchange, 4*, 26–29.

Kurtz, R., & Garfield, S. (1978). Illusory correlations: A further exploration of Chapman's paradigm. *Journal of Consulting and Clinical Psychology, 46*, 1009–1015.

Lilienfeld, S. O., Wood, J. M., & Garb, H. N. (2000). The scientific status of projective techniques. *Psychological Science in the Public Interest, 1*, 27–66.

Murstein, B. I. (1963). The relationship of expectancy of reward to achievement performance on an arithmetic and thematic test.*Journal of Consulting Psychology*, *27*(5), 394–399.

Palmer, L., Farrar, A. R., Valle, M. et al. (2000). An investigation of the clinical use of the House-Tree-Person projective drawings in the psychological evaluation of child sexual abuse. *Child Maltreatment*, *5*(2),169–175.

Piotrowski, Z. A. (1957). *Perceptoanalysis: A fundamentally reworked, expanded and systematized Rorschach method*. Macmillan.

Rorschach, H. (1927). Rorschach test – Psychodiagnostic plates. Hogrefe.

Veltman, M. W. M., & Browne, K. D. (2002). The assessment of drawings from children who have been mistreated: A systematic review. *Child Abuse Review*, *11*, 19–37.

Wildman, R. W., & Wildman, R. W., II. (1975). An investigation into the comparative validity of several diagnostic tests and test batteries. *Journal of Clinical Psychology*, *31*, 455–458.

Williams, S. D., Wiener, J., & MacMillian, H. (2005). Build-a-Person Technique: An examination of the validity of human-figure features as evidence of childhood sexual abuse. *Child Abuse and Neglect*, *29*, 701–713.

Wood, J. M., Nezworski, M. T., Lilienfeld, S. O., & Garb, H. N. (2003). *What's wrong with the Rorschach?* Jossey-Bass.

15 Demonic Possession and Disorders

Christopher C. French

Demonic possession may be defined as the alleged phenomenon whereby an external spiritual being, in this case a demon, takes control of a person's body and mind. Demons are said to be supernatural beings, typically with malign intent. The specific character-istics of demons vary from culture to culture. In Christianity, demons are said to be the agents of the devil (also known as Satan), the latter being a fallen angel who established the kingdom of Hell. It is further claimed that the afflicted person may be required to undergo an exorcism ritual in order for the demon to be forced to leave. Within Christian communities, the exorcist may be a specially trained priest officially appointed by the Catholic Church but a large number of exorcisms are also carried out by maverick priests, evangelical ministers, and others (Cuneo, 2001). While some exorcisms may involve nothing more than exhortation, ritual praying, and chanting, others may involve more extreme measures, such as beating and starving, in an attempt to drive out the demon or demons thought to be possessing the affected individual.

Throughout history, and even up to the present day, believers claim that there are a number of different ways whereby a person may become possessed, including taking part in occult rituals or engaging in practices such as the use of Ouija boards. It is also believed that witches can cause their enemies to become possessed by demons. Demonic pos-session may manifest itself in a variety of ways including violent and lewd behavior, convulsions, blaspheming, self-harm, hallucinations, repetitive behavior, and contempt for and aversion toward religious items such as holy books and symbols. In some cases, supernatural phenomena such as levitation, speaking in languages unknown to the possessed individual, preternatural strength, the vomiting of foreign objects, and knowing others' secrets have also been reported (Spanos, 1996). The possessed individual is often said to be completely amnesic for the events occurring during the possession when they return to normal consciousness.

Detailed discussion of the concepts of possession and exorcism across a wide range of religions is beyond the scope of this short chapter. However, it is important to note that there is considerable variation from one culture to another regarding the claimed effects of possession. To give one example, belief in possession by *jinn* (singular, *jinni*) is common amongst Muslims. In contrast to Christian demons, some jinn are said to be benign al-though most accounts focus upon the actions of the malignant ones. Possession by a jinni may entail similar symptoms to those described above but jinn may also be responsible for causing a wide range of other more common afflictions including "back pain, anxiety, depression, mood swings, hallucinations, delusions, gynaecological and sexual problems" (Lim et al., 2015, p. 21). This chapter will mainly focus upon possession and exorcism in a Christian context but even within this context, considerable variation can be found

DOI: 10.4324/9781003107798-15

(Levack, 2013; Spanos, 1996) with the details of the behavior demonstrated by the possessed individual generally corresponding to the specific teachings of that individual's religious beliefs. It is worth pointing out that Islam and Christianity have demons and possession at their core: it isn't a fringe belief or an add-on. Jesus' ministry repeatedly consisted of exorcising people, from exorcising a mute man to the incident with the Gerasene swine.

As pointed out by French (2017), demonic possession is but one of a number of phenomena in which an individual's behavior and personality appear to be radically altered. Others include channeling (during which a medium allegedly allows their body to be temporarily taken over by the spirit of a deceased individual) and so-called *dissociative identity disorder*, a rare and highly controversial psychiatric diagnosis formerly known as *multiple personality disorder*. Individuals labeled as suffering from dissociative identity disorder display at least two distinct personalities, each allegedly with their own self-consciousness and even memories. Other situations where a person's behavior and personality appear to change dramatically include a number of hypnotic phenomena such as age regression, past-life regression, and hypnotic suggestions during stage shows in which individuals, in response to suggestions from the hypnotist, appear to temporarily become animals, aliens, or celebrities (Spanos, 1996). This suggests that the psychological processes underlying these phenomena may sometimes be the same as those involved in alleged cases of possession. It is also worth noting that spiritual possession is sometimes welcomed and deliberately induced such as, for example Christians "speaking in tongues" (technically known as *glossolalia*), allegedly as a result of being taken over by the Holy Spirit, and shamans being "possessed" by the spirits of animals and mythical creatures.

Examining the Claims

Pop Psychology, Pop Culture, and Public Perception

Public understanding of the concepts of demonic possession and exorcism is largely based upon media coverage on the one hand and the stated views of religious leaders on the other. Regarding the former, possession and exorcism are popular topics for horror movies, with more than one claiming to be "based upon a true story." The most famous of these is *The Exorcist*, released in 1973. The inspiration for the movie was the 1971 bestselling novel of the same name by William Peter Blatty. This book was itself based upon an allegedly true account of the demonic possession of a teenage boy over two decades earlier. There is, however, strong circumstantial evidence to suggest that this spectacular case may be based upon nothing more than a hoax carried out by the alleged victim himself (Nickell, 2013; Opsanik, 2000). In addition to portrayals in movies and TV dramas, other cases are featured in documentaries and reality TV programs, often of dubious reliability. In reality, cases of alleged possession are typically much less dramatic than these sensationalized cases would suggest.

Arguably much more influential than such media portrayals, at least amongst a substantial proportion of the world's population, are the actions and official statements of recognized religious leaders. For example, in 2014, Pope Francis formally recognized the International Association of Exorcists, consisting of 250 priests spread across 30 countries. The association was co-founded by Father Gabriele Amorth who was the Chief Exorcist of the Vatican. He performed many thousands of exorcisms during his long career as a priest and his views on exorcism and possession were influential within and beyond Catholicism.

Belief in the literal reality of Satan and demons is obviously a prerequisite for belief in possession and exorcism. It is thus worth noting that widespread belief in the former is at the root of the Satanic panic of the 1980s and 1990s and its recent resurgence as one element of the so-called QAnon movement (Rothschild, 2021). Opinion poll data show that 22% of American adults believe that demons "definitely exist" with a further 24% saying that they "probably exist" (Ballard, 2019).

Levels of belief in the UK are much lower but even here 18% reported that the devil exists and that he can possess people (Jordan, 2013). The majority of British adults (65%) deny that the devil exists or that he can possess people, with 17% undecided. In contrast, this poll found that 57% of American adults believed in the devil and 51% believed that people can be possessed by the devil or "some other evil spirit." Systematic survey data are not available from most of the rest of the world but it seems highly probable that high levels of belief in possession would be found in most highly religious countries.

The Evidence

The only evidence that has ever been put forward to support the claim that demons exist and are capable of possessing people is anecdotal in nature. It consists entirely of reports from individuals, often with strongly held religious beliefs, attempting to explain phenomena for which they have no better explanation. In fact, as we shall see, more plausible explanations do indeed exist for a wide range of phenomena that are often explained by believers in terms of demonic possession. No convincing evidence has ever been produced in support of allegedly paranormal effects associated with possession.

French (2017) argues that the majority of cases of alleged possession, excluding the small minority that are based upon deliberate hoaxes, fall into two broad categories: neuropathological (including psychiatric; Beyerstein, 1988, 1996, 2007) and sociocognitive (Spanos, 1996).

It is understandable that the concept of possession was often used by our ancestors to explain bizarre behavior which we would now recognize as symptomatic of neuropathological conditions (Beyerstein, 1988, 1996, 2007). For example, a range of different symptoms may be caused by the paroxysmal neural firing of an epileptic seizure. These include sudden loss of consciousness, convulsions, and incontinence. Although Hippocrates himself (c. 460–370 BCE) argued in *On the Sacred Disease* that the behaviors, sensations, and emotions associated with epilepsy were due to a condition of the brain and not possession by demons, his insight was forgotten by many subsequent generations.

Another condition that was often viewed as evidence of possession we would now recognize as Tourette's syndrome, a condition characterized by numerous physical tics and at least one vocal tic. This would be most likely to occur in the minority of cases (around 10%) in which the sufferer is prone to obscene vocal outbursts. Interestingly, it is thought that the first detailed description of a case of Tourette's syndrome is that found in the book *Malleus Maleficarum* ("Witch's Hammer") written by Jakob Sprenger and Heinrich Kraemer in the late 15th century as a guide to the identification and prosecution of witches.

Possession by jinn is often the preferred explanation amongst Muslims for a range of unusual symptoms and behaviors. Lim et al. (2015) reviewed the medical literature on this topic and identified 47 relevant case histories. In their words (pp. 23–24):

The psychiatric symptoms listed were hallucinations, delusions, anxiety, aggression, mutism, anorexia, sleep disturbances, catatonic posturing, and self-mutilation. The somatic symptoms comprised epileptic seizures, alcohol withdrawal, knee injury, paralysis of a limb, personality changes after a *trauma capitis* [head injury], and typhoid fever.

Almost two-thirds of these cases received a definite psychiatric diagnosis and, of those that did, 45% were diagnosed with schizophrenia spectrum disorders.

However, a strong case can be made that a sizeable proportion of cases of alleged possession are not based upon neuropathological or psychiatric disorders at all. The late Nicholas Spanos (1996) argued that such cases are better explained in terms of the sociocognitive approach. According to this perspective, those involved in such cases – the allegedly possessed individual, the exorcist, and others – are often simply behaving in line with what they believe to be expected of them in each of their respective roles. As Spanos points out:

> The characteristics of possession displays in other cultures ... vary greatly both among societies and within societies. Possession is not a unitary phenomenon and differs dramatically depending on the status of the possessed person, the context in which the possession occurs, and the meaning attributed to the possession both by the possessed individual and by his or her audience. (1996, p. 147)

In other words, those involved are adopting rule-governed roles that must be learned, either by explicit instruction or by observing others. This is not to say that those involved are simply play-acting. The process is subtler and more nuanced than that with those involved typically convinced that possession is a genuinely supernatural phenomenon. What are the benefits to those involved in the different roles in this dramatic situation? The exorcist is seen by others in the community as a hero of the highest order, taking on the forces of supreme evil and defeating them through the strength of their faith in, in the case of Christianity, the one true God. Official Catholic exorcists will have received detailed training in how to carry out exorcisms. Unofficial exorcists will have learned what to do by observing others carrying out the ritual. When exorcisms appear to work, as they sometimes do, the local community is rewarded by this confirmation of their faith in the one true religion; that is, the one that they already embrace.

Initially, it might be harder to understand why anyone would willingly take on the role of the possessed individual but in fact that role also confers benefits in some contexts (Cuneo, 2001; French, 2017). Those who are said to be possessed are not held responsible for previous immoral behavior as it will be accepted that it was the demon who possessed them that should be blamed. Once they been through a successful exorcism, they will be welcomed back into their community as saved and pure.

The behavior of the possessed individual while they are allegedly possessed will depend upon a number of factors. Initially, they will already have some preconceived notions about what is involved based upon general knowledge and possibly explicit religious teachings but their behavior may well be modified somewhat once they begin to interact with, say, members of the clergy. Spanos (1996) illustrates this point with reference to the allegedly possessed children involved in the Salem witch trials of 1692. Initially, the children had behaved in a variety of odd ways such as adopting unusual positions, running around wildly, and crawling under furniture. However, the more they interacted with clergy and neighbors, the more their behavior corresponded to what was expected from a possessed individual such as claims of being bitten and punched, "seeing" the specters of attacking witches, and convulsions.

Possessed individuals can engage in behavior that would be totally unacceptable in other circumstances. Lewis (1987) made an important distinction between what he called *central* and *peripheral* possession. Central possession involves the possession of a respected member of society, such as a shaman, by a major deity and their behavior while possessed serves to validate the central values of the community. The person possessed in a case of peripheral possession, on the other hand, is a low status member of the community, with little power and few resources. The possessing spirit (or demon) is amoral and capricious. Lewis argues that in such cases the possession provides a means for such socially marginal individuals to express their resentment, frustration and anger toward their superiors without fear of retribution.

Understanding Beliefs

If children grow up in religious communities, it is not surprising that they are likely to adopt the religious beliefs of that community. For example, many studies (Martin et al., 2003; Milevsky et al., 2008) demonstrate the importance of parental views in influencing the religious views of their offspring. For those holding particular religious beliefs, their religion provides a framework to understand the world around them. As already discussed, for large proportions of society, both historically and currently, possession appears to provide a satisfactory explanation for a wide range of bizarre behaviors and beliefs that modern psychology would explain in terms of neuropathological and/or psychiatric conditions. As also already discussed, many cases of alleged possession may not involve any underlying neuropathology or psychiatric condition but are best understood in sociocognitive terms. By adopting the various roles involved in this psychodrama, there are benefits to the exorcist, the wider community, and even to the allegedly possessed individual themselves.

However, belief in demonic possession is also associated with many harmful consequences. In some societies, the notion of being possessed carries less societal stigma than that of mental illness. Therefore, those seeking solutions to problems of mental health may prefer to initially consult religious leaders and request an exorcism in preference to seeking medical treatment. This decision may well be supported by family members, friends and religious leaders. In some cases, especially those where there is no underlying neuropathological or psychiatric problem, undergoing the exorcism may actually have a beneficial effect as already described. Unfortunately, there appears to be no systematic outcome studies of how often this is actually the case. What is more certain is that such a course of action will sometimes lead to delays in seeking medical diagnosis and treatment which may well have a negative effect on outcome (Lim et al., 2015; Pietkiewicz et al., 2021), particularly in cases of suspected psychosis (Albert et al., 2017).

It should be noted that those who believe in the possibility of demonic possession typically do also accept that mental health problems are sometimes caused by underlying neuropathology and/or psychiatric disorders. It is simply the case that they do not believe that all such problems can be explained in terms of the models of Western medical science. In the context of jinn possession, Dein and Illaiee (2013, p. 293) offer the following advice:

Mental health professionals should be aware of the explanatory models adopted by their patients and there is a need for these professionals to collaborate with imams in the provision of holistic mental health care which incorporates biological, psychological and spiritual factors. Whereas mental health professionals can teach imams to recognise mental illness, Islamic religious professionals can in turn educate health professionals about the importance of religious factors in psychiatric disorders. Clinicians must be careful to distinguish between culturally sanctioned belief in spirit possession and obvious psychotic symptoms lest the patient be treated unnecessarily with antipsychotics. On the other hand, clinicians must exercise caution and not assume that all unusual beliefs in a patient from an unfamiliar culture are culturally sanctioned lest psychosis goes undetected and untreated.

In discussing the historically uneasy relationship between religion and medicine within the Roman Catholic Church, Bauer (2022, p. 10) makes the following observation:

> What characterizes this branch of modern exorcism practices in the Roman Catholic Church is the explicit integration of medical expertise. Medical concepts are included to legitimize religious practice. This also gives the religious experts supposed "medical" competence. Modern exorcists seek to emphasize their credentials by interacting with modern medicine and psychology. Demonic possession is, they claim, a separate phenomenon to mental illness, and the exorcist steps in where the psychiatrist cannot help. This argument helps to establish the practice of exorcism not only as equal to the world of medicine, but even as superior, as an exorcist provides a service when modern medicine fails.

There are of course anecdotal reports in the literature of improvement in symptoms following participation in such practices but, in the absence of systematic outcome studies, there is no strong evidence to support any claim that the practice of exorcism is superior to conventional psychiatric treatment. Although within the Roman Catholic Church the official line is that exorcisms should only be carried out once potential underlying neuropathological and psychiatric conditions have been conclusively ruled out on the basis of a full clinical assessment, it is unclear how often this actually occurs in practice given the large number of unofficial exorcisms (Giordan & Possamai, 2017; Pietkiewicz et al., 2021).

A report by the Christian thinktank Theos warned of the dangers posed by the recent increase in the number of exorcisms performed in the UK (Ryan, 2017). Describing exorcisms as a "booming industry" in the UK, the report calls for "an analysis of the burgeoning exorcism scene in the UK in the light of concerns over how it is being used and its possible negative consequences" (p. 26). It warns of the risk of "Christian over-spiritualising," that is "a tendency to ascribe anything and everything to spiritual causes when other medical ones may exist" (p. 25).

Tragically, there have been numerous cases of serious injury and even deaths occurring as a result of extreme physical abuse being inflicted in misguided attempts to drive demons from the bodies of allegedly possessed individuals. One of the most notorious cases is that of Anneliese Michel, a young German with epilepsy who died in 1976 having undergone 67 Catholic exorcism rites in the year before her death. Anneliese had been persuaded to abandon the conventional medical treatment for her epilepsy and a local bishop, citing Jesus's admonition that demons should be exorcised through prayer and fasting, approved starving Anneliese in order to save her soul. She weighed only 68 pounds when she died. In 1978, her parents and two German priests were convicted of negligent homicide. They received suspended sentences (Beyerstein, 1996). This case inspired a number of movies including *The Exorcism of Emily Rose* (2005), *Requiem* (2006), and *Anneliese: The Exorcist Tapes* (2011).

Similar tragedies have been reported in the UK. In February 2000, 8-year-old Victoria Climbié, originally from the Ivory Coast, died in north London having endured months of torture at the hands of her guardians, Marie Therese Kouao and Carl Manning. Her guardians believed she was possessed by an evil spirit as did their church leaders. They were jailed for life for her murder. In 2005, in North London, three adults were convicted of child cruelty. In this case, an 8-year-old child from Angola had chilli peppers rubbed in her eyes as well as being beaten, starved, and cut with a knife because it was believed that she was possessed.

Summary and Conclusion

Belief in demons that can possess the minds and bodies of their victims is widespread both geographically and historically. There is considerable variation between and even within different cultures regarding the details of the effects of demonic possession upon behavior and personality. Within a Christian context, possession typically is said to entail the complete taking over of an individual's consciousness, possibly resulting in convulsions, screaming, swearing, and violent and lewd behavior. In contrast, within a Muslim context, although possession by jinn may have similar results, it may also result in a wide range of other psychiatric and somatic symptoms. It is claimed that demons can be expelled by undergoing a process of exorcism. There is considerable variation with respect to what is involved in such rituals ranging from prayers, exhortation, and chanting on the one hand, up to severe physical abuse on the other.

The dramatic changes in behavior and personality seen in some cases of possession are similar to those seen in a variety of other contexts including channeling by mediums, so-called dissociative identity disorder (formerly known as multiple personality disorder), and various hypnotic phenomena.

With the exception of rare cases based upon deliberate hoaxing, most cases of alleged possession fall into one of two broad categories: those based upon underlying neuropathological and psychiatric conditions and those best understood in sociocognitive terms. With respect to the former category, individuals suffering from a wide variety of disorders, including epilepsy, Tourette's syndrome, and schizophrenia, were often and, to a lesser extent, still are viewed by those around them as being the victims of demonic possession. In some cases, the afflicted individual will themselves accept that this is indeed the case.

A strong case has been made that in many cases of alleged possession there is no underlying medical condition. Such cases are best explained in sociocognitive terms. This approach emphasizes the fact that each of those taking part in the powerful psychodrama of possession – the exorcist, the possessed individual, and others – takes on a role that must be learned, either by explicit instruction or else by observation. Each of those involved gain benefits from their roles: the exorcist gains respect and kudos; the possessed individual is not held responsible for previous immoral behavior and is welcomed back into the community; the wider community receives confirmation that their religion is the one true religion.

Public understanding of the concepts of possession and exorcism are largely based upon portrayals in the media, on the one hand, and teachings of religious leaders on the other. The former typically presents a sensationalized account of both possession and exorcism.

Belief in possession and exorcism can and does result in serious harmful consequences. In cultures where possession is less stigmatized than mental illness, those labeled as possessed may delay seeking medical treatment with negative consequences for clinical outcome. Clinicians dealing with such cases must have an awareness of their patients' beliefs regarding possession if they are to achieve optimal outcomes.

Tragically, there are a number of cases of severe physical abuse, sometimes with fatal results as a consequence of belief in possession. Such senseless loss of life is inexcusable in the 21st century.

References

Albert, N., Melau, M., Jensen, H., Hastrup, L. H., Hjorthoj, C., & Nordentoft, M. (2017). The effect of duration of untreated psychosis and treatment delay on the outcome of prolonged early intervention in psychotic disorders. *NPJ Schizophrenia, 3*, 1–8.

Ballard, J. (2019). Many Americans believe ghosts and demons exist. *YouGovAmerica*. Retrieved from https://today.yougov.com/topics/lifestyle/articles-reports/2019/10/21/paranormal-beliefs-ghosts-demons-poll

Bauer, N. M. (2022). The devil and the doctor: The (de)medicalization of exorcism in the Roman Catholic Church. *Religions, 13*, 87.

Beyerstein, B. L. (1988). Neuropathology and the legacy of spiritual possession. *Skeptical Inquirer, 12*, 248–262.

Beyerstein, B. L. (1996). Possession and exorcism. In G. Stein (Ed.), *The encyclopedia of the paranormal* (pp. 544–552). Amherst, NY: Prometheus.

Beyerstein, B. L. (2007). The neurology of the weird: Brain states and anomalous experience. In S. Della Sala (Ed.), *Tall tales about the mind and brain: separating fact from fiction* (pp. 314–335). Oxford: Oxford University Press.

Cuneo, M. W.(2001). *American exorcism: Expelling demons in the land of plenty.* New York: Doubleday.

Dein, S., & Illaiee, A. S. (2013). Jinn and mental health: Looking at jinn possession in modern psychiatric practice. *The Psychiatrist, 37*, 290–293.

French, C. C. (2017). Possession and exorcism. In D. Groome & R. Roberts (Eds.), *Parapsychology: The science of unusual experience* (pp. 34–47). London & New York: Routledge.

Giordan, G., & Possamai, A. (2017). *Sociology of exorcism in late modernity.* London: Palgrave Macmillan.

Jordan, W. (2013). 18% of Brits believe in possession by the devil. *YouGov*. Retrieved from https://yougov.co.uk/topics/politics/articles-reports/2013/09/27/18-brits-believe-possession-devil-and-half-america

Levack, B. P. (2013). *The devil within: Possession & exorcism in the Christian west.* New Haven: Yale University Press.

Lewis, I. M. (1987). *Ecstatic religion.* Routledge.

Lim, A., Hoek, H. W., & Blom, J. D. (2015). The attribution of psychotic symptoms to jinn in Islamic patients. *Transcultural Psychiatry, 52*, 18–32.

Martin, T. F., White, J. M., & Perlman, D. (2003). Religious socialization: A test of the channelling hypothesis of parental influence on adolescent faith maturity. *Journal of Adolescent Research, 18*, 169–187.

Milevsky, I. M., Szuchman, L., & Milevsky, A. (2008). Transmission of religious beliefs in college students. *Mental Health, Religion and Culture, 11*, 423–434.

Nickell, J. (2013). *The science of miracles: Investigating the incredible.* Prometheus.

Opsanik, M. (2000). The haunted boy. *Strange Magazine, 20*. Serialized at http://strangemag.com/exorcistpage1.html

Pietkiewicz, I. J., Klosinska, U., & Tomalski, R. (2021). Delusions of possession and religious coping in schizophrenia: A qualitative study of four cases. *Frontiers in Psychology*, *12*, 628925.

Pietkiewicz, I. J., Klosinska, U., Tomalski, R., & Van der Hart, O. (2021). Beyond dissociative disorders: A qualitative study of Polish catholic women reporting demonic possession. *European Journal of Trauma & Dissociation*, *5*, 100204.

Rothschild, M. (2021). *The storm is upon us: How qanon became a movement, cult, and conspiracy theory of everything*. Monoray.

Ryan, B. (2017). *Christianity and mental health: Theology, activities, potential*. Theos.

Spanos, N. P. (1996). *Multiple identities & false memories: A sociocognitive perspective*. Washington, DC: American Psychological Association.

16 Energy Psychology and Therapy

Carmen P. McLean and Madeleine Miller

Can tapping on the body relieve emotional distress? Practitioners of energy psychology (EP) claim that tapping techniques, typically combined with standard psychotherapy approaches, can yield remarkably rapid and lasting relief from a range of psychological disorders, physical health conditions, and life problems. Energy psychology is an umbrella term for a collection of treatments designed to help shift targeted emotions, cognitions, and behaviors by manipulating human "energy fields" (Gallo, 2004). According to energy psychology theory, psychological disorders and other health conditions are associated with disturbances in the body's electrical energies and energy fields (Feinstein, 2008). Energy psychology treatments typically combine cognitive-behavioral and supportive therapy approaches with the stimulation of specific points on the skin. These points, referred to as "acupoints," are thought to correspond to energy systems associated with non-Western methods for healing and spiritual development (Callahan & Callahan, 2000). Among the more prominent energy psychology approaches are Thought Field Therapy (TFT)™, the Emotional Freedom Technique (EFT)™, and the Tapas Acupressure Technique (TAT)®, although dozens of other variations of energy psychology have been identified.

Examining the Claims

TFT was introduced to the public in 1985 through the book, *Five Minute Phobia Cure* (Callahan, 1985). A clinical psychologist who had studied applied kinesiology reportedly developed TFT after experimenting with tapping while treating a client with a treatment-resistant phobia of water. Inspired by the success of this case, he and his wife subsequently developed a series of tapping "algorithms" to treat various presenting problems (Callahan & Callahan, 2000). In TFT, clients focus on the problem that is distressing them while tapping specific parts of their bodies, following the specific algorithms. Clients are also sometimes asked to engage in additional body stimulation such as eye movements or humming thought to facilitate the correction of the energy perturbation. The tapping sequence is typically repeated until the client's subjective distress is eliminated. A related website proposes that applying TFT to various problems addresses their underlying causes by delivering a healing code, and balancing the body's energy system, thereby eliminating negative emotions within minutes.

A popular variation of TFT is EFT, developed by an engineering graduate who was trained by the developer of TFT. Rather than using specific tapping algorithms for different problems, EFT prescribes a universal 12-point sequence for treating all presenting problems. In EFT, clients focus on a distressing memory while tapping and

DOI: 10.4324/9781003107798-16

verbalizing an affirmation such as "Even though I have (stated problem), I fully and completely accept myself" (Clond, 2016).

Another popular energy psychology is the Tapas Acupressure Technique (TAT). TAT was developed by a licensed acupuncturist and uses self-administered pressure, rather than tapping, on a small set of points near the eyes, above the nose, and behind the head. Holding one's fingers on this set of points is referred to as the TAT pose. In TAT, clients focus on a series of statements aimed at healing and resolving barriers in a problem area while holding the TAT pose (Elder et al., 2012). Although energy psychology is most commonly associated with tapping, TAT involves applying constant pressure to specified points. Other variants of energy psychology, known as "chakra methods," purport to manipulate energy without tapping or pressure (e.g., by holding a hand over specific areas of the body without physically touching).

Across variants of energy psychology, proponents claim that treatment leads to rapid, profound relief from a variety of psychological problems, including anxiety, depression, phobias, posttraumatic stress, substance use, eating disorders, guilt, shame, jealousy, anger, as well as physical ailments such as chronic pain, vision problems, weight loss, among others, and to improve athletic performance and one's ability to love and succeed in life. Energy psychology is also purported to reduce medication side effects and boost medication efficacy for those with arthritis, cancer, heart disease, and other physical conditions. In general, energy psychology treatment claims are marked by an absence of clear boundary conditions (Hines, 2003). Related websites and materials assert that energy psychology can *eliminate* negative emotions within minutes, and its benefits are claimed to be proven, being a cure for several conditions (Callahan, 1985, 2001).

Proposed Therapeutic Mechanisms

What are the suggested mechanisms that cause energy psychology to work? Early formulations proposed that somatic stimulation of acupoints modulate "energy fields" or "thought fields" (Callahan & Callahan, 1996). These energy systems are not easily detected or measured (Collinge et al., 1998) but have long been discussed in non-Western cultures. Energy systems include energy pathways (e.g., "meridians"), energy centers (e.g., "chakras"), and energy fields surrounding the body (e.g., "biofield" or "aura") that can be disturbed or unbalanced by emotional difficulties. Psychological problems are believed to be associated with perturbations in the energy system. Modulation of these systems, through acupoint stimulation such as tapping, is proposed to correct the perturbations in the energy system and bring it into balance again, thereby resolving the emotional or physical problems. More specific explanatory models have also been proposed.

One prominent explanation of energy psychology suggests that acupoint stimulation sends deactivating electromagnetic signals directly to relevant brain areas. Certain points on the body are thought to connect with physiological pathways which may be embedded in the fascia, part of the body's connective tissue, more so than adjacent points (Bai et al., 2011). Through these physiological pathways, it is proposed that acupoint stimulation sends activating or deactivating signals to specific brain regions involved in the client's emotional problem (Feinstein, 2019). In the treatment of anxiety-related problems, acupoint stimulation is said to send deactivating signals directly to the amygdala (Feinstein, 2019), a brain structure that is central to threat detection, fear expression, and fear learning (Milad et al., 2009). By combining acupoint stimulation with imaginal exposure (i.e., mentally focusing on an anxiety-provoking image or memory), it is proposed that the amygdala receives conflicting information: activating signals from the exposure and deactivating signals from the acupoint stimulation (Feinstein, 2019).

Imaginal exposure is a technique used in several effective treatments for post-traumatic stress disorder (PTSD) and other anxiety-related disorders. The therapeutic mechanisms of exposure are relatively well conceptualized through learning, emotional processing, and inhibitory learning theories (Craske et al., 2008; Foa & Kozak, 1986; Mowrer, 1960). The pairing of exposure techniques with body tapping, which is not part of standard exposure therapy, is proposed to fast-track corrective learning as clients engage with the anxiety-provoking image or memory without experiencing high arousal (Feinstein, 2021).

Additional, complimentary models of how energy psychology works have also been proposed. One model suggests that acupoint stimulation increases the amplitude of delta waves in brain areas associated with fear and memory, which disrupts the activated memory networks, possibly though the depotentiation of receptors in neural circuits activated by fear memories (Harper, 2012). This depotentiation is thought to effectively deactivate amygdala arousal and quickly reduce distress (Feinstein, 2012). Another model focuses on "organizing fields" of neural activity, suggesting that acupoint stimulation promotes balance and harmony in the body's energy pathways (Feinstein, 2012). This model assumes "subtle energies" exist throughout the body, carry information (including psychological information), and can be modulated through acupoint simulation to influence health and mental health (Feinstein, 2012). It is also proposed that some people are able to clairvoyantly "see" subtle energies throughout the body that others cannot, giving them unique healing abilities (Gerber, 2001).

Energy Psychology in Popular Culture

Energy psychology has been embraced by the popular culture and many influential figures and media sources including therapists on TV, prominent newspapers, and popular magazines (Jones, 2016; Kelly, 2008; Trespicio, 2014). Energy psychology practices have also been recommended by prominent academics, best-selling authors, and psychiatrists (Mollon, 2007). In 1998, the Association for Comprehensive Energy Psychology (ACEP) was formed as an international organization to promote research, training, and ethical principles amongst those who practice energy psychology (Mollon, 2007). The ACEP sells training courses and certification in EFT and comprehensive energy psychology (CEP).

Energy psychology has a long history of fighting for recognition as an evidence-based treatment. Some have argued that EFT and TAT meet the American Psychological Association (APA) Division 12 criteria as a "probably efficacious" treatment for specific phobias and maintaining weight loss, respectively (Feinstein, 2008, 2012, 2019). To our knowledge, Division 12 has never commented on any energy psychology treatments. Although ACEP has been approved by the APA as a provider of continuing education (CE) credits since 2012, this does not indicate that the APA endorses energy psychology. The APA offers CE credits for training in many controversial therapies, which has been a point of criticism from clinical scientists for some time (Coyne & Kok, 2014; Thyer & Pignotti, 2016).

A Review of the Evidence

Research on energy psychology lagged behind its practice for many years, but has increased considerably since 2001, when the *Journal of Clinical Psychology* published six papers on TFT (Callahan, 2001a, 2001b, 2001c; Johnson et al., 2001; Pignotti & Steinberg, 2001; Pignotti (2005) later redacted their article; Sakai et al., 2001). The papers were not peer reviewed but were published alongside six critiques (Herbert & Gaudiano, 2001a; Kline, 2001; Lohr, 2001; McNally, 2001; Rosen & Davison, 2001; Rosner, 2001). The supporting papers cite improvements in heart rate variability as a measure of TFT's success, while critiques question the reliance on heart rate over a standard psychiatric measure.

In 2008, Feinstein reviewed evidence for energy psychology, including many anecdotal reports, systematic observations, case studies, and a few uncontrolled trials and randomized controlled trials. Feinstein (2008) concluded that the evidence met APA Division 12 criteria for a probably efficacious treatment. This review was criticized for this optimistic assertion as well as for omitting what are arguably the most important studies of energy psychology to date (Bakker, 2013; McCaslin, 2009b; Pignotti & Thyer, 2009). The omitted studies were the only two randomized controlled trials of energy psychology that have tested "sham" tapping controls (Pignotti, 2005; Waite & Holder, 2003). Both studies found that the treatment and sham tapping conditions led to equivalent therapeutic change.

In the first study, Waite and Holder (2003) compared EFT with two sham conditions tapping on non-EFT points on the body and tapping on a doll, as well as a waitlist condition. The study found no differences between the three active conditions. Thus, counter to theories of how EFT works, which suggest that tapping on specific areas of the body representing energy meridians promotes recovery, this study suggests that the benefits of treatment are unrelated to the tapping itself. In the second trial, Pignotti (2005) found that the effect of tapping following a sequence of meridian points used in the most advanced level of TFT was not different than tapping in randomly selected sequences. Contrary to the claims that energy psychology works by stimulating specific acupoint locations and that specific sequences of tapping yield unique therapeutic benefit, these studies suggest that the location and sequence of tapping makes no difference, and thus could not be considered an active component of treatment.

In 2009, Feinstein responded to the critiques about the omission of these studies, citing paper length as a primary justification and also claiming that the data from the omitted studies actually support the efficacy of tapping, and that "strict adherence to original tapping protocols is considered by most practitioners to be unnecessary" (Feinstein, 2009, p. 263). Indeed, Feinstein and others have argued that tapping is beneficial even with significant variation in provider implementation (Feinstein, 2009, p. 269). Feinstein referred to the Waite and Holder (2003) sham tapping groups as "variations" of EFT and only the waitlist as the control condition, when in fact the "variations" were sham controls, and their efficacy represents evidence against EFT claims. Others have argued that the sham tapping conditions were effective because the study therapists inadvertently stimulated energy points on the *fingertips* when the tappers' fingers tapped other points on the body or the dolls (Feinstein, 2009), thus reinterpreting the findings as supporting EFT claims. Some energy psychology proponents have even proposed a variation of energy psychology in which the practitioner taps on themselves, referred to as "surrogate tapping" or "long distance healing" which moves the practice even further from any plausible therapeutic mechanism.

In 2012, Feinstein reviewed energy psychology evidence again, reporting 18 controlled trials. Feinstein excluded the Waite and Holder (2003) and Pignotti (2005) randomized controlled trials on the basis of not using "full randomization." Pignotti (2005) alternated each second participant to the experimental and control groups, and Waite and Holder (2003) similarly alternated assignment to groups. While these design choices may legitimately be criticized, they are forms of randomization and do not warrant dismal of the study findings.

In the past two decades, research on energy psychology has increased. There are now numerous randomized controlled trials covering various energy psychology protocols for a wide range of ailments. Meta-analyses of energy psychology, which mostly focus on EFT and include a range of clinical outcomes, have found moderate effects for energy psychology compared to waitlist (Gilomen & Lee, 2015). Others report large within-group effects for EFT (Church, 2018; Clond, 2016) but did not report the effects relative to comparison conditions. One meta-analysis found large effects for EFT compared to waitlist and treatment as usual but no effect compared to active psychotherapy for PTSD (Sebastian & Nelms, 2017). Among randomized controlled trials comparing EFT to active conditions, energy psychology was found superior to sleep hygiene education for insomnia (Lee et al., 2015) and superior to deep breathing for physical and psychological symptoms related to body stiffness/pain at follow up but not post-treatment (Church & Nelms, 2016; Church et al., 2020). EFT was also and not superior to cognitive-behavioral therapy (CBT) for agoraphobia (Irgens et al., 2017), and was not superior to eye-movement desensitization and reprocessing (EMDR) for posttraumatic stress (Karatzias et al., 2011; note that EMDR is also a similar and highly controversial type of treatment).

Overall, these results suggest that EFT may be efficacious for reducing symptoms of some common mental health problems. Critically, however, this does not mean that tapping is an active ingredient in EFT. Like other energy psychology protocols, EFT includes several standard psychotherapy components used in first line evidence-based psychotherapies. These include establishing therapeutic rapport, identifying treatment goals, providing a treatment rationale, cognitive restructuring, mindfulness, and imaginal exposure, all of which are components of well-established therapies. Indeed, EFT is an "exposure-based treatment" (Feinstein, 2008). Exposure is a robust and powerful therapeutic tool. As such, we would expect any intervention that uses exposure as a primary therapeutic component to show beneficial effects, regardless of whether complimentary techniques (i.e., techniques that don't interfere with exposure) are included as part of the treatment protocol or not. So, while EFT is associated with therapeutic change, this does not necessarily mean that tapping has anything to do with the effects. Treatments that combine an effective component (e.g., exposure) with an implausible nonessential component (e.g., wearing a purple hat during therapy) are sometimes referred to as *purple hat therapies*, especially when the nonessential ingredient appears to be emphasized over the effective component (Rosen & Davison, 2003).

Given the demand characteristics of the therapy, only studies using a sham placebo control condition, in which both therapist and patient are blind to the theorized tapping locations and sequences, can accurately evaluate energy psychology claims (Herbert & Gaudiano, 2005). Studies using other designs cannot rule out the possibility that energy psychology is simply a redundant elaboration of exposure therapy – which is already known to be effective. Some studies have compared energy psychology to a similar exposure protocol without tapping (Fox & Malinowski, 2013) in an attempt to dismantle energy psychology and isolate the contribution of tapping.

However, such designs do not control for demand characteristic or therapist bias. Researchers have called for sham placebo controlled studies of energy psychology for over a decade (McCaslin, 2009a), yet to our knowledge, Waite and Holder (2003) and Pignotti (2005) remain the only sham placebo controlled trials of energy psychology that have been conducted to date.

What is lacking for energy psychology is evidence of specific efficacy (Lilienfeld, 2011). That is, despite evidence that energy psychology works better than nothing, and comparably to some other interventions, what is needed is evidence that acupoint stimulation has anything to do with the observed effects. This is particularly true given the questionable theoretical plausibility of energy psychology's purported mechanisms. We are not aware of any evidence supporting the existence of energy meridians, or any other energy systems in the human body that energy psychology purports to manipulate (Bausell, 2007). The fact that these elements cannot be detected or measured renders the theory underlying energy psychology unfalsifiable. When a theory cannot be falsified, it is unscientific (Popper, 1959).

Understanding Beliefs

How can we understand the popularity of energy psychology, especially given the lack of evidence to support fundamental claims around the existence of energy systems? We propose that there are a number of factors at play that may influence the general public, clients, and practitioners to believe energy psychology claims.

Similar to a number of complementary and alternative therapies such as Reiki and yoga, energy psychology is represented as having roots in non-Western medicine. Proponents claim that the theories underlying energy psychology are derived from ancient Chinese medicine (Elder et al., 2007; Herbert & Gaudiano, 2001; Hooke, 1998; Wells et al., 2003). This appeal to "ancient wisdom" implies that if something has been around for thousands of years, then it must be effective. However, it's easy to think of examples of incorrect ideas, like the earth being flat, that persisted for a long time (in addition, see Colquhoun & Novella, 2013) for a summary of the history of acupuncture's varied popularity). The "ancient wisdom" underlying energy psychology is often contrasted with conventional Western medicine, thereby couching the controversy within the larger "clash of paradigms" (Feinstein, 2009) of Eastern-holistic-traditional vs. Western-modern-conventional medicine.

Relatedly, leaders of energy psychology are often described as mystic healers with unique abilities. This serves as an appeal to authority and implies that if energy psychology claims seem implausible, this is because most people don't have access to all the information or ways of knowing that the energy healer possesses.

At the same time that some energy psychologists reject Western medicine and its focus on measurable phenomena, others use findings and established concepts from modern neuroscience to describe hypothesized mechanisms of energy psychology. For example, in defense of the existence of subtle energies, Feinstein (2003) makes an analogy to gravity, suggesting that because subtle energy and gravity are alike in some ways (i.e., that they are both invisible), then they are also alike in other ways (i.e., they are both real – ignoring the fact that unlike subtle energy, gravity can be measured objectively, described mathematically, and its effects are observable). This appeal to scientific credibility can involve misrepresenting the evidence for acupoint stimulation, suggesting that the database is far stronger than is actually the case.

A similar tension exists with energy psychology's relationship with mainstream psychology. On one hand, some energy psychology proponents describe themselves as outsiders, bucking the narrowmindedness of mainstream psychology. On the other hand, others have sought, and continue to seek, scientific credibility by claiming that energy psychology meets the APA's criteria for designating a treatment as "probably efficacious." In contrast to the skeptical or status quo scientists, energy psychology proponents are described as open to new ideas and being at the forefront of a paradigm shift within psychotherapy (Stapleton et al., 2019).

Reviews of energy psychology, as well as many energy psychology websites, demonstrate an overreliance on anecdotal evidence supporting energy psychology. Anecdotal evidence is a weaker form of evidence heavily prone to bias. In fact, as Pignotti and Thyer (2009) point out, the more people know about energy psychology and the extraordinary claims associated with it, the greater the risk that expectancy and confirmation biases influence perceptions of change. When therapists and clients are expecting a miraculous therapeutic transformation, they will be biased toward interpreting the therapy experience in this way. However, when someone experiences benefit from energy psychology or hears about others' benefitting from the approach, they will likely attribute the benefit to energy manipulation, in line with the information they receive about the approach from websites, books, and practitioners.

Therapists are prone to biases too. In general they tend to overestimate their therapeutic success (Miller et al., 2014) such that they perceive treatment as more helpful than it actually was. This is particularly likely when the practitioner is not routinely gathering clinical outcome data from reliable and valid clinical assessment tools as part of treatment (i.e., measurement-based care), and is relying instead primarily on client report and clinical judgment. While it's not clear how common measurement-base care is among energy psychology practitioners, several trials of energy psychology have been criticized for relying on clients' subjective reports rather than validated tools, which tend to be highly influenced by demand characteristics and expectancy bias (Pignotti & Thyer, 2009).

What Is the Harm?

One of the potential harms associated with energy psychology relates to presenting the treatment as a "miracle cure." Research has found that when therapy isn't successful, clients may be less likely to seek care again in the future (Taber et al., 2015). The more a treatment is pitched as working extremely well for nearly everyone, the more a client may personalize a treatment failure. The use of the term "cure" is misleading for any mental health treatment. Even our best psychological treatments don't come close to producing remission for all clients (Meichenbaum & Lilienfeld, 2018).

Summary and Conclusion

Energy psychology blends efficacious psychotherapy approaches, most notably exposure, with acupoint stimulation techniques that are based on unsupported and unscientific ideas about energy fields. Given that energy psychology treatments include a combination of supported and unsupported techniques, studies that compare energy psychology treatments to waitlist or other treatments do not address the controversial claims made by energy psychology about the causes and solutions to mental health problems. As such, the current body of evidence supporting energy psychology treatments is largely uninformative. The treatments seem to work, but the only studies to date designed to properly test whether acupoint stimulation is related to therapeutic changes suggest that it is not.

When evaluating whether a therapy "works," the theoretical plausibility of the treatment matters (Lilienfeld, 2011). Given that the idea of invisible unmeasurable energy fields impacting our wellbeing contradicts our existing scientific understanding, it is reasonable to require that energy psychology produce more convincing research evidence than would be required for treatments based on well-established theory (Atwood, 2008). When theoretical plausibility is low, as is the case with energy psychology, the evidentiary bar must be high. At present, the evidence supporting energy psychology falls below this bar.

Despite the lack of evidence supporting energy psychology claims, energy psychology is popular among providers and the public. Much of the appeal of energy psychology is likely to be connected with interest in complementary and alternative medicine in general, which has been increasing over the past several decades (Ernst et al., 2001). It is also relevant that even our most effective psychotherapies have considerable room for improvement; many clients fail to complete treatment and/or fail to benefit adequately from treatment. In this context, a treatment that promises to cure almost every ailment quickly, permanently, and with almost no client discomfort is understandably appealing. However, based on the evidence to date, there is no compelling reason to expect energy psychology to be more helpful than, other, better supported approaches such as CBTs.

Clinical innovation is needed in the field of mental health. New approaches, however, must be examined critically. This is particularly true when proponents exaggerate claims of treatment effectiveness, claim that treatment "fits all," propose change mechanisms that lack "connectivity" with extant science, explain away negative findings, and minimize the role of non-specific factors (Meichenbaum & Lilienfeld, 2018), as many energy psychology proponents do.

References

Atwood, K. (2008). *Prior probability: The dirty little secret of "evidence based alternative medicine."*. Retrieved September 28, 2010, from http://www.sciencebasedmedicine.org/?p=48

Bai, Y., Wang, J., Wu, J. P., Dai, J. X., Sha, O., Tai Wai Yew, D., Yuan, L., & Liang, Q. N. (2011). Review of evidence suggesting that the fascia network could be the anatomical basis for acupoints and meridians in the human body. *Evidence-Based Complementary and Alternative Medicine.* doi:10.1155/2011/260510

Bakker, G. M. (2013). The current status of energy psychology: Extraordinary claims with less than ordinary evidence. *Clinical Psychologist, 17*(3), 91–99.

Bausell, R. B. (2007). *Snake oil science: The truth about complementary and alternative medicine.* Oxford University Press.

Callahan, R. (1985). *Five minute phobia cure: Dr. Callahan's treatment for fears, phobias and self-sabotage.* Enterprise Publishing.

Callahan, R., & Callahan, J. (1996). *Thought field therapy and trauma: Treatment and theory.* Thought Field Therapy Training Center.

Callahan, R., & Callahan, J. (2000). *Stop the nightmares of trauma: Thought field therapy, the power therapy for the 21st century.* Professional Press.

Callahan, R. J. (2001a). The impact of thought field therapy on heart rate variability (HRV). *Journal of Clinical Psychology, 57,* 1153–1170.

Callahan, R. J. (2001b). Raising and lowering heart rate variability: Some clinical findings of thought field therapy. *Journal of Clinical Psychology Review, 57,* 1175–1186.

Callahan, R. J. (2001c). Thought field therapy: Response to our critics and a scrutiny of some old ideas of social science. *Journal of Clinical Psychology, 57*, 1153–1170.

Church, D., & Nelms, J. (2016). Ain, range of motion, and psychological symptoms in a population with frozen shoulder: A randomized controlled dismantling study of clinical EFT (emotional freedom techniques). *Archives of Scientific Psychology, 4*(1). doi:10.1037/arc0000028

Church, D., Stapleton, P., Kip, K., & Gallo, F. (2020). Corrigendum to: Is tapping on acupuncture points an active ingredient in emotional freedom techniques: A systematic review and meta-analysis of comparative studies. *The Journal of Nervous and Mental Disease, 208*(8), 632–635. doi:10.1097/NMD.0000000000001222

Church, D., Stapleton, P., Yang, A., & Gallo, F. (2018). Is tapping on acupuncture points an active ingredient in Emotional Freedom Techniques? A systematic review and meta-analysis of comparative studies. *The Journal of Nervous and Mental Disease, 206*(10), 783–793. doi:10.1097/NMD.0000000000000878.

Clond, M. (2016). Emotional freedom techniques for anxiety: A systematic review with meta-analysis. *The Journal of Nervous and Mental Disease, 204*(5), 388–395.

Collinge, W., Yarnold, P. R., & Raskin., E. (1998). Use of mind/body selfhealing practice predicts positive health transition in chronic fatigue syndrome: A controlled study. *Subtle Energies & Energy Medicine Journal Archives, 9*, 171–190.

Colquhoun, D., & Novella, S. P. (2013). Acupuncture is theatrical placebo. *Anesthesia & Analgesia, 116*(6), 1360–1363.

Coyne, J. C., & Kok, R. N. (2014). Salvaging psychotherapy research: A manifesto. *Journal of Evidence-Based Psychotherapies, 14*(2), 105–124.

Craske, M. G., Kircanski, K., Zelikowsky, M., Mystkowski, J., Chowdhury, N., & Baker, A. (2008). Optimizing inhibitory learning during exposure therapy. *Behaviour Research and Therapy, 46*(1), 5–27.

Elder, C., Ritenbaugh, C., Mist, S., Aickin, M., Schneider, J., Zwickey, H., & Elmer, P. (2007). Randomized trial of two mind-body interventions for weight-loss maintenance. *Journal of Alternative and Complementary Medicine.* doi:10.1089/acm.2006.623

Elder, C. R., Gullion, C. M., DeBar, L. L., Funk, K. L., Lindberg, N. M., Ritenbaugh, C., Meltesen, G., Gallison, C., & Stevens, V. J. (2012). Randomized trial of tapas acupressure technique for weight loss maintenance. *BMC Complementary and Alternative Medicine, 12.* doi:10.1186/1472-6882-12-19

Ernst, E., Pittler, M. H., Stevinson, C., & White, A. (2001). *The desktop guide to complementary and alternative medicine: An evidence-based approach.* Mosby International Ltd.

Feinstein, D. (2003). *Energy psychology interactive self-help guide.* Innersource.

Feinstein, D. (2008). Energy psychology: A review of the preliminary evidence. *Psychotherapy: Theory, Research, Practice, Training, 45*(1), 199.

Feinstein, D. (2009). Facts, paradigms, and anomalies in the acceptance of energy psychology: A rejoinder to McCaslin's (2009) and Pignotti and Thyer's (2009) comments on Feinstein (2008a). *Psychotherapy: Theory, Research, Practice, Training, 46*(2).

Feinstein, D. (2012). Acupoint stimulation in treating psychological disorders: Evidence of efficacy. *Review of General Psychology, 16*, 364–380. doi:10.1037/a0028602

Feinstein, D. (2019). Energy psychology: Efficacy, speed, mechanisms. *Explore, 15*(5), 340–351. doi:10.1016/j.explore.2018.11.003

Feinstein, D. (2021). Six empirically-supported premises about energy psychology: Mounting evidence for a controversial therapy. *Advances in Mind-Body Medicine, 35*, 17–32.

Fox, L., & Malinowski, P. (2013). Improvement in study-related emotions in undergraduates following emotional freedom techniques (EFT): A single-blind controlled study. *Energy Psychology: Theory, Research, and Treatment, 5*, 1–5.

Foa, E. B., & Kozak, M. J. (1986). Emotional processing of fear: Exposure to corrective information. *Psychological Bulletin, 99*, 20–35.

Gallo, F. (2004). *Energy psychology. Explorations at the interface of energy, cognition, behavior, and health* (2nd edition). CRC Press.

Gerber, R. (2001). *Vibrational medicine.* Bear & Company.

Gilomen, S. A., & Lee, C. W. (2015). The efficacy of acupoint stimulation in the treatment of psychological distress: A meta-analysis. *Journal of Behavior Therapy and Experimental Psychiatry*, *48*, 140–148.

Harper, M. (2012). Taming the amygdala: An EEG analysis of exposure therapy for the traumatized. *18*(2), 61–74. doi:10.1177/1534765611429082

Herbert, J. D., & Gaudiano, B. A. (2001a). The search for the holy grail: Heart rate variability and thought field therapy. *Journal of Clinical Psychology*, *57*(10), 1207–1214.

Herbert, J. D., & Gaudiano, B. A. (2005). Moving from empirically supported treatment lists to practice guidelines in psychotherapy: The role of the placebo concept. *Journal of Clinical Psychology*, *61*(7), 893–908.

Hines, T. H. (2003). *Pseudoscience and the paranormal* (2nd edition). Prometheus.

Hooke, W. (1998). A review of thought field therapy. *Traumatology*, *3*(2). doi:10.1037/h0101050

Irgens, A. C., Hoffart, A., Nysæter, T. E., Haaland, V. Ø., Borge, F.-M., Pripp, A. H., Martinsen, E. W., & Dammen, T. (2017). Thought field therapy compared to cognitive behavioral therapy and wait-list for agoraphobia: A randomized, controlled study with a 12-month follow-up. *Frontiers in Psychology*, *8*, 1–14.

Johnson, C., Shala, M., Sejdijaj, X., Odell, R., & Dabishevci, K. (2001). Thought field therapy: Soothing the bad moments of Kosovo. *Journal of Clinical Psychology*, *57*, 1237–1240.

Jones, A. (2016). *Paul McKenna interview: The celebrity hypnotist is launching a new book on the psychology of influence*. https://www.independent.co.uk/news/people/profiles/paul-mckenna-interview-celebrity-hypnotist-launching-new-book-psychology-influence-a6801446.html

Karatzias, T., Power, K., Brown, K., McGoldrick, T., Begum, M., Young, J., Loughran, P., Chouliara, Z., & Adams, S. (2011). A controlled comparison of the effectiveness and efficiency of two psychological therapies for posttraumatic stress disorder: Eye movement desensitization and reprocessing vs. emotional freedom techniques. *The Journal of Nervous and Mental Disease*, 372–378. doi:10.1097/NMD.0b013e31821cd262

Kelly, M. (2008, November 21). Years later, healing the wounds of a stepfather's abuse. *The Washington Post*.

Kline, J. P. (2001). Heart rate variability does not tap putative efficacy of thought field therapy. *Journal of Clinical Psychology*, *57*, 1187–1192.

Lee, J. H., Chung, S. Y., & Kim, J. W. (2015). A comparison of Emotional Freedom Techniques-Insomnia (EFT-I) and Sleep Hygiene Education (SHE) for insomnia in a geriatric population: A randomized controlled trial. *Energy Psychology*, *7*(1), 22–29.

Lilienfeld, S. O. (2011). Distinguishing scientific from pseudoscientific psychotherapies: Evaluating the role of theoretical plausibility, with a little help from Reverend Bayes. *Clinical Psychology: Science and Practice*, *18*(2), 105.

Lohr, J. M. (2001). Sakai et al. is not an adequate demonstration of TFT effectiveness. *Journal of Clinical Psychology*, *57*, 1229–1235.

McCaslin, D. L. (2009a). Comments and rejoinder a review of efficacy claims in energy psychology. *Psychotherapy: Theory, Research, Practice, Training*, 249–256. doi:10.1037/a0016025

McCaslin, D. L. (2009b). A review of efficacy claims in energy psychology. *Psychotherapy: Theory, Research, Practice, Training*, *46*(2), 249–256.

McNally, R. J. (2001). Tertullian's motto and Callahan's method. *Journal of Clinical Psychology*, *57*, 1171–1174.

Meichenbaum, D., & Lilienfeld, S. O. (2018). How to spot hype in the field of psychotherapy: A 19-item checklist. *Professional Psychology: Research and Practice*, *22*, 22–30.

Milad, M. R., Pitman, R. K., Ellis, C. B., Gold, A. L., Shin, L. M., Lasko, N. B., Zeidan, M. A., Handwerger, K., Orr, S. P., & Rauch, S. L. (2009). Neurobiological basis of failure to recall extinction memory in posttraumatic stress disorder. *Biological Psychiatry*, *66*, 1075–1082.

Miller, S. D., Hubble, M. A., Seidel, J. A., Chow, D., & Bargmann, S. (2014). Focus on clinical practice. *Independent Practitioner*.

Mollon, P. (2007). Thought field therapy and its derivatives: Rapid relief of mental health problems through tapping on the body. *Primary Care and Community Psychiatry*. doi:10.1080/17468840701750836

Mowrer, O. H. (1960). *Learning theory and behavior*. John Wiley & Sons. doi:10.1037/10802-000

Pignotti, M. (2005). Thought field therapy voice technology vs. random meridian point sequences. A single-blind controlled experiment. *Scientific Review of Mental Health Practice, 4*(1), 38–47.

Pignotti, M. (2007). Thought field therapy: A former insider's experience. *Research on Social Work Practice, 17.* doi:10.1177/1049731506292530

Pignotti, M., & Steinberg, M. (2001). Heart rate variability as an outcome measure for thought field therapy in clinical practice. *Journal of Clinical Psychology, 57*(10), 1193–1206.

Pignotti, M., & Thyer, B. (2009). Some comments on "Energy psychology: A review of the evidence": Premature conclusions based on incomplete evidence?

Popper, K. R. (1959). The logic of scientific discovery (reprint). Hutchinson.

Rosen, G. M., & Davison, G. C. (2001). Echo attributions" and other risks when publishing on novel therapies without peer review. *Journal of Clinical Psychology, 57,* 1245–1250.

Rosen, G. M., & Davison, G. C. (2003). Psychology should list empirically supported principles of change (ESPs) and not credential trademarked therapies or other treatment packages. *Behavior Modification, 27*(3), 300–312.

Rosner, R. (2001). Between search and research: How to find your way around? Review of the article, "Thought Field Therapy: Soothing the bad moments of Kosovo." *Journal of Clinical Psychology, 57,* 1241–1244.

Sakai, C., Paperny, D., Mathew, M., Tanida, G., Boyd, G., Simons, A., Yamamoto, C., Mau, C., & Nutter, L. (2001). Thought field therapy clinical applications: Utilization in an HMO in behavioral medicine and behavioral health services. *Journal of Clinical Psychology 57,* 1215–1227.

Sebastian, B., & Nelms, J. (2017). The effectiveness of Emotional Freedom Techniques in the treatment of posttraumatic stress disorder: A meta-analysis. *13,* 16–25. doi:10.1016/j.explore.2016.10.001

Spiegel, A. (2006). All things considered. In *Unorthodox therapy raises concern in New Orleans.* National Public Radio.

Stapleton, P., Buchan, C., Mitchell, I., McGrath, Y., Gorton, P., & Carter, B. (2019). An initial investigation of neural changes in overweight adults with food cravings after emotional freedom techniques. *OBM Integrative and Complementary Medicine, 4*(1), 1–5.

Taber, J. M., Leyva, B., & Persoskie, A. (2015). Why do people avoid medical care? A qualitative study using national data. *Journal of General Internal Medicine,* 290–297. doi:10.1007/s11606-014-3089-1

Thyer, B. A., & Pignotti, M. (2016). The problem of pseudoscience in social work continuing education. *Journal of Social Work Education, 52,* 136–146. doi:10.1080/10437797.2016.1151279

Trespicio, T. (2014). Tapping her potential. *Oprah Magazine.*

Waite, W. L., & Holder, M. D. (2003). Assessment of the emotional freedom technique. *Scientific Review of Mental Health Practice, 2*(1), 1–10.

Wells, S., Polglase, K., Andrews, H. B., Carrington, P., & Baker, A. H. (2003). Evaluation of a meridian-based intervention, Emotional Freedom Techniques (EFT), for reducing specific phobias of small animals. *Journal of Clinical Psychology, 59*(9), 943–966.

Postscript: How to Resist False Claims

Anthony R. Pratkanis and Stephen Hupp

In a demon-haunted world full of the latest pop psychology fads, it can be difficult to resist social pressures and sales pitches. In a world of swirling disinformation, it can be hard to check facts. Knowing what is true and what is false often requires expertise, and it's difficult to be an expert in all things. And when we are sold on an idea and make a commitment to it, we can find ourselves in a rationalization trap that is painful and difficult to exit. What can we do to increase our resistance to false claims in pop psychology? Here are a few tips based on some of the work described in this book.

Remember the Basics of Evaluating Claims

Chapter 1 focused on building resistance to false claims. First, many people find it helpful to apply the Sagan Standard – "extraordinary claims require extraordinary evidence." That is, when you begin to evaluate an extraordinary claim, consider the degree to which there is strong evidence to support the claim. Second, be aware of the sources of false beliefs. That is, understanding logical fallacies and cognitive biases can help buffer you from believing in claims with weak evidence. Third, look out for the hallmarks of false claims. Think of these hallmarks as red flags, and be especially cautious when a claim includes several red flags. Finally, Chapter 13 helped you recognize when social influence and the tactics of persuasion are in play. When people use several of these tactics, they may be trying too hard to sell you on something that you really don't need. Table 17.1 provides a list of the sources of false beliefs, the hallmarks of false claims, and the tactics of persuasion.

Ask Questions

The first author of this postscript (Pratkanis) has conducted research on fraud prevention, and one conclusion to be drawn from this research is that the single best defense against a scam is to ask questions (AARP, 2003). That is, when targets of fraud were equipped with questions to ask, their subsequent victimization was reduced by two-thirds. Thus, when you are confronted with a sales pitch it is valuable to explore the motivation and credibility of the source of the message with questions like these:

- *Why is this person telling me this?*
- *What do they have to gain?*
- *Does the person have real expertise or is it a manufactured image?*
- *What is the evidence for this?*

DOI: 10.4324/9781003107798-17

Table 17.1 Basics of Evaluating Claims

Sources of False Beliefs	Hallmarks of False Claims	Tactics of Persuasion
Post hoc ergo propter hoc reasoning	Meaningless jargon	Phantom dreams
Assuming causation from correlation	Untestable idea promotion	Story-telling
Reasoning by representativeness	Anecdote overreliance	Tailored pitches
Argument from authority	Placebo exploitation	Source credibility and authority
False analogy	Data manipulation	Social consensus and social identity
False dichotomy	Burden of proof shift	Scarcity
Nirvana fallacy	Science discreditation	Information control
Grain of truth exaggeration		Self-generated persuasion
Appeal to nature		Commitment
Appeal to antiquity		The rationalization trap
Biased sample misperception		
Selective perception		
Confirmation bias		

Note: The sources of false beliefs and hallmarks of false claims are described in Chapter 1, and the tactics of persuasion are described in Chapter 13.

- *How good is that evidence?*
- *Does the evidence meet scientific standards such as a controlled experiment and reliable observation?*
- *Can the source of the evidence be trusted? Is it from a friend of a friend or someone with real knowledge?*
- *What are the arguments for the other side?*

Three big questions that are particularly helpful are as follows: What else can it be? So, what? What does the evidence say? (Pratkanis, 2017). When confronted with a claim – say, a medium has psychic powers – begin by asking: *What else can it be?* It could be psychic powers, but it could also be many other explanations: the person making the claim is lying or mistaken; the psychic demonstration may be due to a simple explanation such as cold readings or a magic trick; the psychic performance could be a one-off lucky fluke; and so on. Next, ask: *So what?* What are the consequences of the claim? In other words, assume for a moment that a claim is true and consider what the world would have to look like for the claim to be true. For example, if psychic powers existed, then Las Vegas would not be possible; a slight skewing of the odds via paranormal processes would bankrupt the casinos. If a psychic demonstration is a one-off, then you would expect there to be little reliable replications of the phenomenon. Finally, ask: *What is the evidence?* In this case, Las Vegas continues to thrive.

Have a Plan for Evaluating Claims in Order to Keep an Open Mind

One safeguard to falling for false claims is to have a plan for evaluating claims and for changing your mind. A plan for evaluating claims serves at least two purposes: (a) by focusing your attention on the information needed to validate the claim as opposed to the content of the sales pitch; and (b) by allowing you to have an open mind and to be clear on the evidence you would need to change your position.

We suggest using science as a way of evaluating a claim (Pratkanis, 2017). In other words, claims, such as the value of a given therapy or the power of extrasensory perception, should be tested in multiple randomized double-blind experiments. Given the fallibility of human perception and memory, observations should be repeatable and verifiable. The involvement of those with expertise in an area – scientists, magicians, skilled investigators – is useful for evaluating alternative explanations of any findings. Any finding should be replicable by other researchers. The evaluation of a claim should be done with a scientific attitude of bending over backward to prove one's self wrong (Feynman, 1985) and with checks and balances on decision making (Pratkanis & Turner, 2013).

Exit the Rationalization Trap

Obviously, the best way to avoid a rationalization trap is to look before you leap and have a plan for evaluating claims. However, we are all human, we all make mistakes, and therefore we can all find ourselves in such a trap. In order to start to get out of the trap, it's useful to recognize this fact and to realize that just because we do something stupid doesn't mean we are stupid. In fact, admitting a mistake and taking responsibility for it are traits of someone who is smart and moral. It shows you are a capable person who cares enough to avoid spreading false claims to others.

The norms of science provide us with a way to lower our chances of being caught in a rationalization trap and, when we make a mistake, getting out of one. The scientific process is the only way of knowing that actually seeks out reason it might be wrong instead of seeking to confirm what is already believed. This norm is rooted in the fact that as human beings we are fallible, and we do make mistakes. As such, a scientist humbly adopts checks and balances on their thinking as a way of defeating the arrogance of self-righteous dogma. By adopting the mindset of a scientist, it will help each of us gain the needed grace and humility to admit and even embrace a mistake.

If you find yourself exiting the rationalization trap, it might be helpful to know that you are not alone. We've both had to take this exit several times ourselves; almost everyone does from time to time. In fact, many prominent members of the skeptical community have spoken publicly about their exits from the trap. For example, Susan Blackmore, a professor of psychology, used her own scientific research to shift away from believing in parapsychological phenomena such as extrasensory perception (Blackmore, 2001). She wrote about her changing beliefs in a chapter titled "Why I Have Given Up," published in the book, *Skeptical Odysseys: Personal Accounts by the World's Leading Paranormal Inquirers* (Kurtz, 2001). The same book includes several such stories and helps to serve as a model for all the rest of us.

Lastly, thinking in a skeptical way doesn't mean that you believe in nothing at all. Sagan (1996) often emphasized that you can be skeptical while also experiencing wonder. There are so many scientific discoveries every year, that there's no shortage of topics for which one can experience wonder. As a scientific discipline, psychology makes great strides every year. For example, since the 1990s, the American Psychological Association has led in efforts to identify evidence-based treatments for a broad range of issues (see Hupp and Maria (2019) and Hupp and Santa Maria (2023) for an overview of these efforts). Further, the science of psychology still has many exciting discoveries ahead.

Summary and Conclusion

When you're exposed to claims through pop psychology, start from a point of scientific skepticism. Remember the Sagan Standard, the sources of false beliefs, the hallmarks of false claims, and the tactics of persuasion. Ask questions. Have a plan for evaluating claims in order to keep an open mind. And, when needed, exit the rationalization trap.

If you're a scientist, or if you have a scientific mindset, there's a whole community of skeptical thinkers for you. A great starting point is the Committee for Skeptical Inquiry (CSI). Many of our chapter authors are Fellows of CSI (including the book's co-editor – Richard Wiseman). They regularly contribute to CSI's magazine, *Skeptical Inquirer,* and speak at the yearly conference – CSICon – with many of the presentations available for free viewing online. There are many other organizations as well. The Skeptics Society publishes *Skeptic* magazine, and local skeptical groups host other conferences such as the Northeast Conference on Science and Skepticism (NECSS). Conferences outside of the United States include the European Skeptical Congress and QED (Question, Explore, Discover), to name a few (for additional ways to get involved, check out Hupp & Santa Maria, 2019).

References

AARP. (2003). *Off the hook: Reducing participation in telemarketing fraud.* Washington, DC: Author.

Blackmore, S. (2001). Why I have given up. In P. Kurtz (Ed.), *Skeptical odysseys: Personal accounts by the world's leading paranormal inquirers.* Prometheus Books.

Feynman, R. P. (1985). *Surely you're joking, Mr. Feynman.* Norton.

Hupp, S., & Santa Maria, C. (2019). Scientific skepticism and critical thinking about therapy. *Behavior Therapist, 42*(5), 158–162.

Hupp, S., & Santa Maria, C. (2023). *Pseudoscience in therapy.* Cambridge University Press.

Kurtz, P. (2001). *Skeptical odysseys: Personal accounts by the world's leading paranormal inquirers.* Prometheus Books.

Pratkanis, A. R. (2017). The (partial but) real crisis in social psychology: A social influence analysis of the causes and solutions. In S. O. Lilienfeld & I. D. Waldman (Eds.), *Psychological science under scrutiny: Recent challenges and proposed solutions* (pp. 141–163). John Wiley.

Pratkanis, A. R., & Turner, M. E. (2013). Methods for counteracting groupthink risk: A critical appraisal. *International Journal of Risk and Contingency Management, 2*(4), 18–38.

Sagan, C. (1996). *The demon-haunted world: Science as a candle in the dark.* Ballantine Books.

Index